Mind, Immunity and Health

Key Texts in the Psychology of Health and Illness
Edited by Professor Keith Phillips, University of Westminster

Current textbooks in health psychology are limited in their ability to treat the main areas in adequate scope and depth. With this exciting new series each of the core areas of health psychology has a single volume devoted to it. Students will find for the first time a properly comprehensive and in-depth treatment. Particular attention is given to accessibility of style and to providing the necessary apparatus – such as glossaries and recommended reading – that students require.

First titles in the series:

Mind, Immunity and Health:
The science of psychoneuroimmunology
Phil Evans, Frank Hucklebridge and Angela Clow

Pain
Janice Abbott and Jane Smith

Mind, Immunity and Health: The Science of Psychoneuroimmunology

Phil Evans, Frank Hucklebridge and Angela Clow

FREE ASSOCIATION BOOKS / LONDON / NEW YORK

First published 2000 in Great Britain by
FREE ASSOCIATION BOOKS
57 Warren Street, London W1P 5PA

hb 185343 486 8

pb 185343 487 6

A CIP catalogue record for this book is available from the British Library.

Designed and produced for Free Association Books Ltd by
Chase Production Services, Chadlington, OX7 3LN
Printed in the European Union by Athenaeum Press, Gateshead

Contents

List of Figures and Tables

Figures

Tables

Preface

Writing an introductory book on psychoneuroimmunology (PNI) has proven to be quite a challenge. There is no template. Most specialised books, which already exist in this area, come in the form of an edited collection of contributions. Most also assume a knowledge of immunology. PNI is also not so developed a science as to have a straightforward and basic syllabus. How, then, have we attempted to address these issues?

First of all, our experience with trying to convey the key findings of PNI to our students, whether they have been studying on health psychology courses or joining our team as fledgling researchers, has been invaluable. We have taken two important points on board. First, those whose basic discipline is psychology often have, at best, only a very limited acquaintance with the workings of the immune system. Second, a proper understanding, and, more particularly, an ability to interpret the complex findings in this area, has to involve some reasonable knowledge of immunology. What then follows from this? One solution would be to write a book, which assumes prior knowledge, and instruct the reader inwardly to digest an introductory text in immunology prior to approaching our book. For many reasons, this purist approach was ruled out, not least because it would be over-inclusive in terms of the total content addressed in a dedicated immunology text. Another approach would be to use part of our own book to serve the function of familiarising the student with the basics of immunology needed to understand PNI. This indeed is the approach we have adopted.

Thus, after an initial short chapter setting the scene for the book as a whole, in Chapter 2 we give the reader just such an introduction to immunology. The key cells of the immune system and their function are described in a fair amount of detail. The reader, approaching immunology as a novice, may find the chapter heavy-going, so a word of advice is in order. We suggest that Chapter 2 should be seen not just sequentially, but as a key reference chapter, to be returned to as needed. A first reading may allow a basic understanding of the issues arising in later chapters, but further re-reading may provide a deeper understanding. To a certain extent, the same may be said for Chapter 3, where we talk about the channels of communication between brain and immune system, through neural, endocrine and cytokine messengers. Chapter 4 is, we hope, a useful chapter for the reader who wishes to explore primary sources in the PNI literature. We attempt to give a catalogue and overview of the principal types of immune system measures which will crop up in typical research papers. Chapters 5–9 are finally where we review that literature. As we have said, there is no set syllabus for PNI. Instead, we have tried to use chapter headings as means of subsuming areas of PNI where much research has been carried out. All these chapters have some relevance to health issues, but, in view of the placement of this book in a series devoted to health matters, we end in Chapter 9 with a chapter that tries to make health a central focus, pulling strands together.

There may not yet be a template for a book on PNI, but we hope that, whatever else, we have written a book which will convey some of the excitement which we ourselves feel as researchers in this area. That has been a primary aim. Inevitably at times, we have had to simplify some arguments more than we might wish. Some expert readers (although the book is not for them!) may consider we have overstated our case at times. We have consulted with others and sought advice on some points that have arisen. Nevertheless, if oversimplification or overstatement is judged on occasion to have resulted in error, we must shoulder the blame. Interdisciplinary researchers usually develop broad shoulders.

1

Setting the Scene

Psychoneuroimmunology is the conventional name given to an interdisciplinary science which explores the neural and neuroendocrine links between the domains of psychology and immunology. For those of us whose research is by its very nature interdisciplinary, it seems the most natural thing in the world. But in what way exactly is the new science of psychoneuroimmunology (hereafter conveniently shortened to PNI) interdisciplinary?

PNI: A New Interdisciplinary Science?

One view might be that PNI is hardly interdisciplinary at all but is simply a reassertion of an older science, biology. It is true of course that, in our universities, there are few remaining departments of biology, pure and simple. It seems that, in the natural scheme of things, scientists are highly motivated to create new and separate sub-disciplines which then in time become new disciplines. The reasons for such compartmentalising, we would mischievously conjecture, often has less to do with subject matter and more to do with very human concerns: a desire for status and professionalisation, a desire of people of like mind to run their own affairs and, within a university, for example, to accrue their own quotas of senior positions, administrators, courses and dedicated laboratories. This is not a novel conjecture (see Rose, 1997, for example), nor is it entirely cynical if utilitarian benefits of separateness are considered. In any case, it is not a conjecture we need to pursue further in this particular book. Indeed, given that this book is part of a series of books intended to be of relevance to the newly emerging discipline and profession of health psychology it may be impolitic to do so! Rather our point is that, whatever walls some scientists may throw up around their focus of interest, nature certainly does not recognise them. Boundaries between disciplines are naturally permeable and artificial. An analogy, not to be taken too far, would be that boundaries between disciplines are like national frontiers drawn on a land mass. The study of the land mass as a whole is our common subject matter, but the frontier posts are drawn up by groups of human beings, shaped by desires and their own unique collective histories.

To pursue the analogy a little further, we may imagine that behind the frontiers, one bit of land mass is occupied by a particular nation whose citizens have particular rights over it. Visitors require special entry permits or visas, and unless, by hook or by crook, they manage to stay for a sufficiently long time in foreign territory and get to know and influence the right authorities, they will never be recognised as full citizens. Out of this imperfect but somewhat illuminating analogy, we confront one of the hazards faced by interdisciplinary scientists. Read for citizenship, expertise; read for population, population of scientists; read for nation, discipline; and what we confront is the suspicion in some quarters that interdisciplinary scientists (like general medical practitioners as opposed to consultants perhaps?) cannot speak with the full authority of experts.

To counter this suspicion, we need to move beyond the simplest interpretation of this particular analogy. Let us first make the obvious point that interdisciplinary science is seldom conducted by individuals but rather by teams of scientists who collaborate in order to pool their expertise. Our second point, however, takes us back to our opening assertion that in one sense our particular interdisciplinary science – PNI – may not be really interdisciplinary at all, if the old parent discipline of biology is reconstructed out of its fractionated parts. PNI, however interesting it may be to us (and hopefully, after reading this book, to you the reader) is not a truly adventurous foray into interdisciplinary science. It does not combine startlingly different disciplines to reveal stark new insights into natural phenomena. Rather, it represents a coming together of scientists who, in terms of our land mass analogy, already occupy adjacent terrain. If we separate the 'P', the 'N' and the 'I' out of PNI, we find the interested parties: the psychologist, the neuroscientist and the immunologist. The latter two we have no problems subsuming under the umbrella of biology. Psychology we know is the broadest of churches, but psychology is generally recognised (not least by its professional bodies) to be a biological science, as well as a social science, a cognitive science, or whatever else.

Thus any PNI team, while it may pool plenty of individual expertise as stated above, is also likely to share much already. It is true of course that the 'N' of PNI is not in the middle by accident; it is the bridge in the acronym. A general training in psychology, while it contains much about the nervous system, may contain little about immunology (except perhaps nowadays the odd mention of PNI in an optional course of study!). Similarly, nowadays no self-respecting immunology text, even at an introductory level, would be complete without some mention of interactions between the nervous system and the immune system. However, one would not find reference in such a text to much in the way of essentially psychological investigations.

To summarise then, we are saying that PNI is a relatively new interdisciplinary science, but, looked at in a certain context, it is not radically interdisciplinary. What else therefore about the agenda of PNI researchers tends to define the area, or better (since strict 'definitions' of areas are rarely helpful) characterise it? We would venture to suggest that one answer lies in the *approach* of PNI researchers to their subject matter. We cannot speak for all but we certainly speak for ourselves. Moreover, the approach we are about to outline we would guess is that which has reverberated most strongly with that lay public, who, while not in the main a body of trained scientists, has shown great interest in PNI findings as they have been disseminated outside specialist journals and in the wider media.

When an Organism Responds to Events, the Whole Organism Responds

Ignore for a moment the tautologous aspect of this statement. What we want to emphasise is the word 'whole'. In keeping with our belief that the 'P', the 'N' and the 'I' of PNI are all encompassed by biology, so here we might add that it is individuals (be they mice or men) who respond to events and they respond as whole biological organisms. It is not systems making up individuals which respond, whether the system under scrutiny is the central nervous system, the neuroendocrine system or the immune system. We shall see that one of the recurring themes in this book is that such systems, sketched out by humankind for its own convenience, refuse to behave like isolated systems. Indeed, it is becoming increasingly difficult, in the light of recent research, to see clear boundaries between such systems.

An excursion into history may be illuminating at this point. In the last years of the nineteenth century the distinguished psychologist and philosopher William James was among the first to put forward a proper theory of that most difficult (but from our point of view, as we shall see, crucial) construct: emotion. James (1884) effectively linked the psychology of emotion irrevocably to physiological processes. We could say then that James ensured that the future study of emotion would be interdisciplinary. Different chapters of this book will all, explicitly or implicitly, be dealing with how the immune system is influenced by our emotional states, our feeling states: chronic states of stress or depression, or the transient odour of something nice or something nasty. Immunology hardly existed as a distinct science when James first put forward his theory of emotion, yet it is this physiological system which now joins old familiars such as the autonomic nervous system as a window on our emotional life. It is appropriate in this opening chapter to give the reader an overview of how we ourselves construe the concept of emotion. In particular we shall continue to emphasise the importance of seeing the whole organism as reacting emotionally. Thus we should be no more surprised to see the expression of emotion in a measure of immune system functioning as in, say, an autonomic measure, such as a heart pounding in terror or a face red with anger.

In essence William James saw the psychological experience of emotion as our own awareness of, or more precisely, our conscious perception of physiological changes which happen to us in those situations which we know invoke strong emotional responses, notably danger. In what nowadays we would call a good sound-bite, he effectively asked us to reverse our normal way of thinking of emotions and related actions. If we imagine a danger (confronting a bear in the woods), the view espoused by William James was that we become afraid because we run, rather than run because we're afraid. As we might expect, James' theory is no longer fully acceptable in its originally baldly stated terms. After all, a good theory should sow the seeds of its own destruction by suggesting lines of enquiry and experimentation which inevitably will lead to important modifications. However, the view that conscious emotional experience is in some way just part (and perhaps not such an important part – see below) of a wider physiologically evidenced activation of the organism, and not a direct cause of behaviour, is a view which is still essentially correct.

One of the weaker aspects of James' theory, in the light of what we have now discovered about emotional processes, is that it gave too much emphasis on explaining human experience or conscious awareness of different emotions. We shall now take up issues relating to two words in the last sentence: 'human' and 'conscious'.

Much of what we currently know about physiological systems activated in emotionally arousing situations (such as danger) comes from studies of non-human mammalian species, where issues of conscious experience are by necessity irrelevant, given the impossibility of experiential self-reporting and introspection. Nevertheless, in terms of emotionally relevant brain systems, humans share a common mammalian evolutionary heritage. We shall hear much in subsequent chapters of this book about central nervous system mechanisms underpinning emotional responding, the chemical transmitter substances and other hormones which convey and direct neural messages, the autonomic nervous system and neuroendocrine components which often register strong emotional states, as well as the 'emotionally sensitive' immune system. All of these parts of the whole organism are characterised by similarity rather than difference across mammalian species. Decades of research have firmly demonstrated that emotional responding involves many different biological systems and sub-systems, and that is only counting the ones so far intensively investigated. In this scheme of things, the immune system is just one more Johnny come lately to the party. One is virtually compelled to take a holistic view: it is the biological organism as a whole which is reacting in every nerve and sinew. And for what purpose?

Emotion, as the Latin root of the word implies, is really no more than an offshoot of its big cousin: motivation. Motivation in turn is about being programmed with the basics to respond urgently to the challenges of often harsh environments, and to adapt successfully. Good adaptation involves constant adjustment, and constant adjustment is itself a balancing act. That brings us to a key word to have as a constant background in discussing PNI findings, and that word is 'homeostasis'. Just before we turn to homeostasis, however, we need to tie up the loose end of emotion as conscious experience.

Most of us in our personal lives recognise the importance of emotions. After all, positive emotions are what makes life worth living, and intense negative ones by contrast can lead some to the view that life is not worth living. The following assertion may therefore appear paradoxical. Consciousness, at least in relation to emotional experience, is, in our view, a somewhat over-inflated stock. That is not to deny its importance. We would simply point out that people's global appraisal of emotionally laden information is not necessarily always accompanied by florid conscious experience of an emotion. Some of the most interesting findings of psychologists are those which show how our emotional behaviour can be unconsciously influenced, and how independent it can be of conscious cognition. A few examples will suffice.

Patients with so-called 'split brains' where the corpus callosum, which normally connects the two hemispheres of the brain, is cut (usually to relieve massive epilepsy), have provided fertile ground for research on emotion (see LeDoux, 1998). If an emotional stimulus (a word, phrase or picture with pleasant or unpleasant connotations) is presented in such a way that the sensory information only goes to the right cerebral cortex, the information in the stimulus cannot be transferred to the (usually language-processing) left cortex. The patient typically is unable to identify the stimulus. However, the strange finding is that the emotional significance of the stimulus is communicated. The patient 'knows' that something emotional has been presented but does not know what. The reason is that crucial aspects of emotional processing take place in older (in an evolutionary sense) areas of the brain, below the level of the two cerebral hemispheres, and are in an important sense independent of cognition. That is not to deny that in normal functioning, both hemispheres are involved in emotional processing. Indeed, we shall see in a later chapter (see Chapter 8) that lateralisation of function may also be an issue in regard to the effects of affective stimuli on the immune system.

In any event, recognising that full consciousness of emotion is not synonymous with the full impact of emotional stimuli on an individual, does not mean that cognition is irrelevant to emotion. How we recognise, define, speak about and behave in relation to our emotions may be heavily influenced by cognition. This may be especially so for those multitudes of words for emotional states which probably represent subtle gradations and mixtures of feelings and which may even be culturally or historically specific, that is, differentially recognised in different locations and different historical periods. If, for example, one of us were to proclaim that we had fallen 'romantically' in love, we would think that we were communicating something about our emotional life, and indeed we would be doing that. However, a neutral observer might correctly guess that we come from a western or westernised culture, and we ourselves would implicitly be using a whole raft of culturally dependent 'cognitive' information and cultural expectations in arriving at the conclusion that we are 'in love'.

Whenever we use any emotional word, we are always adding a cognitive dimension to a feeling state. In the phrase given currency by the philosopher Ludwig Wittgenstein there can be no private languages to describe any states that we would like to call wholly 'inner states'. Any word in a language must express something that is public and able to be referenced by all persons who make up a linguistic community. It is below this level of 'named' feeling states that we are saying emotion is independent of cognition. It is at the level of basic preference: liking or not liking things.

The psychologist Robert Zajonc has done pioneering work in this area (see Zajonc, 1984, for example) and shown definitively that preferences for simple stimuli (for example, Chinese-type characters) can be established without any conscious appraisal, by first of all presenting them subliminally. Of two characters, for example, the one first presented subliminally is preferred over the novel character, even though the subject sees both as equally novel. Similarly, preferences can be influenced by subliminal 'priming'. If you present subliminally a smiling face prior to one stimulus, and a frowning face prior to another, it will be the former which will be preferred. We will not extend our survey of findings here. One of us has written elsewhere and at length about how cognitive process and emotional processes show both mutual interaction and mutual independence (Evans, 1989), and LeDoux (1998) provides a useful update.

For our purposes, we simply invite the reader to see conscious reports of emotion, when they occur, as solely the tip of an iceberg. The emotionally processing and reacting organism, the whole biological organism, gets on with its emotional business (mouse or man) often regardless of conscious experience. Indeed, it is germane to mention that attempts to control emotional states by bringing them into the full rational glare of consciousness are often flawed. Seeing a fear as irrational does not of itself help anyone with that fear to change their feelings. Advertisers do not get people to 'like' their products by direct persuasion; their messages are implicit, avoiding or at least discouraging conscious recognition, rather like the case of priming stimuli mentioned above.

It will probably not escape the reader's attention that comparing conscious emotional experience to the tip of an iceberg has overtones of an old Freudian psychology in which below the tip of consciousness lies a dynamic and fundamentally emotional unconscious. We do not have to accept all the assorted paraphernalia of psychoanalysis to accept at least one implication of recognising the pervasiveness of unconscious emotional processing: in the case of human beings, what a person says about their emotional state (how strongly they rate themselves as 'stressed' or 'depressed', for example) may not always relate perfectly, and may sometimes be at odds with how their physiology is behaving, including the behaviour of immune system measures. This may be of some importance when we explore in subsequent chapters the extent to which life circumstances, emotional functioning and immune system responding may influence our physical health. The issue of consciousness is also relevant to another later chapter of this book which deals with classical conditioning of the immune system (see Chapter 7). It has long been known that classically conditioned responses do not require consciousness. Indeed, they may take place under conditions of anaesthesia.

To sum up then, we wish to emphasise the following view of emotion, as a concept. Emotional responding is multilayered across several physiological systems and measures, and to limit its scope to human conscious experience would be singularly inappropriate. We now move on to a consideration of what the whole person is doing when they respond emotionally. We take up the concepts of adaptation and homeostasis.

Meeting Challenges and Maintaining Balance

We have already expressed the view that emotion and motivation are part and parcel of the same set of phenomena. Let us be a bit more precise about the circumstances in which such phenomena are apparent. The recognition (not necessarily conscious recognition) of, on the one hand, biological needs and, on the other hand, external environmental contingencies is certainly the foundation for those emotional and motivational states which appear common to at least all higher organisms, and which will provide much of the focus for subsequent chapters of this book. At base, an organism needs to have elements of programming which efficiently ensure that it survives long enough to propagate its genes into the next generation. Essentially, it must be motivated to approach some situations and avoid others.

Since the kinds of links which will be the basis of this book (between the domains of psychology, neuroscience and immunology) were clearly not laid down overnight, but developed over an evolutionary time course, it seems sensible to divide up emotion and motivational phenomena in this relatively simplistic way. Thus positive emotions associated with approach motivation can be seen in turn to be associated with basic essential activities: eating, sexual activity and, certainly in higher animals, social and affiliative activity which can be shown to have survival value. Negative emotions, by contrast, are associated with avoidance behaviour in the case of fear, or aggression in the case of anger, and are in turn linked to activities associated with threat.

It is periodically mentioned that a search of emotional words in databases, such as Psychological Abstracts, will inevitably throw up more scientific papers on negative states such as fear rather than positive ones such as joy or euphoria. It should therefore be no surprise that this is the position in regard to the physiology of emotion, adaptation and homeostasis. Unfortunately, it is a bias which is evident in PNI research too, although we have attempted at some points in this book (notably Chapter 8) to consider both positive and negative affect in relation to effects on the immune system. Nevertheless, the concept of 'threat' was certainly central stage in the theory of so-called emergency motivation which was developed by the distinguished physiologist Walter Cannon in the early decades of the twentieth century.

Cannon took up the insight of William James, whose theory we have already discussed. Cannon, like James, saw physiological processes at the heart of emotional phenomena. However, unlike James, he did not see emotional experience as a direct result of conscious feedback from physiological activity. In particular, Cannon was singularly critical of the view that feedback from the peripheral autonomic nervous system was what actually constituted awareness of emotion, pointing out, among other things, that such feedback was too slow and too general across different emotional states. Instead, Cannon was among the first to point out how adaptive were the autonomic responses engendered in primitive responses to threat. In short the adaptation is summed up in the well known phrase, the fight or flight response. We shall consider the physiology of this response in more detail in subsequent chapters, particularly when we examine the effects of stress on the immune system. It is sufficient for present purposes to point out that both running away and fighting involve a massive use of energy over and above that used by the organism at rest. The sympathetic branch of the autonomic nervous system is wonderfully capable of orchestrating all the different bodily systems and organs which play a role in providing and directing energy to where it is needed.

In terms of our present knowledge about how organisms meet environmental challenges and, in particular adapt to stressful circumstances, Walter Cannon's contribution was, in the middle decades of the twentieth century, complemented by that of Hans Selye, a medic with a profound interest in the apparently common effects of a whole range of different sources of stress. He put forward the notion of a General Adaptation Syndrome (GAS), which he thought encapsulated the common elements which typically characterise an organism under threat and meeting an emergency. Once again we shall discuss elements of Selye's GAS in more detail in later chapters, but for present purposes we need to emphasise its basics only. The major point to make is that Selye, like Cannon, saw the organism's predominant response to a perceived threat as adaptive. In addition to the autonomic reactions that characterise feeling threatened and responding to an emergency, Selye also drew attention to the activation of another physiological system, namely the so-called hypothalamic-pituitary-adrenal (HPA) axis. This hormone-driven neuroendocrine axis will receive much attention in later chapters since it is not only responsive to psychological inputs, it also releases, as its end products, steroid hormones with significant influences on the immune system.

Clearly in later chapters we shall discuss many of the physiological measures, and particularly the chemicals and hormones, which are associated with the motivational and emotional systems first sketched by Cannon and Selye and much elaborated on by others who followed in their wake. We simply emphasise here that, in the short term at least, the activation of such systems from an evolutionary point of view is indeed adaptive. Essentially, all of the many co-ordinated changes we see should in principle help an organism in its natural habitat to survive. (As an aside you might want to ask yourself whether and to what extent current human societies still constitute a natural habitat for human bodies – an important issue to be discussed later.)

The sort of adaptation processes originally outlined by Cannon and Selye were meant to be short-lived. In terms of the need for energy expenditure which the systems described are meant to serve, the organism has its limits and when those limits are reached there is exhaustion, a failure of adaptation, dysfunction and ultimately death. Thus Selye's GAS can be imagined as a graph (see Figure 1.1) in which the ordinate is the resistance of the organism to withstand a challenge to its integrity and the abscissa is time. Initially the organism is thrown out of balance, it lacks the energy and resources to meet the challenge. This stage Selye refers to as shock.

Usually, however, this danger period is short-lived. The body mobilises rapidly to counter the shock, and resistance goes up, but as more time goes by and the challenge or threat does not go away, or is not successfully met, the organism passes into the stage of exhaustion, which, as we have indicated, may lead ultimately to death.

One of the key investigators, during the 1970s and 1980s, of the hormones involved in strong emotional states including stress processes, was Marianne Frankenhauser. She used a very apt term to describe the entirety of all the different processes involved. She talked about an organism 'raising the body's thermostat' in order to function efficiently to meet a challenge. The phrase is apt because it provides an obvious link from adaptation to homeostasis. She

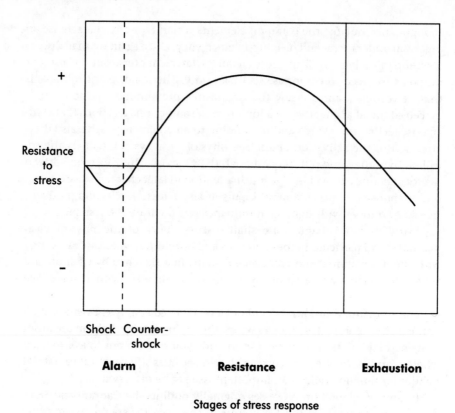

Figure 1.1   Selye's General Adaptation Syndrome

was clearly using the term 'thermostat' metaphorically, and not referring to heat as such. The point is that a thermostat is a particular kind of homeostat. Despite short-term fluctuations, the body must restore its overall balance in due course.

Any homeostatic system contains negative feedback loops in which changes in one parameter ultimately feed back to prevent further change. An example in terms of just one hormone would be insulin. When the body detects levels of blood glucose to be higher than a certain desirable set-point, insulin is released (insulin production is said to be up-regulated) which helps to reduce blood sugar levels. As blood sugar levels then fall, the effect is to turn down (down-regulate) insulin production. But this example is a mere microcosmic instance of one negative feedback loop. Within any wider system, such as the HPA axis, which is central within PNI, there are several. But can we isolate just one system, such as the HPA axis? The answer is no. The HPA system at its highest representation in the brain we shall see is linked to the control of autonomic activation. And still we cannot stop there. The immune system, as we shall discover in Chapter 3, not only receives information from and is influenced by the nervous and neuroendocrine systems, it also sends information to and influences the nervous system. Thus there are loops, and where there are loops there can be both negative and positive feedback.

And this finally is where this chapter has been resolutely heading. Future chapters will give the reader the 'meat' of PNI; this chapter is designed to suggest how that meat should be approached, digested if you will. When it comes to interpreting PNI findings, there can be no clear division of systems. All systems speak to each other. Wherever we look, there is cross-talk and mutual influence. We cannot sensibly talk about any one system in isolation maintaining its balance, its homeostasis. We cannot sensibly extend homoeostasis to a collection of systems – the boundaries are too fluid and new findings inevitably add to the scope of mutual influence. We are left reasserting our position that in regard to motivation and emotion, adaptation, and now homeostasis, the only sensible system to consider is the whole organism. We must assume that the processes we study in PNI, as a normal rule, are functional; ultimately that they enhance rather than detract from survival. We shall also need to alter some of the characteristic ways that we think of certain phenomena. If the immune system 'speaks to' the nervous system, as well as being spoken to, we shall need to include in our embrace the notion that the immune system can be as much a sense organ as our eyes, ears and nose. Take, for example, the event of an immune system cell encountering a foreign microbe. The microbe's presence is indeed 'sensed' by the immune system and, as we shall see in future chapters, the immune system can send chemical messages to the nervous system which are just as capable of inducing behaviour (feeling sick and lying down, for example) as the sight of a bear in the woods can lead to the behaviour of running away.

There are significant implications of PNI research for our state of health, and we shall certainly be keenly addressing such issues in later chapters of this book. Can prolonged stress or depression harm your physical health by making you less resistant to infections, or even certain cancers? These are interesting questions but answers are likely to involve discussion of maladaptation and dysfunction of biological systems. We ourselves are strongly of the opinion that it is impossible to have a proper understanding of dysfunction without also having some idea of normal function. We hope that this first chapter will have persuaded you of that belief also.

We have purposefully emphasised the fact that the immune system cannot be seen in isolation, as a hermetically sealed system. Nevertheless, it is likely that many readers of this book will not have a working background knowledge of the structure and function of the immune system, so in the next chapter we attempt to provide some of the essential elements of immunology essential to the understanding of the PNI research which follows.

2
Introduction to the Immune System

Introduction

The immune system is the body's cellular and molecular defence force. It keeps a careful eye on the body's cells and tissues in order to guard against detrimental cell damage and invading foreign organisms. The principal cells of the immune system are represented in the circulation as the white blood cells or leukocytes, and we shall consider many types of these cells in this chapter at different points. These are of five general types: lymphocytes, neutrophils, monocytes, basophils and eosinophils. The general appearance of these cells and their normal representation in peripheral blood is illustrated in Table 2.1.

Although these are circulating cells they can mass in tissues in response to infection and also populate lymphoid organs such as the spleen and lymph nodes in order to communicate and co-ordinate their activities. Because these cells can be easily harvested from the peripheral circulation and their behaviour observed to some extent in tissue culture, the view has grown that the immune system is autonomous, requiring no direction from other sensory modalities. In fact, as we shall soon see, there are many channels of communication between the nervous system and immune system and the talk is in both directions. Before this cross-talk can be examined and its significance appraised it is necessary to understand what the immune system is and what it does.

At the most fundamental level, the immune system responds to foreign molecules, which are expressed on cell surfaces or are released as soluble products. These are termed antigens. They have no legitimate business in the body and could be harmful. How the immune system recognises antigen is a complex business and it is done in a number of ways and at different levels. In essence, recognition of foreignness at a molecular level does not differ from other forms of molecular recognition that are required for cellular communication, such as communication between nerve cells through chemical

12

Table 2.1 Appearance and proportional representation of cells of the immune system in human peripheral blood

Cell type	Size μm	Number per μl	Percentage of total leukocytes
Neutrophil	10–12	2800–5250	40–75%
Eosinophil	10–12	70–420	1–6%
Basophil	9–10	0–70	< 1%
Lymphocyte	7–8	1400–3150	20–45%
Monocyte	14–17	140–700	2–10%

Note: Basophils and monocytes are found in the circulation. In tissues they are referred to as mast cells and macrophages respectively.

transmitter substances at synapses, an example which should already be familiar to most readers. The job of the immune system is to co-ordinate information regarding the emergence of foreign molecular species and mount defensive action to eliminate the intruder. Defence is achieved by what are called effector mechanisms and these follow two different routes.

Humoral versus Cell-Mediated Immunity

The immune system can mount antibody defence. Antibodies are secreted protein molecules capable of specifically binding to antigen and, via a number of ancillary mechanisms, clearing it from the body. This route involves what we call humoral immunity. Alternatively, a more appropriate response may be to recruit aggressive cells that have cell-destroying (so-called 'cytotoxic') capacity. On making contact with their target antigenic cell, again as a result of specific binding, they are capable of destroying it. There are a number of cell types with this capacity but collectively this route involves what is called cellular or cell-mediated immunity. On the whole, antibody-mediated immunity is effective against microbes which exist outside the body's cells (extracellular organisms) and against their toxic products, which are readily accessible. Cell-mediated immunity, on the other hand, defends us against organisms such as viruses which can live and replicate inside our cells. In this case, infected cells are usually killed. Elegantly in both cases the molecules that are used in the initial recognition event are also employed as binding molecules to target and focus these effector mechanisms. The decision as to which of these two courses of action predominates in response to antigen challenge is an important one and has much bearing on disease and the resolution of disease. Of great importance in the context of this book, the nervous system plays no small part in the necessary decision making.

The Discrimination of Self and Non-Self

The immune system protects the cellular integrity of the body. To do this it must distinguish Self from Non-Self. Self is healthy, functional integrated cells and tissue; Non-Self (that is, antigen) is unhealthy, dysfunctional, non-integrated tissue and of course foreign invading organism. The body devotes considerable resources to this vital task.

The immune system has a number of innate defences. They are called innate because they are always in place regardless of whether the body is facing any particular challenge. These range from physical barriers, like the skin, which micro-organisms cannot easily penetrate, to cellular defences such as are provided by phagocytic cells (macrophages, the tissue equivalent of circulating monocytes and neutrophils), which guard our organs and tissues. These cells have the innate capacity to recognise the surface features of bacteria. Once identified the bacterial cell is engulfed and phagocytosed (eaten). Recognition is the key event, the ability to distinguish Self from Non-Self, and here it is based upon 'pattern recognition' – the general organisation of surface molecules which distinguishes a bacterial cell from a mammalian cell (see Mahoney and Gordon, 1998).

However, as evolutionary forces drove animal life to greater complexity, longevity and metabolic activity, pattern recognition as the basis for Self versus Non-Self discrimination was no longer sufficiently precise to cope with all eventualities. Greater subtlety was required in order to recognise organisms that had learned how to avoid direct detection on the basis of broad 'pattern recognition'. Moreover, protection based upon cell to cell defence (hand to hand combat, as it were) was no longer sufficient, given the cosy environment for microbial activity that the vertebrate body now provided. Means would have to be found to recruit and marshal more potent defensive resources. The immune system developed the capacity to scan precise molecular detail in making Self versus Non-Self discriminations. Warm-blooded vertebrates (birds and mammals) mark a culmination in these developments. In addition to the rather general innate molecular recognition exhibited by such cells as phagocytes, triggering of immune responses became based upon so-called epitope recognition. The term 'epitope' is a key term for this chapter and one the reader will need to become familiar with. Epitopes are small details of molecular structure. A bacterial cell may fool a phagocyte into considering it to be Self on the basis of its general surface appearance but it cannot avoid more specific epitope recognition: from your general demeanour, I thought you were my brother but now I see your face I know you are not.

Molecules can express epitopes in two ways: surface configurations revealed by the three-dimensional conformation of the molecule and internal linear sequences of chemical subunits (see below). Many different types of molecule can express surface epitopes but only protein molecules can provide the appropriate sequence information for epitope recognition.

All organisms are composed of macromolecules, which sometimes form associations such as membranes. Each macromolecule in turn is made up of subunits; nucleic acids, amino acids, sugars and lipids – the building blocks of life. Hence every macromolecule carries a defining fingerprint described by the epitopes it expresses. External epitopes are literally the electron clouds of groups of atoms forming lumps and bumps on the molecular surface, like the craters on the moon. Internal epitopes are amino acid sequences forming the primary structure (peptide chains) of protein molecules. The cells of the immune system that see the molecular world of an organism to this degree of resolution are lymphocytes. To understand how this is done proved one of the most fascinating stories in biology, but it is also a story which should deepen the understanding of anyone interested in the interdisciplinary findings of PNI research.

Cells of all types receive most of their information about the world that surrounds them through the expression of specific receptors. Receptors are proteins whose three dimensional folding pattern provides a receptor site (or paratope). Into this site can fit a signalling molecule (or ligand). Ligand–receptor interaction then, through various signalling systems influences the behaviour of the cell. Ligands can be free soluble molecules as is the case with neurotransmitters and hormones or they can be expressed on the surface of other cells. If the latter is the case then communication requires cellular contact.

The information that lymphocytes receive about the world of Non-Self (antigens) is of like nature. Uniquely for lymphocytes the antigen receptors expressed on their surface are designed to recognise epitopes. Herein lies a conceptual difficulty. It is easy to appreciate that, for instance, a liver cell expresses a surface receptor for insulin in order to be responsive to the hormone. There is only one insulin molecule and the liver cell knows exactly how to construct a receptor that will selectively bind to it. The epitopic universe is virtually infinite. How does the lymphocyte population know how to make receptors that can recognise this vast diversity of molecular triggers?

Two possibilities were considered. The lymphocyte, as a result of contact with an antigen might gain information about its epitopic make up, so as to synthesise the appropriate receptor specificity. This view of things is expressed by the so-called 'instructional hypothesis' where the epitope in some way provides a template to direct the construction of the specific receptor site. Alternatively, each lymphocyte may only express one predetermined receptor specificity. Contact with an epitope that can bind to the specific receptor site would trigger an immune response. Clearly, if this model is correct, then specificity for any particular epitope would only be expressed by a tiny proportion of the lymphocyte population. Hence, before an effective immune response can be mounted it would be necessary for these selected clones to proliferate and expand the response. This in essence is the clonal selection hypothesis, which was refined and developed by Burnet, Jerne and Talmadge in the 1950s (see Kuby, 1997). Fundamentally, the lymphocyte contribution to immune defence is indeed organised in this way.

Clonal expansion requires time: time for the initially tiny proportion of lymphocytes with the correct receptors to meet the specific epitopes of the foreign antigen, and time also to proliferate and produce clones of themselves. Thus it is several days following infection before lymphocyte responses can contribute to protection. During this time the body relies upon innate defences such as the spontaneous activity of macrophages and a bacteriolytic enzyme cascade called 'complement' and the induction of what is known as 'the acute phase response' before the forces of lymphocyte-mediated immune defence can be marshalled. Infection results in the release from local tissue of inflammatory mediators. These induce a whole host of adaptive physiological and behavioural responses. The liver is stimulated to release acute phase proteins into the circulation. These proteins in a number of ways can damage bacteria. Body temperature rises by a few degrees. This 'fever' enhances the rate at which lymphocytes proliferate but inhibits bacterial growth. Sickness behaviour is induced. There is general withdrawal from social activity, loss of interest in feeding and sexual behaviour, which require exploration and energy expenditure; instead there is a shift towards rest and energy conservation. The acute phase response and its implications for brain–immune system interactions is discussed in more detail in future chapters.

   Although clonal expansion delays the recruitment into the fray, of lymphocyte-mediated defence forces it does mean that once they have been mobilised they are considerable and exact. Large numbers of cells are now armed with a precise recognition molecule that can be used in the identification and destruction of the cellular enemy. In addition, clonal expansion not only results in large populations of effector cells but also memory cells. Memory cells are small resting cells that remain dormant until alerted again by challenge with the same antigen that triggered the initial response. This secondary challenge does not encounter a naïve lymphocyte population but one reinforced with expanded populations of memory cells, all with the capacity to recognise the epitopes that characterise the challenge. We have seen this enemy before and there are numerous cells with the capacity to

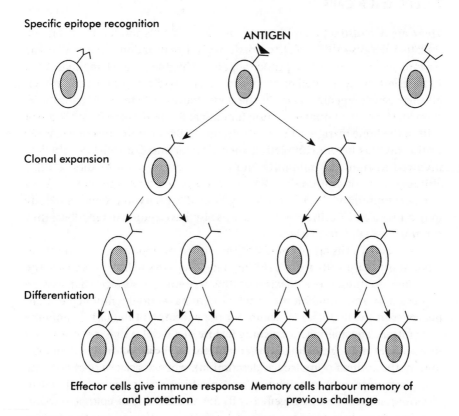

Figure 2.1   Clonal proliferation of lymphocytes driven primarily by antigen, which follows two pathways to produce an expanded population of short-lived effector cells, and also an expanded population of long-lived memory cells retaining specificity for antigen

respond. The response is quantitatively and qualitatively different; it is more precise, more potent and more rapid. This of course is the physiological basis of vaccination and underlies the phenomenon that for many infectious diseases we can develop sterile immunity, suffering sickness (the acute phase response) only on the first wave of infection.

This happy state of affairs unfortunately does not apply to every challenge to the immune system. In relation to many pathogens, all the immune system can perform is a holding operation, restraining the virulence of the organism to tolerable levels. The balance is often delicate and, as will be seen in future chapters, much influenced by psychological processes.

The basic concept of clonal selection is illustrated in Figure 2.1.

T Cells and B Cells

There are two distinct lymphocyte populations, T cells and B cells. T cells are so-called because they need to go through a maturational process in the thymus and are therefore dependent upon it. The thymus is a lymphoid organ in the chest cavity situated just above the heart. B cells by contrast go through all their developmental stages in the bone marrow where all blood cells are formed. Hence in mammals mature functional B cells develop from precursor cells in the bone marrow whereas T cells must migrate from the bone marrow to the thymus before completing their development. B cells are crucially involved in humoral immunity and are the source of antibodies. T cells, although they do not produce antibody, do play a vital supporting role in humoral immunity. B cells have a very limited capacity to produce antibody in the absence of T cells. However, T cells also have cytotoxic functions: they can find and kill target cells.

B cells and T cells are not easily distinguished by appearance. In the circulation most of the cells are in a resting state; they are small and compact. The smallness of these cells maximises the recognition surface that can be expressed by the population as a whole. We have more lymphocytes than neurones in the brain, an indication of the enormity of the task of immune recognition. The main distinguishing feature of a B cell is that it expresses on its surface immunoglobulin (another term for antibody but more commonly used in the context of molecular description), whereas a T cell does not. The B cell's surface immunoglobulin is the all-important receptor that can recognise an epitope of antigen. T cells are also capable of epitope recognition but do so in a different way and employ a different receptor for the purpose. B cells not only express surface immunoglobulin but can also be driven, as a result of epitope contact and recognition, to proliferate and differentiate into a population of plasma cells. Plasma cells bear all the characteristics of cells specialised to produce large amounts of protein for export. The protein they secrete is a modified version of their surface immunoglobulin. This then is the antibody which appears in body fluids and, by binding to antigen as an effector molecule, plays a key role in humoral immune defence.

The Structure of Antibody

The structure of the antibody molecule has been very well characterised, and, since antibody measures are referred to throughout this book, it is useful to provide a simple description of the sort of molecule which is measured. Immunoglobulin, the antibody molecule, is protein; protein consists of chains of polypeptides; and polypeptides in turn are made from smaller building blocks called amino acids. Fundamentally, immunoglobulin consists of four polypeptide chains. Two are 'heavy' chains (each composed of about 450 amino acids) and two are 'light' chains about half that long. The two heavy chains, arranged alongside each other, are joined together by various bonds and a light chain joined to each heavy chain but only along half its length. The molecule could be envisaged as having a Y-shaped structure, the two arms of the Y are the regions where the heavy and light chains overlap and the tail of the Y is formed by the additional sequence of the heavy chains alone. In any given molecule the two heavy chains are identical, as are the two light chains. The regions of epitope recognition (antigen binding) are restricted to the arms of the Y whereas the tail mediates various effector functions. It is a bifunctional molecule, the arms targeting antigen and the tail delivering the killer punch. This structure is illustrated in Figure 2.2.

The chains are not just linear sequences of amino acids but each is folded in a defined way into what is known as the 'domain structure', each domain encompassing about 110 amino acids. Light chains express two such domains, and heavy chains, usually, four. The domain is the level of organisation that gives the molecule its functional capabilities. We need not trouble ourselves with the details of domain structure here but some appreciation of the organisation of domains on an antibody molecule is necessary. In recent years the 'immunoglobulin domain' has been recognised as a feature of many protein molecules that play recognition roles in the immune system (and other tissues) but do not have antibody activity. Antibody (immunoglobulin) is now considered to be just one member (although a rather special member) of this immunoglobulin superfamily.

There is a considerable degree of variability, comparing one molecule with another, in amino acids composing certain parts of the antigen-targeting arms of the Y as might be expected, since different amino acids have different shapes and different shapes fit different epitopes. Hence the domains in which this

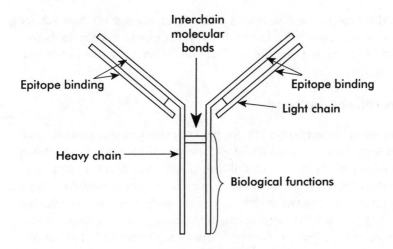

Figure 2.2   The polypeptide chain structure of the bifunctional antibody molecule. The arms of the Y formed by both light and heavy chains bind epitopes (and hence antigen–antibody binding sites). The heavy chain tail directs biological activity including effector functions

variation is expressed are called variable domains (one on the light chain and one on the heavy). The light and heavy chain variable domains are oriented together to form a single antigen binding site. The other domains are called 'constant' because they have fixed biological roles. Their job is to support the variable domains on the arms of the Y, and in addition the heavy chain domains, that extend into the tail of the molecule, determine its effector function and distribution within the body. There are five major variants of the heavy chain tail domains which give rise to the different antibody classes or isotypes called IgM, IgG, IgA, IgD and IgE, each with its special role in immune defence. Which class of antibody predominates in an immune response depends upon the nature of antigen challenge (including psychological influences) and the part of the body suffering invasion.

The typical organisation of domains in an antibody molecule is illustrated in Figure 2.3.

IgM and IgG are the dominant forms of antibody in the blood and both can focus blood defences on to a target antigen. Relevant defences include phagocytosis, which we have already mentioned where antibodies locked on to antigen can amplify the innate recognition ability of phagocytic cells. These antibodies can also promote complement activation. Complement, we will recall, is an enzyme cascade which when triggered and targeted can destroy bacterial cell walls. Complement is part of our innate defences since it can be

IgG

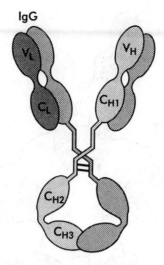

Figure 2.3 A more realistic representation of an antibody molecule (IgG), showing also the constant (C) domains (numbered 1–3) and variable (V) domains. Also shown are the heavy (H) and light (L) chains (adapted from Kuby, 1997)

triggered by bacterial surface membrane features alone. The contribution of IgM and IgG antibody is to focus and markedly enhance complement activation. IgA is produced by the mucosal immune system and defends the body's internal surfaces: gut, lung and urinogenital membranes. IgE has a special role in inducing allergic responses. IgD is expressed on the B cell surface as an epitope receptor but is thought not to have an effector function as a secreted antibody.

Antibody can exist as single Ys, as it were, or they can be joined together as composite molecules. Thus IgM is 'pentameric', that is, it consists of five identical Ys. IgA can be formed as a monomer (a single Y) or a dimer, trimer, tetramer or pentamer, though as we shall see later it exists in mucosal secretions largely as two joined Ys (that is, in dimeric form). The other classes only exist in the monomeric form. The advantage of more 'arms' to a molecule is that there is more to hang on to at an antigenic surface. For antibody classes which are monomeric this advantage is outweighed by greater precision in epitope binding ('affinity') and the requirement to be small and mobile. IgM is the dinosaur of the antibody family appearing early in evolution and also early in an immune response. In essence it is useful but clumsy. Its individual sites have less affinity but the large molecule is sticky, as it were, and can effectively immobilise antigen (so-called 'avidity'). The domain structures of pentameric IgM are illustrated in Figure 2.4.

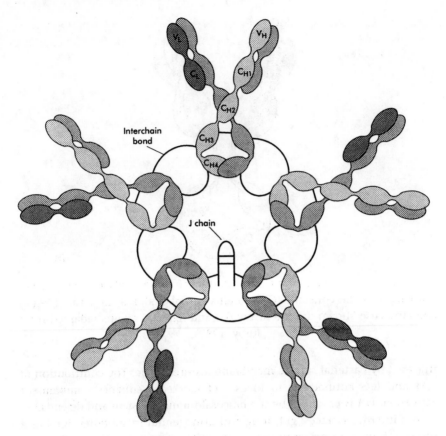

Figure 2.4 A representation of the IgM molecule, showing how individual Ys are joined to form a 'pentameric' overall structure (adapted from Kuby, 1997)

Generation of Antibody Diversity

We have said already that immunoglobulin is a bifunctional molecule. Evolution has generated and expanded variability in the variable domain to facilitate epitope recognition but the constant domains direct biological function and are relatively stable. If a complete gene were required to encode each immunoglobulin polypeptide chain with all the variants that constitute the recognition repertoire (once the prevailing view), many metres of genetic information would be required – far more than is available within the entire human genome.

What if different genes are responsible for encoding the variable domain as opposed to the constant domain? This was the radical idea proposed by Dryer and Bennett in 1965. It was envisaged that a process of gene rearrangement must take place during a B cell's development to bring together a randomly selected 'variable gene', encoding the variable domain with an appropriate 'constant gene' encoding the constant domains to form a continuous message. This would be very efficient since only a few genes would be required to encode the different constant domains, which make up the bulk of the molecule. The variable domains would require a large library of genes but only encoding the amino acid sequence of the variable domain. This notion of how the variable domain is generated turned out to be essentially correct and a huge saving in terms of the coding information required.

The impact of these molecular biology findings was stunning. It was a complete revelation that genes could be shuffled around like a pack of cards and dealt out in the immune system's game of poker. Just as in poker, there is a small leeway to change one or two cards but once the hand is decided the cell is committed. The cell makes productive gene rearrangements which are expressed on the surface as a unique receptor. The cell is said to be 'mono-specific'. Every antibody molecule the cell makes, either expressed on the surface as a receptor or released as an effector molecule, will have identical variable domains, the product of the unique gene rearrangement for that cell.

There are winners and losers. The hand that the cell has been dealt determines its fate. Some will be invited (by antigen) to participate in an immune response, simply because their receptor specificity happens to fit. Others will be redundant and never called up in the body's defence. Still others are dangerous because they express a Self specificity, that is, they recognise Self as antigen. These the body must delete.

Monoclonal Antibodies

The monospecificity of antibody-producing cells has been exploited techni-cally. In a physiological immune response many B cells are recruited since many different epitopes are seen on the antigen surface. Thus naturally produced antibody is always polyclonal with many specificities represented. If it were possible to persuade an antibody-producing cell to grow and divide in culture then a population of cells could be derived from a single cloned cell. Antibody-producing cells do not live long and die in culture. Techniques were devised to immortalise them. This was first achieved by Millstein and Kohler in 1979. It is now possible to harvest antibodies in culture from a single cloned pure cell line. These are called monoclonal antibodies. Because they are mono-specific they reliably identify a single epitopic determinant. Their applications have revolutionised medicine and biology (see Ritter and Ladyman, 1995). One application is to identify particular cell types by using monoclonals that selectively bind to characteristic cell surface markers (so-called CD molecules). The different populations and subpopulations of the immune system are characterised in this way. Much application has been made of this approach in PNI research in order to determine the representation of different immune cell populations in relation to psychological processes.

The T Cell Receptor

What of the T cell receptor? Immunoglobulin could not be detected on the surface of T cells so the T cell receptor (TcR) had to be different. Also, T cells are restricted in the way they recognise antigen. Cytotoxic T cells can respond to a virally infected cell and kill it but they cannot bind free virus or viral antigen. It seemed they could not respond to native antigen in its natural form, they could only respond to processed antigen presented on the body's own cell surfaces.

So the T cell receptor had to be different, but characterising its structure proved to be difficult. The main problem was that T cells don't mass produce their TcR and secrete it into body fluids in any way analogous to antibody. There was no material to work with. Sophisticated techniques to explore the molecular surface of the T cell had to be developed before the TcR could be described. Eventually it was tracked down and characterised. This receptor belongs to the immunoglobulin superfamily of recognition molecules which we have previously mentioned. It consists of just two distinct chains, each anchored to the surface membrane of the T cell, but extracellularly each chain is composed of two immunoglobulin domains. There is a variable domain, which takes part in epitope recognition, and there is a constant domain. The genetic basis of the generation of TcR diversity is comparable to that of immunoglobulin.

Why should the T cell, using similar genetic mechanisms to generate diversity, utilise a different but related molecule to recognise an antigenic signal? The answer is simple. It sees a different kind of epitope. The B cell surface immunoglobulin recognises the surface features of an antigenic molecule whereas the TcR recognises 'information' about the amino acid sequence of peptides. Since only proteins are composed of amino acid sequences, T cells can only respond to protein-derived epitopes. Moreover, the B cell recognises epitopes on the surface of the native antigen in its natural form. Peptide sequences within a protein molecule must be made accessible to the T cell before they can be recognised. Other cells are required to process the protein into its peptide sequence components and display these peptide epitopes on their surface where they are exposed to the T cell. The essential point, in other words, is that T cells can only see an epitope displayed on the surface of another cell.

More than this, T cells can only see an epitope displayed upon a Self cell – one that legitimately belongs in the body. This is crucial since the T cell must recognise and interact with Self cells. The relevant molecules for Self recognition are known as MHC molecules. (The acronym derives from the fact that they are encoded in a genetic locus called the major histocompatibility complex, or MHC.) Each individual expresses a more or less unique set of MHC molecules upon their cell surfaces. We inherit a particular set of genes to encode for these molecules from a very large gene family in the human gene pool. Inheritance of these genes and expression of their products defines the individuality of a person's cells. T cells are educated to recognise only foreign peptide displayed by the individual's own particular MHC molecules.

The Role of MHC Molecules

There are two important types of MHC molecule: class I and class II. Class I MHC molecules are displayed on the surface of every nucleated cell. The expression of class II molecules on the other hand is restricted to cells of the immune system, principally B cells and macrophages. Class I MHC molecules display foreign peptides usually derived from the protein synthesis activities of a virus that is infecting the cell. On the other hand, class II molecules display peptides derived from proteins that originate outside the cell, exogenous protein. In this latter case the cell must first internalise the foreign protein. Both B cells and macrophages exhibit this capacity. There are two very different types of T cell designed to recognise these different signals and respond accordingly; helper T (Th) cells and cytotoxic T cells (CTL). As the name implies, helper T cells are designed to facilitate the activity of other immune system cells, such as B cells or macrophages. Cytotoxic T cells, by contrast, kill a cell that reveals the foreign peptide with class I MHC signal. This is appropriate since one of the most effective ways of dealing with a viral infection is to kill cells that harbour the virus.

Cytotoxic T Cells

Cytotoxic T cells are characterised by their expression of a surface molecule called CD8. The CD8 molecule performs an adhesion function, binding to the class I MHC molecule and thus helps to stabilise the contact between the cytotoxic T cell and its target. They are therefore often referred to as CD8+ T cells. These cells perform the role of immunosurveillance. Cells that begin to manufacture an unusual protein are potential targets. Such cells will display the peptide products of aberrant protein synthesis as T cell epitopes for CTL recognition. Normal healthy cells also display peptide products of endogenous protein synthesis but the T cell recognition repertoire is blind to these signals. Unusual protein synthesis reveals an abnormal cell. The cell may have acquired new gene coding sequences or a defunct regulatory system may lead to the expression of otherwise dormant genes. This is commonly the case in viral infection or the development of cancer cells. Sometimes this may actually be the same thing since the insertion of viral genes into the cell's genome may trigger cellular transformation and cancer development. Whatever the mechanism for the genesis of dysfunction, an important role for our CTL population is to flush out diseased cells of this nature and eliminate them.

CD8+ cells not only respond to the foreign peptide + Self MHC signal but also to foreign MHC such as would be found on the cells of an unrelated ('allogeneic') person. 'Allograft' rejection is a concern in organ transplantation. Where possible, attempts are made to match the donor to the recipient such that MHC differences are relatively inconspicuous. Immunosuppressive drugs are targeted at the aggressive CTL response. Remarkably, evidence has accumulated over recent years, in animal models, that this kind of immunosuppression can be classically conditioned such that immunosuppression can be transferred from drug to conditioned stimulus. This aspect of brain–immune relationship is discussed in detail in Chapter 7.

The natural context in which the immune system is provoked by 'alloantigens' is their expression on foetal membranes, which are exposed to the maternal immune system in the placenta. The maternal immune system must engineer its own immunosuppression to prevent immunological rejection, which would result in spontaneous abortion. Hormone changes during pregnancy are thought to play a major role in directing the immune system away from aggressive cell-mediated responses (Raghupathy, 1997), what we now call a shift in the Th1/Th2 balance (see below). This is an interesting example of the immune system's sensitivity to physiological changes and will be touched upon again in future chapters.

Helper T Cells and the Th1/Th2 Balance

Helper T cells express the surface molecule CD4. In like fashion to CD8 its function is to form an attachment to the class II MHC during cellular association. In this case, however, the associating cell is not a target to be hit but a co-operative cell to be helped. Help signals are delivered in the form of cell surface ligand–receptor interactions but also in the form of secreted molecules of communication. These secreted molecules, which can extend the range of communication to neighbouring and even distant cells, belong to a family of proteins called cytokines. It is tempting to liken them to hormones, although their effective range is usually not as far as classical hormones which are carried to distant target cells in the circulatory system. This kind of more local communication is referred to as paracrine rather than endocrine. The distinctions, however, are blurred.

A major advance in understanding the immune system in recent years has been the recognition that there are two types of Th response. The responses are distinguished by the pattern of cytokine production (for review see Romagnani, 1997, and also Murray, 1998). A T helper type 1 (Th1) response is characterised mainly by the secretion of interleukin 2 (IL-2) gamma interferon (IFN-γ) and tumour necrosis factor beta (TNF-β). These activate macrophages, promote macrophage-mediated inflammatory reactions and are stimulatory to CTLs and Natural Killer (NK) cells. NK cells are also cytotoxic cells but have the innate ability to recognise target cells by pattern recognition rather like innate recognition capacity of macrophages. All these processes are broadly referred to as cellular or cell-mediated immunity. A different cocktail of cytokines is secreted in a T helper type 2 (Th2) response. These are inter-leukin 4 (IL-4), IL-5, IL-6, IL-10 and IL-13. These stimulate humoral immunity, including preferential secretion of IgA and IgE. Activated macrophages produce IL-12 which sustains the Th1 response and both CTLs and NK cells can produce type 1 cytokines, thus promoting their own activity. The distinction is not absolute and there is a further population of cells T0 that can produce a mix of both Th1 and Th2 cytokines, nor is it clear whether a particular T cell is irrevocably committed to the Th1 or Th2 subset, although recent evidence suggests that this is probably the case. What is clear is that the two types of T cell are counter-regulatory. IL-4 and IL-10 inhibits the activity of Th1 cells and INF-γ inhibits Th2 cells. Hence the immune system is balanced between cell-mediated and humoral immunity. How this balance is set depends upon the prevailing nature of pathogen challenge and the environment within which T cell help is activated. This can change and there is abundant evidence that prolonged experience of psychological stress shifts the balance away from Th1 activity in favour of Th2 (see Chapter 5 in particular).

It is thought that Th1 responses are provoked by intracellular micro-organisms. Certain organisms can escape phagocytic killing and therefore live inside the macrophage. A strong Th1 response with the accompanying inflammatory process and macrophage activation stabilises the infection and favours macrophage clearance. One form of IgG, sometimes referred to as cytotoxic antibody, is actually stimulated by the Th1 cytokine, IFN-γ. The general distinction between Th1 – cellular immunity, and Th2 – humoral immunity, still holds since this form of antibody contributes to cellular defence. Th1 domination and CTL and NK cell stimulation is effective against viral infection during the intracellular phase and is also thought to be important in defence against cancer.

By contrast, humoral immunity is most effective against extracellular organisms, most notably helminthic parasites that can gain entry to the body. An effective immune response to helminthes (certain forms of worm, mostly parasitic) is associated with Th2 activation, which promotes IgE synthesis,

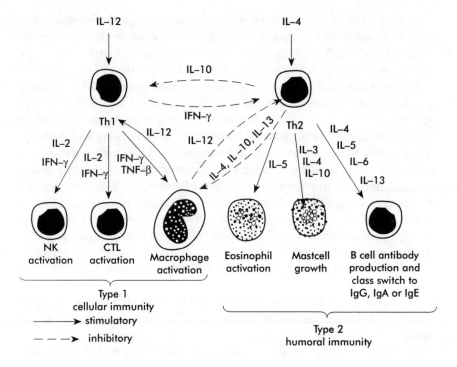

Figure 2.5   The influence of Th1 and Th2 cytokines
and counter-regulatory pathways

mast cell growth (cells which when stimulated by IgE produce the powerful inflammatory agent called histamine) and the growth and differentiation of eosinophils, cells which are particularly adapted to the killing of antibody-coated parasites. These latter two cell types play important roles in immune defence against helminthes. The Th2 immune system, driving IgA production, is also important in mucosal defence.

Inflammation is a response to microbial invasion and tissue damage. Initially it can be generated very rapidly as a result of the recruitment of mediators that are part of innate defence, the acute phase response. Th1 cells promote macrophage involvement in inflammatory processes. Macrophages present antigenic peptide to Th1 cells, and Th1 cells in turn produce macrophage stimulatory cytokines, most notably IFN-γ and TNF-β. Activated macrophages release inflammatory cytokines such as IL-1 which, amongst other adaptive changes, signal to the brain to induce fever and sickness-related behaviour. Hence fever and feelings of sickness or malaise are associated with Th1 activity.

Another kind of inflammatory process is associated with Th2 activation. This is the infiltration of tissue by eosinophils and basophils stimulated by IgE-promoted degranulation of mast cells (a form of basophil). This is the allergic response seen in atopic individuals. Although Th1 and Th2 responses can be seen as opposite ends of a spectrum both can result in inflammatory tissue damage. Examples can be seen in two lung diseases, tuberculosis and asthma. The Th1-mediated macrophage inflammatory response is important in defence against tuberculosis. This can result in damage to the lung but is important in preventing bacterial colonisation and stabilises the infection. By contrast, in asthma an overactive Th2 response resulting in IgE-mediated inflammation is responsible for pathology. Psychological stress pushes the immunological balance towards Th2 domination. Hence during sustained periods of stress, such as might be experienced in war zones, there is a resurgence of tuberculosis due to loss of Th1 control and an increase in the incidence of asthma as a result of overly active IgE-mediated processes (Rook, 1997). Paradoxically, although steroidal anti-inflammatory drugs are effective (and commonly used) in alleviating the acute symptoms of asthma and other forms of allergy, in the longer term their use may be detrimental since, as will be seen later, they promote Th2 immunity, the imbalance that underlies the atopic condition (Blotta *et al.*, 1997).

The counter-regulatory influence that Th1 and Th2 cells exert upon each other means that certain kinds of immune activity are incompatible (immune deviation). For instance, individuals who develop juvenile onset (type 1) diabetes, a Th1-driven inflammatory disease in which healthy tissue is damaged, are less prone to develop asthma, a Th2-driven atopic disorder (Douek *et al.*, 1999). An inherited bias in the immune system is intimated since protection from asthma is also seen in siblings of diabetics who do not themselves develop type 1 diabetes. Support for this cross-regulatory influence over disease susceptibility is drawn from animal models. An inbred strain of mouse with the genetic characteristic to develop type 1 diabetes is protected by exposure to helminth worm larvae, which stimulate a strong Th2 response. Appreciation of the importance of these reciprocal influences opens new possibilities for therapeutic intervention (for reviews see Abbas *et al.*, 1996; Rocken *et al.*, 1996; Rook, 1997).

The Th1/Th2 balance is subject to regulation by the neuroendocrine system (see Rook and Lightman, 1997). One reason for this is that, in order to prevent polarisation, the Th1/Th2 balance oscillates between nocturnal Th1 domination and diurnal Th2 domination (Petrovsky and Harrison, 1995; 1997). This is adaptive since the fever, malaise and loss of function associated with Th1 inflammatory processes are appropriately directed to a period of sleep and inactivity. As might be expected, sleep deprivation (only partial deprivation) adversely effects Th1 immunity (Irwin *et al.*, 1996). Neuroen-

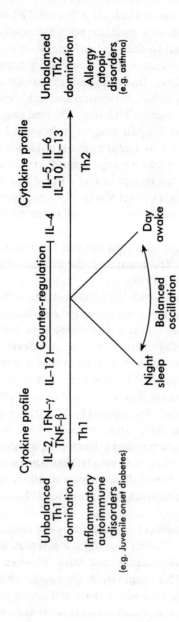

Figure 2.6 The Th1/Th2 balance of the immune system

Unbalanced
Th1
domination

Inflammatory
autoimmune
disorders
(e.g. Juvenile onset diabetes)

Cytokine profile

Th1

IL-2, IFN-γ
TNF-β

IL-12

Counter-regulation

IL-4

Night
sleep

Balanced
oscillation

Day
awake

Th2

IL-5, IL-6
IL-10, IL-13

Cytokine profile

Unbalanced
Th2
domination

Allergy
atopic
disorders
(e.g. asthma)

docrine systems which exhibit pronounced circadian patterns in relation to sleep and the nocturnal/diurnal cycle are thought to regulate Th1/Th2 activity in relation to this cycle. Of particular importance in this respect is the hypothalamic-pituitary-adrenal (HPA) axis, the neuroendocrine system, which we shall see in Chapter 3 is crucially involved both in stress responding to psychological inputs but also in immune regulation. Hence, superimposed upon the circadian cycle, psychological inputs can prejudice the Th1/Th2 balance. This has important implications for infection and the progress of disease and will be discussed in more detail in later chapters.

The counter-regulatory balance in Th1/Th2 immune system activity and some of the consequences of imbalance are illustrated in Figure 2.6. As will be seen in Chapter 5, chronic experience of stress pushes the balance in favour of Th2 immunity whereas acute stress challenge is often associated with a 'transient' up-regulation of Th1 cellular immunity. Pregnancy also promotes Th2 domination.

Central Tolerance

Recall that a T cell, from whatever subpopulation, responds to two signals: Self MHC together with Non-Self peptide. Yet the mechanisms of gene rearrangement that generate the required extensive repertoire of receptor specificities do so with no or little cognition of this requirement. A truly vast repertoire of TcR specificities, estimated at about 10^{15}, is generated by gene rearrangement. These cells then go through a selection process to test if they meet the requirements, first to recognise Self MHC. This is positive selection and these cells are saved. Cells that fail to do this are killed. After this selection process cells are tested for their ability to recognise Self MHC plus Self peptide. Any such cell would be autoreactive (autoimmunity) and have the dangerous ability to react against normal healthy cells if released into the periphery. These are also killed. This is called negative selection. The vast majority of T cells fail to meet these two selection criteria and are deleted. Although the thymus is the T cell nursery and the environment it provides facilitates T cell differentiation and development, it is a major site of T cell death. The immune system can afford to generate billions of cells with different specificities and then select in favour of those that are functional (can recognise Self MHC) and also delete those that are dangerous (can recognise Self peptide expressed by Self MHC, that is, a normal healthy cell).

Negative selection ensures tolerance towards healthy Self cells. Hence Self reactive T cells are eliminated and the periphery is populated only with T cells that recognise Self MHC and foreign peptide, CD4+ cells that recognise foreign peptide expressed by class II MHC and CD8+ cells that recognise class I MHC plus foreign peptide.

B cells also undergo a selection process but since there is no requirement of B cells to recognise Self MHC only negative selection is involved and the whole process takes place in the bone marrow. B cells that express autoantibodies against Self antigens present in bone marrow are killed. It is estimated that only 10 per cent of manufactured B cells make it into the circulation. Many are lost because of failure to negotiate negative selection in the bone marrow. In this way the immune system develops tolerance to Self antigens. Forbidden clones of autoreactive cells are deleted. This is often referred to as central tolerance since it takes place in the primary, or central, lymphoid organs, the bone marrow and thymus.

Peripheral Tolerance

An important development was the demonstration that tolerance can also be induced peripherally, that is, in lymphocytes that have survived central selection to become immunocompetent and have joined the peripheral re-circulating pool. Under certain circumstances exposure to what otherwise would be an antigenic stimulus can result in the selective deletion of the immune response. This is selective since responses to other unrelated antigenic stimuli are not impaired. It will already be apparent to the reader that activation of an immune response depends upon a complex cascade of signals and cellular interactions. If everything is in place a potent immune response will ensue. Absence of a key trigger may result not just in failure of the response but paralysis of the reacting cells. These findings had far-reaching implications for immunotherapy: those circumstances where it is desirable to up-regulate, as in vaccination, or down-regulate, as in prevention of organ graft rejection, the microenvironment in which activation takes place and the presence or absence of stimulatory signals from associated cells determines the direction of immune responsiveness or unresponsiveness. It is the aim of immunosuppressive therapy (as in preventing organ graft rejection) to accurately target specific activation events and tip the response towards tolerance without upsetting the balance of the immune system as a whole. There is a growing body of evidence that both immunogenicity (up-regulation) and tolerogenicity (down-regulation) can be promoted by classical conditioning (see Chapter 7). As specified some years ago (Marx, 1985) 'The immune system belongs in the body' and we cannot fully understand it if we overlook this simple adage.

Secondary Lymphoid Organs

Secondary lymphoid organs, lymph nodes, spleen and mucosal associated lymphoid tissue provide the environment in which these complex cellular interactions, in response to antigen, take place. Antigen in tissues is carried to the nearest draining lymph node. Antigen in the blood circulatory system is trapped in the spleen and the organised mucosal associated lymphoid tissue (OMALT) intercepts antigens penetrating the mucosal surfaces. These organs have a structure that enhances cellular signalling and interaction with antigen.

Fluid that seeps from the blood into tissue spaces collects into lymphatic capillaries. The lymphatic circulation then carries it back towards the heart where it rejoins the blood circulatory system. Foreign antigens that gain access to tissues tend to be carried into this lymphatic circulation that drains all tissues of the body. Lymphocytes also circulate within the lymphatic system. Strategically placed along this system are lymph nodes, which are crucial places in the mobilisation of immune responses to antigen.

As it enters a lymph node, antigen encounters a network of antigen-trapping macrophages and dendritic cells. Dendritic cells are of the same lineage as macrophages and have fine, finger like projections to maximise cellular contact and interaction. There are also T cell areas and B cell areas and regions where T and B cells can interact. The cellular architecture within a lymph node facilitates the key business of antigen processing and presentation and triggering of both Th1 and Th2 type responses. Plasma cells migrate to the inner region of the node (medulla) where, now independent of T cell help, they get on with the job of secreting antibody which is carried away into the circulation.

The organisation of the lymphoid compartments of the spleen is essentially analogous but unlike lymph nodes, antigen is brought to the spleen via the blood circulatory system and is trapped by lymphoid tissue. Antigen is trapped in a T cell-rich area in order to be presented to T helper cells. Activated T helper cells can in turn stimulate B cells. Antigen challenge stimulates development of rapidly proliferating B cells just as in lymph nodes and these differentiate into plasma cells. CTL activation is also orchestrated in T cell areas of the spleen. On a daily basis more lymphocytes recirculate through the spleen than through all of the lymph nodes combined. Modulation of this splenic trafficking will markedly influence the absolute and relative proportions of lymphocyte populations in the peripheral circulation. Measurement of this index of lymphocyte trafficking is a common variable used to indicate psychological influences over immune activity (see Chapters 4 and 5 particularly).

The mucosal associated lymphoid tissue (MALT) protects the internal mucosal linings of the body. These include the bronchio-respiratory tract–lung, the gastrointestinal tract–gut and the urinogenital tract. Together these tracts represent a massive surface of about 400 square metres of only a single epithelial cell barrier against pathogen colonisation and penetration. This is the most vulnerable portal of pathogen entry and many infectious diseases originate at the mucosa. The only major exceptions are diseases that are carried by blood-feeding insect vectors that penetrate the skin (some parasitic worm larvae can also burrow through the skin directly), or infection consequential to traumatic injury and damage to the skin.

The immune system devotes considerable resources in defending mucosal surfaces. The number of plasma cells engaged in antibody production to protect these vulnerable surfaces far exceeds the plasma cell capacity of all other lymphoid tissue combined. Specialised cells which trap antigen are liberally represented among the mucosal epithelial cells. These cells trap micro-organism and antigenic particles on their surface and internalise them. Antigen is transported across the cell and released across the basal surface, which contains dense aggregates of B cells, T cells and macrophages. The key processes of antigen presentation and cellular interaction result in the activation, pro-liferation and differentiation into plasma cells that secrete the IgA isotype. This is very much Th2 immunity. However, IgA secretion is not local, since first the cells traffic into the circulatory system to colonise remote regions of the mucosa. This cellular traffic results in dispersal of the effector response so the entire mucosal surface can benefit from antibody protection regardless of the local site of antigen penetration. Thus plasma cells colonise what is referred to as the dispersed mucosal associated lymphoid tissue, or DMALT.

The epithelial cells really direct the show. These produce cytokines that finally drive the plasma cells to secrete IgA in its secretory form, predomi-nantly as a dimer (see above). In this form the antibody molecule can bind to a specialised receptor called the poly-Ig receptor. The IgA receptor complex is taken into and transported across the epithelial cell to be released on to the outer surface of the epithelial cells. Release involves cleavage of some of the poly-Ig receptor to cut away the major component, now known as the secretory component, still attached to the sIgA molecule. The secretory component is thought to be protective against enzymatic degradation of the antibody in the harsh mucosal environment. The dimeric IgA molecule together with the secretory component derived from the epithelial cell is referred to as secretory IgA ,or sIgA. As we shall see in later chapters, sIgA has been a much used measure in PNI research. The presence of sIgA in mucosal secretions such as saliva was first described by Thomasi in 1965 (see Thomasi, 1991). By binding to antigen the antibody contributes to immune exclusion of pathogens from mucosal surfaces. The organisation of the mucosal associated lymphoid tissue is illustrated in Figure 2.7.

Branches of the autonomic nervous system densely innervate lymphoid tissue and immunocytes lie in close proximity to nerve endings. Moreover, the microenvironment of lymph organs includes exposure to both locally produced and circulating hormones. Immune cells express specific receptors for the various neurotransmitters and hormones to which they are exposed during the activational processes that take place in lymphatic organs and

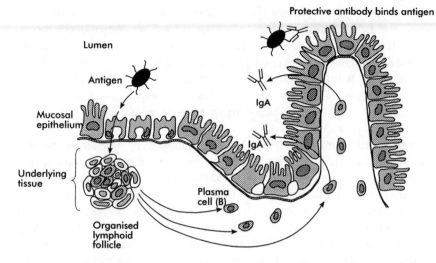

Figure 2.7 The role of sIgA in the defence of the mucosal epithelium. Antigen is trapped by specialised cells in the epithelium and transported to lymphoid cells in the underlying tissue. After stimulation plasma cells traffic to disperse the response. IgA is transported back across the epithelium to protect the mucosal surface (adapted from Kuby, 1997)

tissues. This is therefore an example of important pathways by which the brain can influence activity in the immune system. Afferent pathways also exist by which immune activity in lymphoid organs can influence the brain (see Chapter 3).

Immunoglobulin Class Switching

The mammalian humoral immune system does not become committed to the production of a single antibody class in response to any particular challenge. In the circulation the predominant isotypes are IgM and IgG which are effective against bacterial infection. Both can activate complement once they have bound to an antigenic surface and therefore enhance the spontaneous capacity for complement activation at bacterial cell surfaces. In the course of an immune response IgM appears early, peaking within a few days. IgM production subsequently declines and IgG levels begin to rise. Antibody-producing cells are able to switch from one class to another as the immune response matures. The basic, and primitive, isotype is IgM, but depending on the lymphoid microenvironment of activation, the nature of antigen challenge and the signals they receive from Th cells (predominantly Th2 cells), antibody-producing cells can switch to IgG, IgA or IgE. Class switching is more effectively and rapidly achieved after induction of memory. Hence in the blood, while the IgM response to a second immunological challenge by a previously recognised antigen is unchanged, IgG appears more rapidly and rises to much higher levels. It is considered that IgG represents an evolutionary advancement since it has higher 'affinity' for antigen binding, its small size allows it access to tissue spaces, and it is actively transported across the placenta to confer foetal protection.

In the mucosal immune system the dominant isotype is secretory IgA. It is specifically adapted for its defensive role at mucosal surfaces. Monomeric IgA, which is present in blood, cannot bind to the poly-Ig receptor and is therefore not transported across the epithelial lining. Various aspects of the structure of sIgA together with its secretory component equip it for its role in binding to and blocking microbial penetration and colonisation. Since the poly-Ig receptor can also bind to IgM this isotype can also be transported across the epithelial cellular barrier, but in normal individuals it probably makes only a limited contribution to mucosal defence.

Under certain circumstances a strong isotype switch to IgE characterises the response to antigen challenge. This is very much a Th2 dependent process and is driven by the Th2 cytokine IL-4. The role of IgE is unusual. It is in very low concentrations in the blood but becomes bound, via specific receptors, to the surface of mast cells and basophils. Subsequent interaction with antigen to this cell-bound antibody triggers degranulation and the release of a variety of pharmacologically active mediators, such as histamine, which give rise to the manifestations of allergy. This has been mentioned already but bears repetition. Allergic conditions such as hay fever and asthma are induced by this pathway. It may seem strange that some individuals show this hypersensitive response to what are fairly innocuous antigens in the environment, such as pollen. The biologically important stimulus is provided by helminthic parasites. The mediators released have anti-parasite effects and also recruit cells, important in defence against parasites, to the site of activation. Some individuals are said to be atopic since they respond in this way to inappropriate challenge.

The mechanisms of gene rearrangement that generate variable domain diversity also facilitate class switching. The immune system has the versatility to associate the gene system encoding the variable domain with a new heavy chain constant domain sequence, which we have seen is the basis of antibody class. Thus antibody can be produced with different biological functions without sacrificing the specificity of the response. The important point, however, is that class switch mechanisms and the T cells that direct them are thought to be influenced by psychological variables.

Conclusions

The immune system, over the past few decades, has been explored in enormous detail. Not surprisingly, it is pivotal between life and death, health and disease. Our understanding of it at the cellular and molecular level has grown at a fantastic pace. The molecular exploration of immunoglobulin gene rearrangement was a turning point. Questions that had puzzled immunologists for many years were beginning to be explained in the most refined detail. The description in this chapter is the barest outline. Molecular biology was driving immunology, and immunology was driving molecular biology. The reductionism approach was triumphant and biologists interested in the immune system's behaviour within the whole organism were marginalised. Nonetheless, evidence for both afferent and efferent channels of communication between the nervous, endocrine and immune systems continued to accumulate. Now, one of the most exciting areas of immunology is to understand the nature and relevance of this communication. This is the focus of our next chapter.

3
Channels of Communication

'Thought defeating fire' is an intriguing phrase fashioned by Shakespeare and put into the mouth of King Lear. It is something which works in both directions. Taken actively, thought is something which can extinguish fire; taken passively, thought is something which can be overcome by fire. Given that we often associate the brain with thinking, and that one of the prime characteristics of immune activation is inflammation, Shakespeare's phrase serves particularly well to introduce the important topic of brain–immune system relationships. Communication is bidirectional. Pathways of communication include signals from the brain to the immune system and messengers from the immune system in turn feed back to the brain, and, as we shall see, can affect mood and behaviour. There is a complete regulatory loop. We shall need to jump into that loop somewhere, so let us first consider brain influences over immune function.

Brain Influences over Immune Function

The brain directs physiological processes via two pathways, neural and endocrine. The first involves (efferent) neurones which innervate the various organs and glands of the body; the second involves the brain communicating with target cells by stimulating the production of circulating hormones. Skeletal muscle is innervated by the somatic or motor nervous system, but just about everything else, including smooth and cardiac muscle, is influenced by fibres of the autonomic nervous system (ANS), called autonomic because for the most part it runs itself without cognitive processes. The ANS is probably familiar to most readers but we shall briefly outline some of its basic features for those to whom it is not. The ANS has two divisions: the sympathetic nervous system (SNS) and the parasympathetic nervous system (PNS). On the whole sympathetic and parasympathetic neurones exert opposing influences. Sympathetic activity prepares the body for action and energy expenditure (catabolic activity) in response to emergency situations, and challenges to homeostasis; parasympathetic activity, by contrast, mediates rest and energy conservation (anabolic activity).

Sympathetic activation tends to be highly co-ordinated, influencing the whole body at once – the mass preparation for fight or flight. Parasympathetic activation is more localised and discrete. Neural pathways of both systems are composed of two peripheral neurones, a preganglionic neurone emerging from the central nervous system (CNS) which synapses in a ganglion (collection of neurone cell bodies) with a postganglionic neurone, which innervates the actual target tissue. Sympathetic ganglia tend to be close to the CNS such that postganglionic neurones are long, fanning out to broaden and co-ordinate the pattern of influence. Parasympathetic ganglia are situated within the target tissues with short discrete postganglionic fibres. The key neurotransmitters that influence target tissue function are acetylcholine in the case of postganglionic parasympathetic fibres and noradrenaline in the case of sympathetic fibres. Hence postganglionic parasympathetic fibres are cholinergic and postganglionic sympathetic fibres are adrenergic. Both types of fibre can also co-release physiologically active peptides (relatively short chains of amino acids which can also act as neurotransmitters). The sympathetic nervous system has developed a specialisation in the form of the adrenal medulla of the adrenal gland. This important collection of cells sits in the middle of outer layers which make up the adrenal cortex. We shall revisit the adrenal cortex very shortly since it produces its own important hormones, in particular so-called glucocorticoids. Increased glucocorticoid secretion is so much part of the body's response to stress (see later chapters) and so much linked to immune function that it will be a central consideration in this book. But for now let us stay with the adrenal medulla. The medulla is a sympathetic ganglion but the postganglionic neurones do not project axonal outgrowths to innervate target tissue directly. Instead they simply secrete their neurotransmitter into the blood as a hormone.

The anatomical location of the adrenal medulla is no accident. The high concentration of glucocorticoids to which it is exposed from the surrounding adrenal cortical tissue activates an enzyme. This enzyme converts the normal neurotransmitter noradrenaline to perhaps the best known 'stress' hormone: adrenaline (which has a broader range of catabolic influences). Furthermore, this glucocorticoid-rich environment inhibits neuronal development. Without this environment, adrenomedullary cells can be induced to develop axonal projections, just like normal postganglionic sympathetic fibres.

The intimate relationship between the adrenal cortex and the SNS extends beyond these developmental niceties. Emotional challenge is registered and interpreted by a co-ordinated sympathetic adrenomedullary system (SAM). This system was first described by the great American physiologist Walter

Cannon in the early decades of the twentieth century. Cannon used dogs to frighten cats and noted the increase in circulating adrenaline in the emotionally disturbed animals. Some years later Hans Selye drew attention to the adrenal cortex and its major glucocorticoid hormone cortisol (in the human species). Cortisol secretion was seen to characterise physiological responses to psychological and physical challenges (and intriguingly, immunological challenge). In short, the adrenal cortex participates in a stress-neuroendocrine cascade called the hypothalamic-pituitary-adrenal (HPA) axis. The HPA axis is so crucial to many of the PNI studies mentioned in this book that we shall spend some time outlining its main features.

Stimulatory signals may originate in a number of brain areas but focus upon the control centre which is the paraventricular nucleus (PVN) in the hypothalamus. The central neurotransmitters involved in activation are monoamines, specifically noradrenaline and 5-hydroxytryptamine (5HT) (also known as serotonin). Parvocellular cells in the PVN produce a peptide called corticotrophin releasing factor (CRF) which drives the axis. Another peptide produced in the PVN, arginine vasopressin, also plays a stimulatory role under certain circumstances. These regulatory peptides are secreted into a blood vessel, which carries them the short distance to the anterior pituitary gland which, although outside the brain, lies just beneath the hypothalamus. CRF stimulates the release of the pituitary hormone adrenocorticotrophin (ACTH). This circulates peripherally to arrive at the adrenal cortex and stimulate the production of corticosteroids, notably glucocorticoid compounds such as cortisol. CRF lies at the centre of the stress response. Not only is it released to stimulate the pituitary, it acts as a central neurotransmitter to influence mood and emotion and emotion-related behaviours. It also plays a role in stimulating activity in the SNS by stimulating the control centre in the locus coeruleus (for review see Tsigos and Chrousos, 1996). Although SAM and HPA are often treated as separate systems responsive to emotional input, they are better seen as the peripheral limbs of a single central 'stress response system'.

The basic organisation of the 'stress response system' is illustrated in Figure 3.1.

Many psychologists, biologists and certainly immunologists are deeply suspicious of the term 'stress' (coined by Selye) since it is so difficult to define and there is so much cognitive overlay resulting in marked individual differences in response to any particular situation or stimulus. Despite these difficulties which are rehearsed in Chapter 5, the complex and sophisticated neuronal and endocrine circuitry that underlies the stress response system is central to the concerns of this book. Among the target cells that respond to activity in this circuitry are cells of the immune system. Although the SAM and HPA are integrated at many levels it is convenient to deal with each in turn in considering their roles in immunoregulation. We shall first describe the HPA axis.

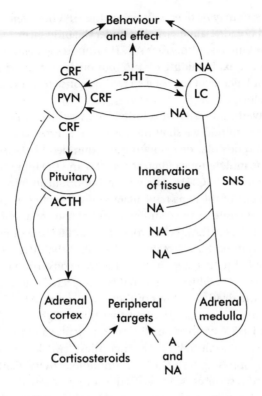

Key:
A   = Adrenaline
ACTH = Adrenocorticotrophic hormone
CRF   = Corticotrophin releasing factor
5HT   = 5-Hydroxytryptamine
LC   = Locus Coeruleus
NA   = Noradrenaline
PVN   = Paraventricular nucleus
SNS   = Sympathetic nervous system

Figure 3.1   The stress response system

The Immunoregulatory Role of the HPA Axis

The adrenal cortex produces steroid hormones (hence the collective term, corticosteroids). All are derived from cholesterol and are synthesised from a common precursor. It is important to realise that steroid hormones are synthesised on demand; they are not stored, as is the case with other messengers such as peptides and monoamines such as noradrenaline. This fact will become relevant in later chapters when we consider the differences between the effects of very short-term acute stress as opposed to more long-term chronic stress. A very acute stressor may be over with before the HPA has even kicked in, while adrenaline and noradrenaline secretion under the influence of SNS stimulation is almost instantaneous. Also, since ACTH promotes general steroid synthesis in the adrenal cortex, including cortisol but other steroid hormones as well, the direction or balance of the total steroid response to stress is potentially of interest (see below).

Anatomically, the adrenal cortex is divided into three zones. The outermost zone (zona glomerulosa) we shall not dwell on. It produces so-called mineralocorticoids responsible for regulating hydromineral balance. The steroids produced by the middle zone (zona fasciculata) and the innermost zone (zona reticularis) respond to ACTH and are both important in immunoregulation. The major product of the zona fasciculata in the human is the glucocorticoid cortisol (corticosterone in mice and rats) and of the zona reticularis is dehydroepiandrosterone (DHEA). Both types of steroid feature in later chapters of this book, so it is important to realise at the outset that ACTH exerts its major influence on only the first step in the sequential conversion of cholesterol to steroids. The degree to which this signal is interpreted into cortisol or DHEA depends upon the relative activity of these two zones. What regulates this is far from clear and it was once thought that there might be a pituitary factor that promotes DHEA synthesis in the zona reticularis but none was found. This is an issue of some relevance since these two key products of HPA activation have opposing influences on immune activity. Cortisol promotes the Th2-directed responses, whereas DHEA (or its metabolites) promote Th1 activity. The two counter-regulatory pathways along which an immune response can be directed were described in the previous chapter.

The pathways of steroidogenesis in the different zones of the adrenal cortex are illustrated in Figure 3.2.

The adrenal undergoes a developmental maturation analogous to the maturation of the hypothalamic-pituitary-gonadal axis that occurs during puberty. This is called adrenarche. It begins at about five years of age and continues into teenage years when adult levels of hormones are achieved. DHEA is a mild androgen and this maturation of DHEA synthesis capacity in the adrenal contributes to the development of sexual maturity. DHEA is responsible for the development of pubic and axial hair during female maturation, influences brain and behaviour, and plays a very important role in the endocrinology of pregnancy. The balancing role that DHEA plays in immune regulation means that in early childhood, in the absence of DHEA, an infant's immune system is biased towards Th2 domination. It is interesting to speculate as to whether this is in any way adaptive. It is possible that in the environment in which humans evolved the chief threat to children derived from large extracellular parasites for which Th2 defence is required. Also, the fever which accompanies Th1-driven inflammatory processes is particularly

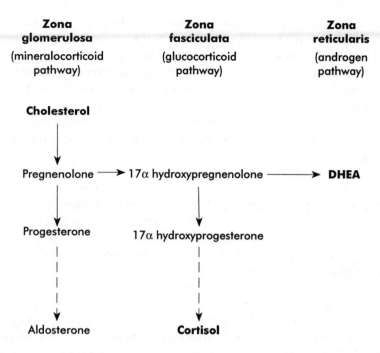

Zona glomerulosa (mineralocorticoid pathway)	Zona fasciculata (glucocorticoid pathway)	Zona reticularis (androgen pathway)

Cholesterol

Pregnenolone $\longrightarrow$ 17α hydroxypregnenolone $\longrightarrow$ **DHEA**

Progesterone   17α hydroxyprogesterone

Aldosterone   **Cortisol**

Figure 3.2   The pathways of steroidogenesis in the zones of the adrenal cortex. Broken arrows indicate that intermediate steroids are omitted. Bold type = referred to in text

dangerous to young infants who have not developed efficient thermoregulatory control in the hypothalamus. In consequence, however, pre-adrenarche infants are vulnerable to pathogens which require Th1 defence. For instance, pre-adrenarche children have little defence against tuberculosis whereas resistance develops as Th1 immunity becomes established (see Rook, 1997).

There is abundant evidence of the opposing roles of DHEA and cortisol in immune regulation (Daynes *et al.*, 1990; Bamberger *et al.*, 1997; Blotta *et al.*, 1997; DeKruyff *et al.*, 1998; Loria and Ben-Nathan, 1998). Receptors for cortisol (there are two types: type 1 and type 2) and DHEA are found on T cells and monocytes (Meikle *et al.*, 1992; Zovata *et al.*, 1996; Foulkes *et al.*, 1997; Miller *et al.*, 1998), the cells that orchestrate the immune response. In stimulated human peripheral blood mononuclear cell (PBMC) cultures (monocytes and lymphocytes) cortisol shifts the balance of cytokine production towards the Th2 pattern and this shift can be reversed by a glucocorticoid receptor antagonist (Agarwal and Marshall, 1998; Visser *et al.*, 1998).

These opposing influences have also been demonstrated in models of infection. Mice exposed to an otherwise lethal viral dose can be protected by

DHEA. Sub-lethal viral exposure becomes fatal when mice are treated with cortisol or subjected to stress. Once again DHEA is protective (for review see Loria and Ben-Nathan, 1998). A metabolite of DHEA, androstenediol (AED) has also been shown to be influential. AED has been found to protect mice from an otherwise lethal influenza virus infection (Padgett *et al.*, 1997). In this study the cellular mechanisms underlying protection were explored. There was an increase in antigen-induced trafficking into the draining lymph node and enhanced antigen specific activation of Th1 cells that control viral pathogenesis.

The focus of cortisol/DHEA influences on Th1 immunity has also been explored in an animal model of delayed type hypersensitivity (DTH). The DTH response is described in detail in the next chapter but for now it is sufficient that this is a good indicator of active Th1 immunity. Experimentation has shown that a DTH reaction is markedly suppressed by the synthetic glucocorticoid, dexamethasone (Dex) and by corticosterone (the principal glucocorticoid in the mouse, as mentioned above); but the reaction is augmented by DHEA (Foulkes *et al.*, 1997).

An illustration of how important the balance between cortisol and DHEA may be clinically, is provided by AIDS. In HIV infection there is a progressive loss of Th1 immunity and a shift towards Th2 with defective production of IL-2 and IL-12 and increased IL-4, IL-6 and IL-10, and increased production of IgE (Norbiato *et al.*, 1997). This shift is accompanied by increased cortisol and decreased DHEA which correlate with the various stages of AIDS progression (Christeff *et al.*,1997). These observations are correlational but do point to links between adrenal steroid output, changes in the balance of the immune system and progress of disease.

The studies described above give some insight into the important role that adrenal steroids play in immunomodulation, and will be central to later chapters which describe the impact of psychological factors on immune system functioning. The patterns of interaction with the immune system are, however, complex. The daily production of cortisol and DHEA by the human adrenal is roughly comparable in healthy individuals, but circulating levels of DHEA are ten to twenty times lower than those of cortisol. The reason for this is that much of the DHEA released is rapidly converted to a different compound, DHEA sulfate (DHEAS). DHEAS builds up in the circulation because of its long half-life and reaches high concentrations (see Miller and Tyrell, 1995). This sulfated form of the steroid is thought to be inactive with respect to immune cell functioning. However, an enzyme present in immune system organs, such as spleen and lymph nodes, can convert it back into DHEA, and in this form it exerts its Th1-promoting activity. This is a classic example of local target tissue being able to modulate a hormonal signal. Thus the important reconverting enzyme is active in lymphoid organs, spleen and lymph nodes, areas which produce Th1-promoting cytokines. By contrast, mucosal associated lymphoid tissue which has a strong Th2 'profile' has little reconverting enzyme (see Foulkes *et al.*, 1997). It is therefore not fanciful to suppose that circulating DHEAS acts as an inactive pool, which can, however, in the right circumstances, provide DHEA to lymphoid tissue so as to maintain Th1 immunity. There is little day to day variation in DHEAS either in terms of a circadian pattern (unlike cortisol) or as a result of psychological challenge because of the large circulating amounts and its long half-life. Hence DHEAS must be seen as exerting tonic, Th1-promoting, control.

Cortisol is the opposite side of the coin. Again most of it circulates in an inactive form; this time not because of conversion to an inactive compound, but because it circulates bound to a specific binding protein called cortisol-binding globulin (CBG). There are clear parallels with DHEA but important distinctions. A key distinction is the dynamics of binding. This is illustrated in Figure 3.3. At total circulating levels up to a certain amount, there is ample binding capacity and therefore very little cortisol is free or unbound. As levels

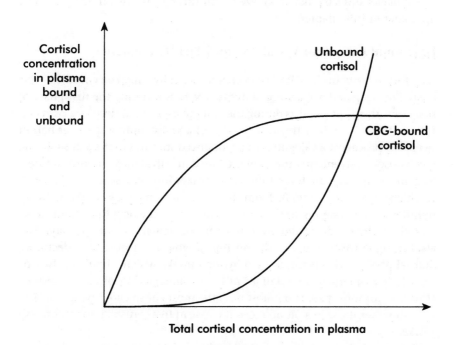

Total cortisol concentration in plasma

Figure 3.3   The dynamics of cortisol binding to CBG. At low total plasma concentrations very little cortisol is free. As adrenal cortisol output increases, the binding capacity of CBG becomes saturated and progressively more cortisol is available to interact with cellular receptors

increase, capacity becomes saturated, and progressively more cortisol is available as free cortisol. Only free cortisol is available to interact with cellular receptors and exert physiological influences.

Hence, unlike DHEAS, levels of free cortisol can increase rapidly in response to increased signalling in the HPA axis. Thus, whereas DHEA promotion of Th1 activity is thought to be tonic, as a result of continual availability of DHEAS to be converted back into DHEA, cortisol's promotion of Th2 activity is more likely to be phasic, determined by increased HPA activity, and subject to psychological influences that drive the axis.

Finally, the immunomodulatory role of cortisol is also partly governed by yet another enzyme which can deactivate it. Its crucial role can be seen in the placenta, where such enzyme activity shields the developing foetus from the harmful effects of circulating maternal cortisol. Spleen and lymph nodes also produce this enzyme so its activity in such tissue is capable of influencing the Th1/Th2 balance. For example, differential presence of this enzyme lies behind differences in the Th1/Th2 balance seen in different strains of inbred mice (see Wilkens and De Rijk, 1997). We revisit this enzyme-driven modulation a little later in this chapter.

Hormonal Circadian Variations and Th1/Th2 Balance

Secretory activity in the HPA axis is characterised by a marked circadian cycle related to sleep and awakening. Activity is very low during the first phase of slow wave sleep but recovers during the latter phase of REM sleep (see Born and Fehm, 1998). On top of this rising phase of activity, during the later half of sleep, the process of awakening is a pronounced stimulus to the axis such that free cortisol (conveniently the form measured in saliva) increases two-to three-fold in about half an hour following awakening (Pruessner *et al.*, 1997; Hucklebridge *et al.*, 1998b). From an early morning peak at about thirty minutes after awakening free cortisol declines over the next three hours or so and then slowly drifts downwards over the remainder of the day. The awakening cortisol response sits on top of what is an otherwise declining diurnal pattern. This is interrupted by food intake which stimulates the axis slightly (post-prandial stimulation) or by psychological or physical stressors. However, for most people on most days the most conspicuous period of HPA activation, resulting in a pronounced increase in free cortisol, is in response to awakening.

The typical diurnal pattern, including the awakening response, is illustrated in Figure 3.4.

This remarkable awakening response is independent of post-awakening activities such as getting up or staying in bed and represents a significant exposure of lymphoid tissue to free cortisol. It has been suggested that this

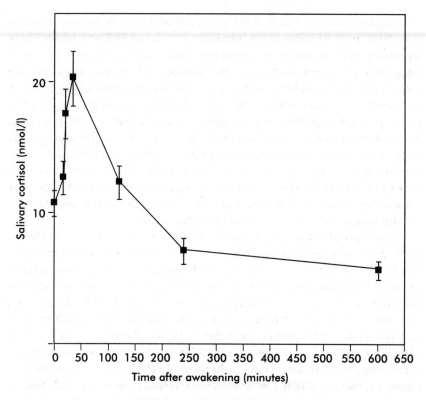

Figure 3.4   The diurnal cortisol profile (free cortisol measured in saliva) showing the response to awakening

plays the important role of biasing the immune system towards daytime Th2 domination (Hucklebridge *et al.*, 1999).

It has been shown that the immune system swings between nocturnal and sleep-related Th1 domination to Th2 domination during wakeful activity (Petrovsky and Harrison, 1995; 1997). Stimulated peripheral blood mononuclear cells harvested during night-time sleep produce a Th1 cytokine profile, whereas daytime samples from wakeful subjects reveal a switch to Th2 domination. It is thought that melatonin (the hormone of sleep), which shows the opposite circadian pattern to cortisol, plays a role in driving night-time Th1 activity since at the peak of Th1 cytokine activity, during the small hours of the morning, Th1 cytokine domination correlates positively with circulating melatonin levels. Administration of cortisol dramatically reverses the night-time cytokine profile (Petrovsky and Harrison, 1997). Thus it seems likely that the increase in free cortisol stimulated by awakening is physiologically important in driving the immune system back into Th2 mode. It has been argued that this circadian rhythm is imposed upon the immune system in order to prevent polarisation into excessive Th1 or Th2 activity. We have repeatedly emphasised the importance of homeostasis and balance in considering immune system functioning. The immune system must stay in balance but it is inherently unstable. Th1 activity inhibits Th2, and vice versa. Hence neuroendocrine systems that are sensitive to night–day, sleep–wake circadian cycles play an important role in preventing polarisation and prolonged domination of one or other face of T cell control. Since Th1 and Th2 are counter-regulatory it only requires a push to shift the balance; the T cells themselves will do the rest. It is considered that the sickness symptoms associated with Th1 activity – malaise, withdrawal, fever, inflammation – are appropriate to a period of rest, night-time sleep. Recovering into daytime activity requires a shift in the immunological balance.

It is also possible that the awakening cortisol response diverts the adrenal cortex away from the production of DHEA. DHEA shows a similar diurnal cycle to salivary free cortisol with morning levels higher than those measured (also in saliva) in the afternoon (Granger *et al.*, 1999). This should not be surprising since both hormones are fundamentally driven by ACTH. It is still possible, however, that patterns of release can become dissociated as a result of other signals biasing steroid production either in favour of cortisol or DHEA. Individuals experiencing high levels of work-related stress show exaggerated cortisol responses to awakening (Schultz *et al.*, 1998). There have been no reports of patterns of DHEA in relation to awakening but it is possible that an enhanced cortisol response is at the expense of DHEA. While this may have very little immediate influence, longer-term deprivation of morning DHEA production could result in significant failure of an important Th1 up-regulating signal to lymphoid tissue. Certainly, prolonged exposure to psychological stress decidedly shifts the balance in favour of Th2 (see Chapter 5) and a shift in the cortisol–DHEA balance might be one mechanism that controls this.

Gender differences may be illuminating in regard to our argument. There is evidence that in females, the immune system is more biased towards Th1 domination (Whitacre *et al.*, 1999). This may partly explain the greater incidence of inflammatory autoimmune disorders such as rheumatoid arthritis (which are Th1 driven) among females. It has also been documented in sociological surveys that females tend to report more symptoms of malaise than males (Wyke *et al.*, 1998), and malaise can indicate Th1 cytokine activity. Finally, females consistently show a more marked and prolonged cortisol response to awakening (Pruessner *et al.*, 1997), which may indicate that a stronger Th1 setting requires a bigger cortisol signal to redress the balance.

It is often claimed, quite wrongly, that cortisol is immunosuppressive. It may be that at high concentrations it inhibits all forms of T cell function but under normal physiological conditions its influence is subtle and multifaceted. Other hormones such as DHEA have counterbalancing influences. Let us not forget that, in the privacy of a lymphoid organ, a lymphocyte will also be receiving regulatory signals from the ANS. What determines its fate will be the sum of all the information it receives. The role of the sympathetic nervous system will now be considered.

Hard Wiring: The Direct Influence of Nerves

The immune system's lymphoid organs are densely innervated by branches of the autonomic nervous system. These are mainly the postganglionic sympathetic noradrenergic fibres which we mentioned at the beginning of the chapter. These fibres go mainly to zones where T lymphocyte and macrophages predominate, and avoid B cell areas. Sometimes nerve terminals actually make slight indentations on the lymphocyte surface (see Stevens-Felton and Bellinger, 1997). This is remarkable considering these synaptic contacts are made with presumably circulating cells. In general this sympathetic input is to sites regulating lymphocyte traffic, sites of antigen capture, antigen presentation and T lymphocyte activation. This is entirely compatible with a regulatory role by which sympathetic innervation can mediate brain influence over immunological events.

There is of course also evidence that lymphocytes can receive this SNS stimulation. Lymphocytes do indeed have (β-adrenergic) receptors, the activation of which, in turn, strongly promotes a Th1/Th2 shift (for review see Straub *et al.*, 1998). The precise relationship between receptor function and SNS signals may be subject to other signals received within the microenvironment of lymphoid tissue. For instance, cortisol has been shown to increase the density of SNS receptors on immune cells. Recently it has also been shown that T lymphocytes and certain other immune cells can synthesise their own adrenaline and noradrenaline and therefore it is possible that autocrine (self-stimulation) and paracrine (stimulation of neighbouring cells) production contributes towards the information flow within a lymphoid organ (Bergquist *et al.*, 1998).

There is ample evidence that direct stimulation of the sympathetic innervation to lymphoid tissue results in the release of the neurotransmitter noradrenaline and over 99 per cent of nerve endings terminating at immune cells make synaptic-like contacts. Hence the evidence is overwhelming that the brain can influence the activity of immune cells in lymphoid tissue by direct neuronal contact.

Studies in which the sympathetic innervation is stimulated support the view already espoused on the basis of molecular and cellular evidence: that sympathetic activity promotes a shift towards Th2 domination. Hence such stimulatory studies result in suppression of T cell proliferation, suppression of

NK cell cytotoxic activity and suppression of production of key Th1 promoting cytokines such as IL-2 and IFN-γ production. To summarise a great deal of evidence: if we block the SNS receptors, we block these influences (see Friedman and Irwin, 1997).

In humans, chronic elevation of sympathetic activity is associated with congestive heart failure (CHF). Patients treated with β-adrenoceptor antagonists ('beta-blockers') show immune changes consistent with a shift towards Th1-type immunity. These include more intense delayed type hypersensitivity (DTH) responses, increases in circulating NK cells and increased IL-2 production from stimulated PBMCs (Maisel, 1994). These findings suggest that the chronic sympathetic activation associated with CHF exerts a down-regulatory influence on Th1 immunity which is reversed by β-adrenoceptor blockade.

In addition to the influence that sympathetic nerves are thought to exert over lymphocyte activity within lymphoid organs, sympathetic innervation plays an important role in regulating the migration of lymphocytes between lymphoid organs and the cardiovascular circulation. Acute stress challenge tasks that stimulate the SNS and increase circulating catecholamines result in differential increases in subpopulations of lymphocytes released into the peripheral circulation. NK cells are particularly sensitive such that the number of NK cells in the periphery can increase more than four-fold. Substantial increases can also be seen in CD8+ T cells whereas CD4+ T cells and B cells are much less affected. These changes are transient and usually return to baseline levels within ten to twenty minutes of the provoking stimulus. These acute changes can be blocked by administration of β-adrenoceptor antagonists (for review see Ottoway and Husband, 1994). Similarly, direct infusion of the catecholamines, adrenaline and noradrenaline, produces comparable changes in circulating lymphocyte populations and again these responses can be reversed by β-adrenoceptor antagonists (Schedlowski *et al.*, 1996). It is thought that, in part, this modulation of lymphocyte traffic is due to changes in adhesion processes between lymphocytes and the blood vessel endothelial cell walls. *In vitro* studies have shown that catacholamines can induce detachment of NK cells from endothelial cells (Benschop *et al.*, 1993). Interestingly, the synthetic glucocorticoid dexamethasone has been shown to interfere with lymphocyte adhesion to endothelial cells and lymph nodes (see Ottoway and Husband, 1994). Hence psychological variables operating via stress neuronal and neuroendocrine pathways can modulate the deployment of different lymphocyte populations throughout the body. These phenomena are revisited in Chapters 5 and 7.

A further approach to probe the role of sympathetic innervation to immune cells in lymphoid organs is to interrupt the neuronal signalling and test the influence upon immune responses. This can be done by surgical sectioning of the nerve supply to a particular lymphoid organ, usually the spleen, or by chemical sympathectomy. Surgical intervention is problematic since surgical trauma itself can result in prolonged immunosuppression. Most studies of this nature have adopted the administration of a drug, 6-hydroxydopamine (6-OHDA) which selectively destroys noradrenergic nerve terminals. This drug cannot cross the blood–brain barrier to penetrate the central nervous system and so central noradrenergic processes are not compromised.

In one experimental protocol (described in Kruszewska *et al.*, 1997) two inbred strains of mice were used, the BALB/c, which exhibits a predominantly Th2-biased immune system (see previous discussion of strains, earlier in this chapter) and is therefore vulnerable to intracellular pathogens, and the C57/Bl/6J strain which is Th1-biased. Mice of the BALB/c typically produce Th2 cytokines (IL-4 and IL-10) in response to antigen challenge, whereas C57/Bl/6J produce predominantly Th1 cytokines (IL-2 and IFN-γ). Mice were treated with 6-OHDA to reveal the influence of chemical sympathectomy on these two different strains. While there was little difference between strains for IL-4 (the Th2 cytokine) in relation to antigen challenge, the increase in IL-2 and IFN-γ (Th1 cytokines) following sympathectomy did discriminate the two strains. The Th1-dominant C57/B1/6J strain showed a marked enhancement, whereas there was no change in the Th2-biased (BALB/c) strain. This experimental approach strongly suggests that sympathetic inner-vation exerts a Th1 down-regulating influence on animals, which are already Th1 dominant. The evidence is less clear for an inbred strain of mouse whose immune system is biased towards Th2-mediated responses. It is possible that cortisol is the predominant influence over the Th1/Th2 balance in this strain, since the immune system of this strain is cortisol dominated. This Th2 dominance results from a relative failure to convert cortisol into an inactive form (see earlier).

Given that the mucosal immune system (particularly in regard to sIgA measures) has been extensively studied in PNI research, we should finally add a word or two on the role of sympathetic innervation in this system. Here noradrenergic sympathetic innervation seems to orchestrate immune responses in a remarkably comprehensive manner. In chemically sympathec-tomised animals, naïve lymphocytes (that is, not yet immunologically challenged) fail to populate mucosal lymphoid tissue. Equally, B Cells which have specifically responded to an antigen, and are committed to produce specific sIgA, fail to migrate to the diffuse mucosal associated lymphoid tissue (DMALT) and hence fail to deliver the effector response (Gonzalez-Ariki and Husband, 1998). These studies indicate that lymphocyte traffic, which is so important to the sIgA component of mucosal immune defence, is under the regulatory influence of the SNS. In addition it has recently been demonstrated (at least in salivary glands) that transepithelial transport of sIgA to the mucosal surface is also regulated both by the SNS and the PNS (Carpenter *et al.*, 1998). Our own data (Hucklebridge *et al.*, 1998a) indicate that cortisol may also play a role in regulating this process. These findings emphasise the pervasiveness of neuronal and neuroendocrine control over sIgA mucosal defence. The importance for those interested in PNI is very evident when we consider that it has been repeatedly demonstrated that this aspect of immunity is extremely sensitive to psychological manipulation (see Chapter 5).

The Th1/Th2 balance, which is so important to the progression and resolution of disease, is regulated at many levels by neuroendocrine hormones and direct neuronal pathways. What we hope we have shown here is that the balance at the level of an immune system lymphoid organ will depend upon the delivery of hormones such as adrenaline, cortisol and DHEA, the activity of activating and deactivating enzymes, the local release of neurotransmitters such as noradrenaline from sympathetic terminals and the expression of appropriate receptors on the target cells. The fate of any reactive lymphocyte will depend upon the sum of all of this input signalling, but, at the end of the day, the brain is pulling the strings. Let us now examine how the immune system talks back.

The influence of autonomic and neuroendocrine mediation upon the Th1/Th2 balance is illustrated in Figure 3.5

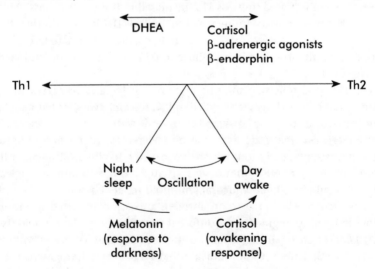

Figure 3.5   Autonomic and neuroendocrine mediators influencing the Th1/Th2 balance

Influence of the Immune System on the Brain

Activation of immune cells induces them to release a host of soluble mediators. We are already familiar with these cytokines, released by macrophages and lymphocytes, that orchestrate the direction of an immune response. Some of these cytokines, however, signal to the brain, like classical hormones. In addition, activated immune cells actually produce classical hormones (the production of adrenaline by lymphocytes has already been noted). The best described of these hormones are ACTH and β-endorphin. Both are secreted by activated macrophages and lymphocytes in physiologically relevant amounts (for review see Blalock, 1994).

We know from Chapter 2 that, when the immune system is challenged by micro-organisms, innate defences hold the fort while time (measured in days) is taken for cellular proliferation to expand the lymphocyte specific response. Chief amongst these innate defences is the innate antimicrobial activity of macrophages. Macrophages are recruited to a site of infection and begin to secrete the pro-inflammatory cytokines, IL-1, IL-6 and TNF-α. A primary role of these cytokines is to mobilise whole body responses, including behavioural changes that are adaptive in the fight against infection. Central to these is the induction of fever.

Fever plays a key role in immune defence. Increase in body temperature slows bacterial growth, prevents formation of bacterial protective coats, accelerates some of the enzymatic antimicrobial systems of the body, and increases the rate of lymphocyte proliferation. To generate fever involves extremely large energy costs. To maintain fever requires about 10–15 per cent increase in energy usage for every additional degree of body temperature. Hence associated with fever is a range of energy-conserving behavioural responses. These include behavioural withdrawal and decreased social interaction, reduced aggression, reduced sexual behaviour, sleep and loss of appetite (to conserve energy not wasted on food searching). All of these adaptations, which we call 'sickness', are orchestrated in the brain (see Maier and Watkins, 1998). It is interesting to note that the behavioural responses described are something which we could see as close to depression and it has been argued that some forms of clinical depression may have immune dysregulation at the heart of their genesis (Maes, 1995; see also Chapter 6).

IL-1 seems to be the key signalling cytokine between the macrophage and the brain during this process. IL-1 injected peripherally or centrally induces sickness behaviour. IL-1 receptors have been located in the brain and activation of these receptors induces sickness, whereas blockade of these receptors in the brain inhibits the sickness response to IL-1 (Maier *et al.*, 1994). IL-1, secreted at a site of infection, circulates in the blood like a hormone and IL-1 is carried to target cells in the relevant brain areas. One small difficulty is that IL-1 is a large protein and cannot penetrate the blood–brain barrier to influence neuronal processes via this route. Remarkably it has been shown that the vagus nerve (a major trunk of the autonomic nervous system with both afferent and efferent fibres) carries IL-1 signals to the brain. The vagus nerve is well adapted for this role. 'Vagus' means wanderer – the nerve goes just about everywhere, and is thus an ideal vehicle for general detection of peripheral IL-1. But why, then, are there IL-1 receptors in the brain, which, when activated, trigger the behavioural response? IL-1 is in fact synthesised centrally in the brain itself. Hence the peripheral IL-1 signal is transduced into neuronal information carried to the brain by the vagus nerve to be retransduced in the brain into IL-1 which finally completes the pathway (for review see Watkins and Maier, 1998; also Dantzer *et al.*, 1997). In addition to the vagal pathway described, lymphoid organs themselves contain afferent nerve fibres which can transmit sensory signals from immune cells to the brain. These fibres have receptors for cytokines and other 'messenger' molecules produced by activated immune cells (see Straub *et al.*, 1998). Figure 3.6 illustrates bidirectional communication pathways between the brain and immune system.

The pro-inflammatory cytokines also potently activate the stress-neuroendocrine HPA axis. Hence administration of a bacterial antigen, lipopolysaccharide (LPS), commonly used in experiments to provoke an immune response, triggers a release of pro-inflammatory cytokines. The cytokines in turn induce a marked and sustained increase in cortisol. This is brain-mediated, involving activation of the PVN of the hypothalamus, which initiates the HPA cascade just as it does in the psychological stress response (Parrot *et al.*, 1995). In fact the nerve pathways in the brain which stimulate the PVN in response to signals of immune challenge are remarkably similar to those for HPA activation by psychological stressors (Dunn, 1998). There are some subtle differences relating to the role of serotonin (Dunn, 1998; Clow *et al.*, 2000) but essentially immunological activation of the HPA axis is mediated by the same central monoamine pathways as psychological activation.

Stimulation of corticotrophin releasing factor (CRF) in the PVN of the hypothalamus is the central event. Intracerebral administration of CRF induces not only HPA axis and SAM activation, but *also* all of the behavioural changes characteristic of sickness (Dunn, 1998). It has been argued (see Maier and Watkins 1998; also Watkins and Maier, 1998) that the *immunological* stress response is evolutionarily older than the *psychological* stress response. In a sense, psychological input can be seen as having hijacked central pathways originally designed to orchestrate an adaptive response to infection and immunological challenge. Behavioural changes are designed to *conserve* energy while HPA axis and SAM activation *release* energy reserves from storage. The net result is availability of energy for raising temperature and fighting

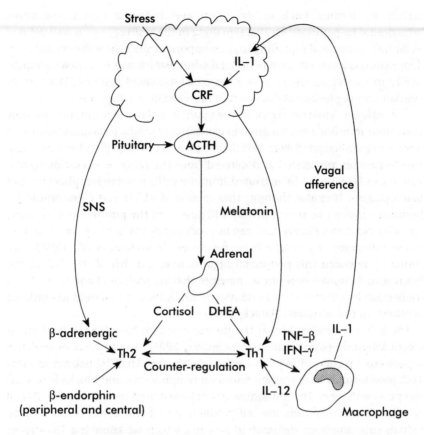

Key:
ACTH = Adrenocorticotrophic hormone
CRF = Corticotrophic releasing factor
SNS = Sympathetic Nervous System

Figure 3.6 Channels of communication

infection. Viewed in this way, not only do the brain and immune systems talk to each other, they are also bed-fellows.

Pathways of communication other than those initiated by pro-inflammatory cytokines also exist. Other cytokines, such as IL-2, also signal to the brain. IL-2 receptors are expressed in different regions of the brain, most potently the hippocampus. IL-2 can be introduced in very tiny amounts into the locus coeruleus of the rat (we may recall that this is the sympathetic noradrenergic brain centre and is also involved in sleep–wake cycles). If this is done, it reduces neuronal activity and promotes sleep (Nistico and De Sarro, 1991). Again we see the importance of a cytokine, produced during cellular immune activation, feeding back to the brain and inducing restful restorative behaviour. The pathways for IL-2 signalling to the brain are not as well defined as for IL-1. Peripheral signalling may be important since drowsiness (and even depression) is a side effect of peripheral administration of IL-2 used therapeutically in cancer patients, to stimulate cell-mediated defence. The role of cytokines in depression is discussed in more detail in Chapter 6.

Not only do cytokines signal to the brain, like classical hormones; we now know that immune cells themselves can actually produce classical hormones (for review see Blalock, 1994). Best described are ACTH and β-endorphin. These two hormones are related and derived from the same precursor molecule, which can be released by activated immune cells, notably lymphocytes and macrophages. It is also thought that release of ACTH and β-endorphin by immune cells can be stimulated by CRF just as in the pituitary (see Weigent and Blalock, 1999). Finally, CRF can be produced by macrophages in lymphoid tissue innervated by sympathetic neurones (Brouxham *et al.*, 1998). The similarity between this peripheral organisation and that of the HPA in the brain is striking. We now know therefore that an additional and more direct route exists by which the immune system can by itself stimulate glucocorticoid synthesis in the adrenals (Blalock, 1994).

The role of β-endorphin in the immune system has also received much recent attention (see Panerai and Sacerdote, 1997). A large body of evidence suggests that β-endorphin plays a role in shifting the Th1/Th2 balance towards Th2. β-endorphin receptors are found on lymphocytes, and blockade of such receptors enhances Th1 inflammatory cell-mediated responses and NK cell activity. In humans, immune cell production of β-endorphin is low in individuals suffering from rheumatoid arthritis, which we know is a Th1-driven autoimmune disease. In animals, β-endorphin administration causes lymphocytes to produce less IL-2 and more IL-4, while blocking receptors for β-endorphin has the opposite effect. These influences are pervasive and are exerted both peripherally and centrally. We know this because we can block β-endorphin action by the attachment of specific antibody to it, rendering it inactive. Vital to the argument is the fact that antibody cannot cross the blood–brain barrier. Nevertheless, such antibody blocking promotes Th1-type responses regardless of whether the antibody is administered peripherally or centrally. Hence β-endorphin exerts a Th2-promoting signalling function both in the brain-influencing central control systems and peripherally at the level of secondary lymphoid tissue. The circle is complete.

For convenience this chapter has been organised into discrete sections. We described first the neuroendocrine pathways of communication, then neural pathways from the brain to the immune system, and finally afferent pathways. However, the cross-talk between the immune system and the brain is so comprehensive that this is somewhat artificial. There are efferent and afferent neuronal pathways of communication and information is also carried back and forth by circulating signalling molecules. The brain has numerous pathways to influence immunoregulation. In recent years much has been interpreted in terms of regulation of the Th1/Th2 balance. No doubt further details of fine-tuning will emerge in due course. In the other direction, immune cells provide signals to the brain, modifying neuroendocrine activity and altering mood, motivation and behaviour.

If we were visitors from another planet and observed the comings and goings, the banter and chatter, between people in a busy street market, we would not understand the language or the mannerisms but it would be perverse not to deduce that communication is happening and that this communication informs and directs motivation and action. We see the brain and immune system from a similar perspective. We don't have to understand a language, even in part, to appreciate its importance in the life of a nation. We are never likely to fully understand the language of communication between the brain and immune system, but we can see it at work. And at work it is contextual. What a signal means will depend upon its context: what accompanies it, what has gone before and what has been learned from experience. Just like an isolated phrase, the same thing may mean something very different in another context: 'Thought defeating fire'.

4
Measures and Interpretation

Studies to explore the relationship between psychological variables and functional status of the immune system must give careful attention to exactly what measures are selected. Most commonly dependent variables are measures of immunological status. A psychological variable is either manipulated or, more often, observed and some facet of immune function is determined. Where essentially psychological and immunological measures are both observations rather than manipulations, the implicit status of the immune measures as being dependent variables can be criticised. A major interest of PNI researchers has indeed been the effects of psychological variables such as stress on the immune system. We have written already enough about reciprocal influences (see Chapter 3) for the reader to be cautious about interpreting essentially correlational information solely in terms of one direction of causal influence.

Measures of immune system status fall into two broad categories: measures of background activity and responses to actual antigen challenge. In studies on human subjects, most commonly background activity is measured since it is not ethical under most circumstances (there are some notable exceptions) to challenge the immune system solely for experimental purposes. Greater freedom is adopted in the approach to animal studies. We shall explore some typical measures of background activity in the first instance.

Circulating Immune Cell Populations and Subpopulations (Leukocyte Enumeration)

One of the most common measures of immune function used in psychophysiology research is the number of cells (absolute and/or relative) representing different immune cell populations in the peripheral circulation. Automated cell counters can enumerate the different immune cell populations in a peripheral blood sample. Cell populations can be expressed as absolute numbers (per ml of blood, for example) or relative proportions. Usually both indexes are of interest. Cell counts are determined by specialised flow cytometry techniques, which detect cells expressing characteristic markers. Cells flow past a detection system and they are interrogated one at a time. Hence a B cell can be distinguished from a CD4+ T cell, CD8+ T cell, NK cell, and so on. The technology makes use of monoclonal antibodies (see Chapter 2) that bind specifically to these surface molecules that characterise and identify the cell. Different monoclonal antibodies that identify different cells can be detected and distinguished because they are tagged with fluorescent dyes. The system is automated and thousands of cells can be analysed in seconds. Although this kind of technology is used for monitoring immunological disturbance in disease states such as AIDS (where CD4+ cells are depleted) it has found its application in PNI research.

The computer-generated scatterplot of such an analysis is shown in Figure 4.1.

PNI findings in regard to leukocyte enumeration are reasonably consistent (they are reviewed and discussed in more detail in later chapters). Negative mood and various forms of prolonged stress and psychopathological conditions such as depression tend, for example, to be associated with reduced numbers, in both absolute and relative terms, of T cells, particularly CD4+ T cells and NK cells in the peripheral circulation. These lymphocyte losses from the periphery are often associated with increased numbers of circulating neutrophils. This pattern of change is consistent with the influence of cortisol (for review see O'Leary, 1990). By contrast, a brief psychological stress challenge such as a public speaking task generally results in a transient elevation of circulating NK cells and CD8+ cells (for example, see Herbert *et al.*, 1994; also reviewed in Evans *et al.*, 1997). There is some evidence that these changes in lymphocyte distribution are mediated by adrenergic mechanisms. They can be mimicked by injection of adrenaline and in one study the acute response to stress challenge was blocked by a β-adrenergic antagonist (Schedlowski *et al.*, 1996).

It is often argued that this kind of approach is uninterpretable. What does it mean if certain immune cell populations are depleted or enhanced in number in the peripheral circulation? The loss of peripheral T cells and CD4+ cells in relation to psychological stress is nothing like that seen in AIDS. In relation to a chronic psychological stress parameter, total T cell loss, and in particular CD4+ T cell reductions can be in the order of 30 per cent (see Hucklebridge *et al.*, 1994) whereas AIDS diagnosis (as opposed to HIV infection) is confirmed when CD4+ cell numbers drop to below 200/µl (about 25 per cent of normal). There is little evidence of loss of functional immunocyte subsets (as in AIDS). More likely what we are seeing is a redistribution of cells between the various compartments of the immune system (spleen, lymph nodes, blood

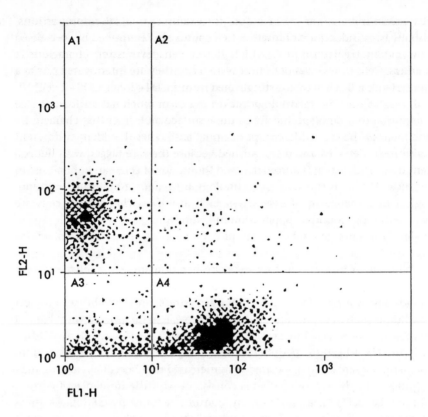

Figure 4.1   Flow cytometry dual fluorescence dot plot of peripheral blood lymphocytes. Cells represented in quadrant A4 are T cells labelled with a monoclonal antibody that binds to a T cell marker. A different monoclonal labelled with a different fluorescent dye identifies B cells, represented in quadrant A1. The cells in quadrant A3 which are negative for both the T cell and B cell marker are probably NK cells. NK cells can be positively identified using appropriate monoclonals, as can subpopulations of T cells.

Source: Kindly provided by Professor P.M. Lydyard, Royal Free and University College Medical School, London

circulation, and so on) The rapid and transient changes seen in relation to an acute stress challenge certainly reflect changes in trafficking, and we have seen in Chapter 3 the important role that the autonomic nervous system plays in regulating lymphocyte trafficking. These studies do of course provide valuable evidence of psychological influences over the distribution of lymphocytes, which may be of physiological and even clinical importance. Indeed, in subsequent chapters we do entertain some speculation about the significance of trafficking changes. However, the fact remains that, in regard to enumerative measures, it is not clear exactly in what way the immune system is being functionally influenced. It follows therefore that differences in enumerative measures of this type should never in isolation be referred to as indicating a general enhancement or suppression of the immune system.

A similar note of additional caution is in order when examining the PNI literature involving lymphocyte population analysis. In the early literature and even in some more recent studies, the CD8+ T cell population is sometimes referred to as cytotoxic/suppressor or even simply suppressor T cell population. It was once thought that there was a distinct population of suppressor T cells that counterbalanced the influence of helper T cells and that these were part of the CD8+ population. It is now thought that most of the immunoregulatory balance resides in the CD4+ Th1/Th2 control. Although some CD8+ cells may exert Th2 down-regulatory influences, it is misleading to associate T cell suppression with the CD8+ population. This is particularly so if any inference is made that a reduction in circulating CD4+ cells and an increase in circulating CD8+ cells in some way indicates an immunosuppressive influence.

Flow cytometry techniques can also be applied to identify various markers of activation in respect to particular cell populations. The expression on the surface of T cells of the MHC class II molecule (discussed in Chapter 2) is an indication of cell maturation and activation, as is the IL-2 receptor. Monoclonal antibodies to identify these activation markers are widely available and this kind of analysis, although originally developed for clinical purposes, is beginning to find its way into PNI research (for example, see Maes *et al.*, 1993; also discussed in Chapter 6). This adds a level of sophistication to leukocyte enumerative analysis, and results can more confidently be interpreted.

Lymphocyte Proliferation Assays

Another way to assess the activational state of lymphocytes is to test their capacity to proliferate. As we have seen in Chapter 2, proliferation is a necessary prerequisite for lymphocytes to participate in an immunological response. Remember only a very small number will be able to recognise any particular epitope. Hence in order to develop functional capacity clonal expansion (proliferation) is required. Lymphocyte proliferation assays enjoy a long history in PNI research and are the most commonly applied tests of 'functional activity' in the immune system. They are still often reported.

The rationale for this approach requires some explanation. The vast majority of lymphocytes, particularly in the peripheral circulation, from where they are most commonly and conveniently harvested, are in an inactive state. They are said to be resting. Activation requires a number of sequential signals.

Although many of these signals are in the form of cytokines and adhesion molecules delivered by associated cells, the primary triggering signal is contact with antigen. One aspect of immune system functioning is to determine how readily resting cells can be driven into activation resulting in proliferation. The difficulty is that only a tiny number of cells harvested from the periphery will respond to any particular previously unseen antigen. This makes a standardised *in vitro* test, using antigen as the primary stimulus, impossible. The solution is to use so-called polyclonal activators. Certain molecules will stimulate all cells of a lymphocyte population regardless of antigen specificity. We need not concern ourselves here with the mechanisms involved. These very general activators are sometimes referred to as lymphocyte mitogens and the most commonly used are two plant proteins: phytohemagglutinin (PHA) and concanavalin A (Con A). These stimulate T cell proliferation in *in vitro* culture.

Procedures vary but typically the test is carried out on peripheral blood mononuclear cells (PBMCs). This population of cells consists of lymphocytes and macrophages isolated from the other cells that are present in a peripheral blood sample. Of the lymphocytes the majority are T cells. These are seeded into small culture wells in a medium to which the mitogen has been added. It is important to note that, although the test is of T cell activation, monocytes are thought to play a supporting role. The concentration of lymphocytes is set up in culture so as to reflect roughly the concentration present in the peripheral circulation. After a few days in culture under environmental conditions, which mimic those encountered in the body, the cultures are tested for rate of cellular proliferation. A radiolabelled molecule is added which is incorporated into cells only when they are busy dividing. The amount of radiolabel incorporated into the cell population is the index of proliferation. Normally, for reliability purposes, the test is set up in triplicate and over a range of mitogen concentrations. For a detailed account of assay procedures see Darko *et al.* (1989). In most studies, response to both PHA and Con A is determined. They usually tell the same story.

A variation upon plant mitogen stimulation recently introduced to PNI research is to use a T cell activating monoclonal antibody. The monoclonal binds to a component of the T cell receptor outside of the antigen-binding site. It therefore bypasses antigen specific recognition but activates the cell via the normal signalling system. This is again polyclonal activation but it can be argued that it more closely simulates the physiological signalling pathway. In a recently reported study (Andersen *et al.*, 1998) this index of T cell activity, measured in patients recovering after surgical intervention to treat breast cancer, was negatively related to the level of psychological stress experienced by the patient. NK cell activity, an index of protective Th1 immunity, was also compromised in relation to stress.

Polyclonal T cell activation tests, using plant proteins, were originally developed as tests for T cell deficiencies. It is perhaps surprising that these tests do reveal some kind of down-regulation of T cell function in relation to psychological negative affect. Consistently in the depression literature and in relation to chronic stress, lowered rates of proliferation, compared with matched controls, are reported. These tests do not distinguish which aspects of T cell function are compromised but they are generally referred to as tests of cellular immunity, implying that they distinguish a failure of Th1 activity. There is little direct evidence for this, although in one study (Bernton *et al.*, 1995; also referred to in Chapters 3 and 5) it was shown that the reduced T cell proliferation in response to mitogen, which characterised a chronically stressed population, could be recovered to normal by the addition of the T cell cytokine IL-2 into the culture medium. In this study also, there was independent evidence of a pronounced shift towards Th2 domination (loss of Th1 activity). More studies of this nature are required in order to probe more accurately which aspects of T cell function are influenced by particular psychological variables

The polyclonal activator pokeweed mitogen (PWM) can be used to stimulate the B cells in PBMCs in culture in a manner similar to T cell stimulation by PHA and Con A. The B cell response to PWM has also been reported in some PNI studies (see Chapter 5). Interpretation of this measure is, however, very problematic. The B cell has a long and complex journey before making a functional contribution to immunity. The B cell has a number of options in terms of antibody isotype and which option is taken depends on signals from other cells. Proliferation is only the very first step. It is therefore uncertain what mitogen driven proliferation of B cells tells us about functional status, particularly since B cells are poorly represented in the peripheral circulation. The signals that drive B cells (including the initial antigen trigger) from rest to antibody synthesis can now be simulated in culture, but this technology has not been applied in PNI research.

Cytokine Measures of Immune Activity: Circulating Cytokines and Markers for Cytokine Activity

The advent of highly specific and sensitive assays for cytokines has made feasible the measurement of cytokines as an index of immunological status. This is done in two ways. Circulating cytokines (and soluble cytokine receptors, see later) can be measured directly in peripheral blood samples. Alternatively, *in vitro* assays of cytokine production and release into cell cultures can be performed. This latter approach is a variation upon lymphocyte proliferation assays except that in this case cytokine release is the index of the activational status of harvested cells, rather than cell division. The cytokine profile in such assays gives a much more detailed picture of immune status (from macrophages as well as lymphocytes) than merely testing for proliferation.

The direct measurement of cytokines in peripheral blood samples has always been of questionable validity in terms of assessing immune status. The argument has been that cytokine communication between immune cells is over fairly short distances (within the milieu of a lymph node, for instance) and peripheral levels will be of little significance. Moreover, cytokines are 'pluripotent': that is to say, the same cytokine exerts different influences over different target cell populations under different contexts. There is no simple interpretation of a cytokine level that can be determined in the peripheral circulation. Notable exceptions are the inflammatory cytokines, IL-1, TNF-α and IL-6. These cytokines derive mainly from activated macrophages at sites of inflammation, do circulate to distant targets (liver, brain; but see discussion of the IL-1–brain afferent pathway in Chapter 3) to initiate the acute phase response, so like hormones their circulating levels do indicate this aspect of immune activation. Indeed, commercial assay systems for IL-6 were primarily developed in order to detect, at an early stage for clinical monitoring, activation of the acute phase response.

Evidence of inflammatory immune activation being associated with major depression derives to some extent from the elevated levels of these circulatory cytokines (particularly IL-6) in the peripheral circulation (see Chapter 6). In addition, circulating levels of the soluble form of the IL-2 receptor were also elevated and this is cited as evidence of excessive cell-mediated Th1 activity (Maes *et al.*, 1995). Paradoxically major depression is also associated with reduced activity in the T cell proliferation assay and reduced NK cell numbers and NK cell activity (see later in this chapter). This seemingly incompatible state of lymphocyte affairs is also discussed in Chapter 6.

Acute Phase Proteins

In addition to the measurement of circulating cytokines in relation to psychological disturbance, stimulation of the acute phase response can be monitored simply by measurement of circulating levels of acute phase proteins. These are routine clinical laboratory assays. One important aspect of the inflammatory acute phase response is that the protein synthesis activity of the liver changes. Synthesis and release of certain proteins, known collectively as positive acute phase proteins (PAPPs), increases, whereas the production of so-called negative acute phase proteins (NAPPs), most notably albumin, declines. The PAPPs play a role in innate immunological defence. For instance, some can bind to microbial surfaces and trigger the complement cascade (just like antibody of certain isotypes, but without the requirement for specific epitope recognition). This shift in the balance of APPs can readily be detected. Normally it is transient since the resolution of inflammation and other homeostatic mechanisms, such as the cortisol response to pro-inflammatory cytokines, redresses the balance. In major depression, however, this system seems to be in a continuous state of activation with heightened circulatory levels of PAPPs and reduced NAPPs (see Chapter 6).

Neopterin

So far, in this chapter, we have sought to introduce and discuss measures which have been widely used in the sorts of PNI studies which will be described in subsequent chapters. At this point, however, we shall allow ourselves a brief digression to highlight a type of indirect measure which has not yet figured much in PNI but may have the potential to do so in the future. Neopterin is an indirect but very useful marker for Th1 activity in the immune system. Neopterin is produced and released by macrophages which are stimulated by IFN-γ (Hammerlinck, 1999). It is sometimes monitored in order to predict aggressive cell-mediated immunological reactions against organ transplants. An increase in circulating neopterin can alert the transplantation team to problems of rejection. Thus, immunosuppressive drug therapy (to encourage tolerance) can be adjusted accordingly. Neopterin levels are also a useful indicator of the maintenance of Th1 resistance to HIV. Neopterin can be measured in both blood and urine; either measure gives a good indication of Th1/Th2 status. Most recently, measurement of neopterin in saliva has been introduced and validated for clinical monitoring (Nishanian *et al.*, 1998). This may prove very convenient for non-invasive PNI work, although for between-subject studies there is a cautionary note. Salivary neopterin levels can be influenced by local inflammatory processes in the oral cavity and therefore in these cases may not necessarily reflect systemic levels. Elevated neopterin in both serum and urine in major depression has contributed to the evidence of an inflammatory Th1-dominated immune system in relation to this particular psychological disturbance (see Chapter 6).

Cytokine Release from Activated Cell Cultures

In addition to measuring cytokines and markers for cytokine activity in the blood or other body fluids, immune status can be determined by the study of cytokine release from cells harvested from the circulation and maintained in culture. Peripheral blood mononuclear cells are set up in culture under much the same conditions as for a proliferation assay. As is the case for a proliferation assay, an activational stimulus is required, usually a mitogen such as PHA. After sufficient time for response, the culture can be sampled and assayed for cytokines released into the surrounding medium by activated cells. These assays have the advantage that the cell population involved and the conditions for cytokine production are reasonably controlled and understood. Again, in depression this approach has revealed elevated macrophage derived pro-inflammatory cytokine production (see Chapter 7).

For some investigatory approaches whole blood is considered preferable to PBMC cultures. Whole blood is thought to more closely approximate the physiological environment in which immunological responses take place, compared with the conditions provided by cell culture medium. The Th1/Th2 balance has been explored in this way. Whole blood cultures can be stimulated by natural antigens such as tetanus toxoid. Most people have been immunologically sensitised to these antigens as a result of prior exposure, so we can expect peripheral cells to respond. Petrovsky and Harrison (1997) used this approach to explore the circadian rhythmicity of Th1/Th2 balance (see Chapter 3). Whole blood samples drawn at intervals during nocturnal sleep produced a greater ratio of IFN-γ to IL-10 in response to *in vitro* antigen challenge than equivalent daytime samples. This indicates Th1 domination of the immune system during nocturnal sleep. Since this was a within subject study, and the final index is a ratio, individual differences in antigenic sensitivity have no bearing

Emergence of Anti-Viral Antibodies

A number of viruses are more or less endemic in the human population. Most notably for PNI research are Epstein-Barr virus (EBV) and the Herpes Simplex virus (HSV). These viruses can remain dormant for considerable periods and are kept in check by Th1 cellular defence. If Th1 immunity is compromised (for whatever reason) the virus can become more active and begins to stimulate Th2 immunity. Anti-viral antibodies appear in the circulation. Hence tests revealing the presence of anti-viral antibodies to these common pathogens are an indicator of some compromise of Th1 immunity. Increased titres of such antibodies have commonly been associated with periods of psychological stress (see Chapter 5). A similar process characterises the progression of AIDS. HIV infection can be restrained by the activity of the Th1 immune system (often for many years). Eventually this defence begins to falter with increased viral activity and load. This shift towards Th2 defence is characterised by increased titres of anti-HIV antibodies in serum and the development of AIDS progression. The pattern of progression, together with the endocrine changes that may underlie it, has already been introduced in the previous chapter and recurs in other contexts later in this book. Opportunistic infections (of a nature rare in healthy individuals, with balanced immune systems) take advantage of the compromised Th1 defence. Since psychological processes have an important bearing on the Th1/Th2 balance they can be influential in determining the progress of morbidity among the HIV-infected (see Chapter 9).

The Delayed Type Hypersensitivity Response

The delayed type hypersensitivity (DTH) response is a Th1-mediated local inflammatory reaction in the skin in response to intradermal injection of certain kinds of antigen. The individual must first have been sensitised by prior exposure as a result of infection or vaccination. The most familiar example is the DTH response seen in most individuals to the intradermal injection of tuberculin (the protein derivative of Mycobacterium tuberculosis). Other commonly used test antigens, which most people have been exposed to as a result of vaccination, are tetanus and diphtheria. The response takes several days to develop, hence the term 'delayed'. This is because although the response is orchestrated by Th1 cells and the release of Th1 cytokines, the inflammatory process requires the recruitment and activation of macrophages, which takes about twenty-four hours to develop. Inflammation (a local area of swelling, redness and irritation) which peaks at about forty-eight hours, is caused by the release from these activated macrophages of enzymes and inflammatory mediators. The DTH response is considered to be a very good indicator of the functional integrity of Th1 immunity. It has often been applied in PNI research and is one of the few examples, in human studies, of the use of antigen provocation to test an aspect of immunological status. There is abundant evidence that this response is compromised in relation to chronic stress but, paralleling the data on immunocyte trafficking, the response to an acute stress challenge is opposite in direction (Dhabhar and McEwan, 1999; also discussed in Chapter 9).

Serum IgE

The DTH response is an indicator of the strength of Th1-mediated immunity. At the opposite end of the T helper spectrum is IgE. Isotype switch to IgE is heavily dependent upon Th2 activity. In normal individuals IgE represents only 0.002 per cent of the total circulating antibody. Increased levels are therefore very conspicuous. Serum IgE is elevated in a number of atopic conditions such as asthma and hay fever, which are manifestations of over active Th2 immunity. The balancing act that our immune systems perform is illustrated by an important study of Japanese children. Children who made poor DTH responses, indicative of the balance tipped in favour of Th2, showed a much greater tendency to develop asthma later in life (Shirakawa *et al.*, 1996; see also Holgate, 1997). A number of studies have shown that sustained periods of psychological stress favour an increase in serum IgE (for example, see

Bernton *et al.*, 1995). Hence, for within subject studies of the influence of chronic stress, serum IgE levels are a useful indicator of the balance of the immune system.

Secretory IgA

In addition to IgE (measured in serum) an antibody isotype of great significance in PNI research is IgA. By contrast, IgA (in relation to psychological variables) is usually measured in saliva. IgA is the main immunological defence of mucosal surfaces: the bronchio-respiratory tract, gastrointestinal tract and urinogenital tract. It is also secreted (actively transported) by a number of glands, including salivary glands, lachrymal glands (tears) and mammary glands (breast milk). For IgA there are two distinct secretory processes. The secretion of the antibody by plasma cells in the mucosal immune system and following this an active transport across the cellular (epithelial) lining of the mucosal surfaces. It is therefore 'secreted' by a process of transport across the mucosal cellular lining to the mucosal surfaces. In this form it is referred to as secretory IgA (sIgA).

The most convenient secretory fluid for the assessment of sIgA is saliva. Usually total IgA is measured as a concentration regardless of antigen specificity. This is equivalent to the measurement of total IgE in serum as an indicator of the balance of the immune system rather than response to a particular antigen challenge.

There has been some controversy over sIgA as a PNI measure so it is necessary to spend a little longer introducing it, compared to other measures. It has been argued that what is more relevant than total sIgA is to measure the specific sIgA response to an orally introduced antigen (ovalbumin) (Stone *et al.*, 1987a). Jemmott and McClelland (1989) countered by arguing that what is really important is the overall activity of the system represented by all specificities (total antibody concentration). Judged by papers published, the consensus has supported this latter view. In fact it has been argued (Mestecky, 1993) that levels of total sIgA measured in saliva are representative of immunological activity in the common mucosal immune system. It can therefore be argued that this is a representative measure of a very important aspect of immune system activity. Most of the antibody production capacity of the immune system is dedicated to sIgA. Along the jejunum of the small intestine alone, there are more plasma cells (producing IgA) than the entire plasma cell population of the spleen and all of the lymph nodes combined (Kuby, 1997)! This phenomenal capacity is required in order to defend the extent of surface involved. For instance, the area of the lungs is roughly equivalent to that of a tennis court. Also these are mostly exchange surfaces and therefore vulnerable to pathogen entry. Most micro-organisms attempt to enter the body by this route and most infectious diseases are as a result of mucosal penetration or colonisation.

Secretory sIgA is structurally different to IgA in serum in that it is linked to a protein chain called the secretory component (see Chapter 2). It has been argued by some that measurement systems should recognise the molecule complete with the secretory component, so that it can be positively identified as sIgA. This may be a valid view if there is reason to suppose that vascular leakage into saliva (perhaps as a result of gum disease) would contaminate sIgA with the higher concentrations of IgA found in the circulation. Most salivary assay systems in PNI published to date merely rely on identification of the alpha chain that characterises this isotype.

The structure of sIgA is illustrated in Figure 4.2.

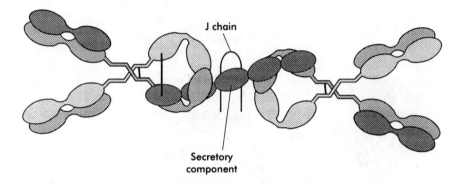

Figure 4.2 Structure of secretory IgA (adapted from Kuby, 1997)

Salivary sIgA has several advantages as a PNI measure. Studies have revealed that it is a reasonably stable trait marker. It shows good repeat measure reliability (Willemsen *et al.*, 1998). Individuals tend to be characterised by their level of production. Sampling is non-invasive and can be taken with little trouble or discomfort to the subject even in an ambulatory setting. These considerations have (unusual in the PNI literature) led to its use in epidemiological studies (Evans *et al.*, 2000). Despite its interindividual stability, numerous studies have also revealed an exquisite short-term sensitivity to acute psychological input (see Chapter 5).

All seems very rosy but there are a few technical considerations to be taken into account when interpreting this measure. Different salivary glands contribute different components to saliva. The parotid, which is not rich in sIgA, responds most strongly to stimulation of salivation. Hence stimulation of salivation has a potential diluting influence. In the most reliable studies stimulation is avoided using passive collection methods and volume collection is controlled for. Salivary sIgA also exhibits a diurnal pattern of activity which seems to have some relation to the HPA cortisol cycle, with elevated levels in the morning, particularly upon awakening (Miletic *et al.*, 1996; Hucklebridge *et al.*, 1998a). Hence time of sampling, particularly in relation to awakening, can be an important consideration. Other aspects of immune system functioning also show circadian and diurnal patterns of activity, often linked to neuroendocrine patterns. This is rarely considered in conventional clinical and molecular immunology, let alone PNI.

Before leaving salivary sIgA it is worth making some comment regarding the oft-quoted criticism that sIgA is measured because it is technically easy. True, but that doesn't make it less revealing. What it reveals requires a very careful consideration of how the mucosal immune system works and its place in

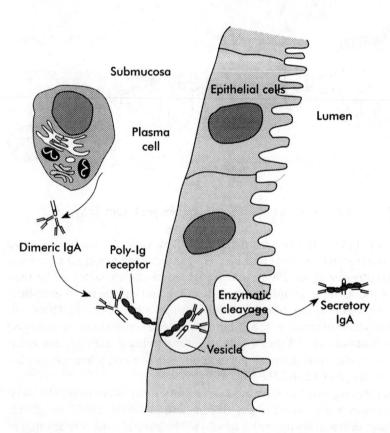

Figure 4.3   Dimeric IgA released from plasma cells in the submucosa is actively transported across the epithelial lining and released as secretory IgA on to the mucosal surface to play its protective role (adapted from Kuby, 1997)

immunological defence as a whole. Although, like most other antibody isotypes, it is a component of Th2 defence, the fact that a transepithelial transport system (the largest protein transport system in the body) has to deliver it to sites where it can function is singular. Both sIgA production by plasma cells, in mucosal lymphoid tissue and transepithelial transport are involved in delivery to mucosal secretions. Levels actually measured will reflect modulation (not necessarily in the same direction) of both processes. Recent studies (see Chapter 3) have revealed that this aspect of immune defence is subject to autonomic regulation at a number of levels. Cortisol may also play a role.

The organisation of the mucosal sIgA immune defence is illustrated in Figure 4.3.

Response to Vaccination

Although it is not ethical to expose people to vaccines for the sole purpose of exploring PNI relationships, a number of studies have exploited ongoing vaccination programmes (see Chapter 6 for details of studies). Most studies have looked at immunological response to influenza virus vaccine. The elderly have been particularly the focus of investigation, since psychologically induced shifts in immune function may be more significant in this already vulnerable group (see Chapter 5). Measures of response to vaccine can include virus-specific antibodies, as well as virus-specific production of various cytokines.

NK Cell Activity

Enumerative studies have demonstrated the sensitivity of NK cell migration to psychological factors. In addition, the anti-tumour activity of NK cells, harvested from the peripheral circulation, has been exhaustively explored. Cytotoxic capacity against tumour cells is stimulated by the Th1 cytokines IL-2 and IFN-γ. Hence, although NK cells are innate, in as much as they don't require priming in response to antigen, they are influenced by and indicative of Th1 activity.

NK cell activity can be determined by assay. These assays involve the loading of a target cell population with a radiolabelled element which can only be released if the cell is attacked and killed. The assay therefore measures the amount of radiolabel released after incubation of NK cells with target cells. Target cell populations are derived from standard tumour cell lines. Since NK cell recognition of tumour cells does not involve associated epitope and Self recognition (as is the case for cytotoxic T cells) the NK cell assay is not restricted to target cells of the NK cell donor. It is thus a relatively simple and convenient assay.

The point has often been made that since psychological factors can powerfully influence NK cell trafficking, changes in cytotoxic NK cell activity may only reflect changes in NK cell distribution and their representation within the cell population which is sampled. To an extent, statistical multi-variate examination of both changes in enumeration and function can help to resolve this source of uncertainty in interpretation. Also, in recent studies rigorous cell sorting has been applied in order to obtain virtually pure NK cell populations for introduction into the assay (for example, see Esterling *et al.*, 1996). In these studies interpretation of genuine changes in functional activity of NK cells circulating in the periphery, can be made with some confidence; and indeed, since there are few contaminating cells and in the example quoted, activating cytokines (IL-2 and IFN-γ) were added to the incubation medium, impairment of function can be attributed to the NK cell itself. Taken together these studies point to a decrement in NK cell activity associated with chronic stress, and also depression.

In addition to their anti-tumour activity NK cells can also recognise and kill virally infected cells (refer to Chapter 2). This aspect of their activity can also be tested in *in vitro* assay systems. In a recently described study of individuals suffering frequently recurrent genital herpes, the capacity of their NK cells to kill a target cell-line, infected with Herpes Simplex virus, was tested (Fox *et al.*, 1999). A psychological intervention, hypnotherapy, increased anti-viral NK cell activity but only when the cells were stimulated with IL-2. The effect was most marked for individuals who reported improvement in their medical condition. There was no change in the overall ability of NK cells to kill tumour cell-line targets in the standard NK cell assay. PNI studies of NK cell activity are important because this measure may have a direct bearing on health outcomes, particularly in relation to viral infection and cancer.

Wound Healing

One of the most recent and provocative indices of immune status to be introduced into PNI research is wound healing. This also has some fairly direct implications for health outcomes, and relevant studies are reviewed in Chapter 9.

The approach is innovative. A small area of skin of standard diameter is excised from a convenient site such as the inner forearm. The wound is dressed and monitored over the succeeding days and weeks to record the progress of healing. Time taken to achieve objective criteria of healing is the crucial variable. Delay in healing will be largely due to early deficits in the recruitment of inflammatory cells. In a recent study analysis of fluid from blister chambers sampled at five hours and twenty-four hours after wound induction revealed that individuals scoring highly for perceived stress had higher salivary cortisol and produced lower levels of key inflammatory cytokines (Glaser *et al.*, 1999). The evidence is of stress-related inhibition of macrophage-mediated inflammatory processes but here measured directly at the site of tissue damage. This is also an example (rare) of deliberate provocation of an immune response in humans in order to examine the influence of psychological variables.

Animal Studies

The main focus of this book is to explore the ways in which human life and experience of the 'outer' world interact with the inner workings of the neuroendocrine and immune systems, and particularly what the implications of this may be for health. Most of the studies described in later chapters will therefore deal with human participants. Although we shall not dwell overly long on animal studies, there are some salient points that need to be made. PNI relationships have been probed in animal studies in ways that simply are not possible with humans, and some may indeed have ethical doubts about using animals in their stead. However, it has to be admitted that most of what has been learned about the pathways of communication between the brain and immune system derives from studies of laboratory rodents in which surgical, pharmacological, morphological and histological examination has been applied. In addition, inbred laboratory strains exhibiting a particular neuroendocrine–neuroimmune bias have been the subject of fruitful study (see Chapter 3). In future, knockout mice (mice with a specific gene deletion) will contribute further to our understanding of brain–endocrine–immune relationships. A brief overview of the role of animal studies is therefore included.

Animal Models

Animal models have been used to explore several areas within PNI: immunomodulation by classical conditioning, inflammatory activation of the stress–neuroendocrine axis, stress induced immunomodulation, in ways and with a degree of control that is not feasible with human subjects. In animal studies pathways of neuroimmune interaction can be explored at the cellular and molecular level and in relation to psychological manipulation, the progress of immune response can be revealed in detail.

A major thrust of animal study has been to explore the neuroimmune response to stress. In human studies there is a reasonable consensus as to what constitutes psychological stress. Threat, unpredictability and lack of control are important components and numerous models of both chronic and acute stress challenge have been explored. In rodent models we do not have such a clear notion of what is a stressor and certainly there is no subjective feedback. The most commonly applied stress procedure is restraint. The animal is placed into a narrow perspex tube, which severely restricts movement. The main indicator that this is a psychological stress is that it is effective in stimulating the HPA axis. A recent study (Sheridan *et al.*, 1998) affords a good example. Mice were infected with either Herpes virus or influenza and then subject to restraint in order to monitor neuroendocrine and ANS regulation over the immune response. There was detailed evidence of failure of cellular immunity in terms of cell trafficking and virus-specific cytokine induction and cytotoxic T cell activity. Pharmacological blockade of the type 11 glucocorticoid receptor reversed the influence of restraint on cell trafficking and cytokine production but did not restore the cytotoxic T cell activity. Additional blockade of β-adrenergic receptors fully restored cytotoxic function. This is a detailed and sophisticated study revealing much about endocrine and autonomic–immune relationships but using a 'psychological' manipulation of questionable ecological validity.

An alternative approach is to manipulate social stress. Male mice are normally solitary and very territorial. When housed together they form social hierarchies. Engineering of housing conditions to disrupt the stable social relationships between individuals increases aggression and social conflict. This model has been used to demonstrate the influence of stress in the mouse on reactivation of latent Herpes virus (Padgett *et al.*, 1998a). Although there is less individual control over such procedures they do involve behavioural responses – avoidance behaviour, submissive postures – which have some psychological validity. Of considerable interest is the fact that simple activation of the HPA axis by restraint, in these studies, did not activate the latent virus.

Most convincing are studies in which the rodent subjects themselves are not directly exposed to a stress challenge but are exposed to the pheromones produced by a stressed individual of the same species (conspecifics). Pheromones are odours that communicate emotional and motivational signals between individuals. Rodents (and many other animals) are very sensitive to the emotional language of pheromones. In this model, it isn't the original stress procedure that is important. It is translated into 'stress pheromones' and this is the key stimulus – inducing immunomodulatory influences via olfactory pathways. Recent studies employing this approach have provided convincing evidence of the Th1/Th2 shift in animals exposed only to the pheromones of stressed (footshock) conspecifics (Cocke *et al.*, 1993; Moynihan *et al.*, 1994) rather than the stressor itself.

The various measures used to determine immune status in PNI studies are illustrated in Figure 4.4. Although not always interpreted as such, many of these measures reveal shifts in the Th1/Th2 balance.

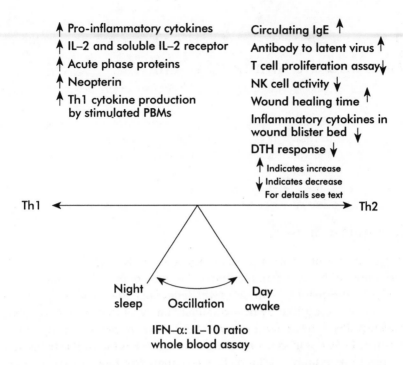

Figure 4.4 Measures of the Th1/Th2 balance of the immune system

Conclusions

Taken together the various approaches to measurement of immune parameters in both human and animal studies indicate that it is not necessarily important to demonstrate that any particular immune response is compromised in relation to a psychological variable. What is more important to know is how the immune system is balanced or set up and the degree to which psychological input influences this balance. This will determine the capacity of the immune system to behave adaptively. The evidence is most persuasive when a combination of these parameters in the same and/or different studies begin to tell the same story. As we shall see in the rest of this book, consensus is beginning to emerge in many areas of PNI.

Traditionally, immunologists have always considered the margins of error for immunological homeostasis to be considerable. Such complacency may, however, be misplaced. The evidence from PNI research is beginning to reveal just how important psychological influences may be on the immune system, and perhaps also vice versa.

5

Stress and the Immune System

The Nature of Stress

A huge number of research papers in the area of PNI make mention of the term 'stress', either as a major theme of the study or an indirect one. Indeed, to judge by the quantity of findings which have relentlessly accumulated, the reader might expect that by now we should know all there is to know about how stress affects the immune system. There is just one problem: people utilise the concept of stress in so many different ways that it is impossible to integrate findings in any simple fashion. It is essential therefore to deal with this complexity at the outset of this chapter, since it is a key consideration in attempting a careful interpretation of the multitude of studies in the area.

Consider some of the different sources of stress which have been investigated in humans in relation to their effects on immune system measures: bereavement, making a speech in public, divorce, exposure to earthquakes or potential nuclear hazards, doing taxing mental arithmetic problems, looking after a spouse with Alzheimer's disease, taking an important academic examination, undergoing minor or major surgery, job pressures, losing one's job, living with life-threatening diagnoses such as cancer or HIV infection, performing a difficult colour-naming task involving interference cues (the Stroop test), sleep deprivation, combat trauma, playing a difficult computer game, accumulated minor hassles over several days, accumulated major life events over a period of months. The list is not exhaustive and does not even include another whole literature on experimentation involving non-human animal species, but it certainly embraces the key methods of investigation used in a good majority of relevant studies of human beings.

What the list shows very clearly is the extreme diversity which has attached to the use of the word 'stress'. Clearly, if we are to look for any patterns in regard to effects on immunity we must recognise this diversity and seek to impose some order on it. For example, one approach would be to categorise the various 'stressors' according to further parameters such as duration and intensity.

Obviously, performing mental arithmetic, however pressurised, in a psychology department laboratory would generally be considered less intense a stressor than having to care for a spouse with Alzheimer's disease. These particular examples of stressors also differ in terms of duration. The former is an acute stressor and is soon over with; the latter is chronic, lasts an indefinite amount of time, and, subjectively, may indeed be perceived as a life sentence.

While the contrast between the two examples just given is stark enough to reveal differences in some parameters, it actually conceals further difficulties which emerge when we consider stressors which may seem more evenly matched on the parameters of intensity and duration, or even when we consider just a single stressor. Psychologists are well aware that different people can react very differently to ostensibly the same stressor. This may be because they appraise the stressor differently, or that they mobilise different coping skills to deal with it. The failure to take such factors into account was of course a key criticism of early work in the area of so-called 'Life Events' research which merely required participants to tick off how many events on a list had happened to them in the last six months or year. If individuals' psychological feelings of being under stress can be modulated by trait-like variables such as characteristic appraisal and coping styles, we might also expect the impact on their immune system to follow suit, and indeed these are issues which have had to be addressed in PNI studies.

Classic Physiological Stress Systems

There is one aspect of PNI work in the area of stress which can provide a unifying framework. Psychological inputs of whatever nature cannot impinge directly on peripheral events. They require neural and, most importantly, neuroendocrine pathways. What unites all of the stressors listed above is their potential, to varying degrees, to stimulate two key systems which we have already outlined in some detail in Chapter 3: the sympathetic adrenomedullary (SAM) system and the hypothalamic-pituitary-adrenal (HPA) axis. Indeed, at one recent conference billed as a 'Stress' conference, it was difficult to find any presentation that did not refer at some point to the HPA axis, and for some researchers it would seem that the capacity to stimulate the HPA axis is almost a definitional requirement of a stressor.

An advantage of keeping these physiological stress systems central stage is that we need not necessarily spend too long and laborious a time working out every nuance of difference which may help to define and refine the complex notion of psychological stress. Suppose that there is empirical evidence which suggests that the activation and mediation of certain *physio-*

logical stress systems are actually required conditions for stressors to have their more distal effects on the immune system. If so we may well conclude that, despite important psychological characteristics which differentiate a range of stressors, their effects are at least 'common' in regard to end-point immunological effects. That is not to deny of course that different psychological stressors may have very different effects in other respects, both psychological and physiological.

While a whole range of psychological stressors may be sufficient conditions for activating physiological stress systems, and bringing certain immunological consequences in their wake, we should not confuse sufficient conditions with necessary conditions. It is of course perfectly possible that the same immune effects mediated by physiological stress systems such as the SAM and HPA systems may be reproduced, using the very same route, by stimuli which we would not normally characterise as psychological stressors at all. It is important to mention this briefly at the outset, since we shall be postulating later on in this chapter that the SAM and HPA systems may in fact have evolved originally in the service of the immune system itself. The systems may only later, and, over a period of evolutionary time, have been 'co-opted' into the response, seen across a variety of species, to what we now call psychological stress (see also Chapter 3).

The Distinction between Chronic and Acute Stressors

To return to the matter of stressors differing in terms of intensity and duration, these dimensions are very likely to be important from an *a priori* point of view. We have seen in Chapter 3 that communications within the immune system and between the immune system, nervous and neuroendocrine systems involve multiple feedback loops. Some of these loops work locally while others work at a distance; some are positive feedback loops which are designed to magnify and maximise activation in the short term; others are negative feedback loops, essential for counter-regulation of necessary but, because of their potency, potentially harmful effects on the body's integrity.

All this means that *timing* of effects is of the essence, and we would not expect uniform effects of stressors which differ completely on *temporal* dimensions. In short, we might expect the research literature on the effects of acute stress on the immune system to tell a very different story from that associated with the effects of long-term chronic stress. We shall shortly discover that this is indeed the case.

Equally, we know from a wealth of evidence that classic acute laboratory stressors differ considerably in their potential to activate the classic SAM and HPA physiological stress systems, mentioned above. For example, we know that laboratory stressors such as paced mental arithmetic or other tasks involving pressurised mental activity are very useful controlled methods of activating the SAM system. This results in well documented effects on cardio-vascular activity consistent with activation of the sympathetic autonomic nervous system. However, the same stressors do not usually result in activation of the HPA axis, except perhaps for those few individuals in any sample who may respond particularly strongly to the situation. Indeed, it takes a lot of manipulation in controlled conditions to produce increases in levels of *cortisol*, which you will recall from previous chapters is the principal hormonal end-product of the HPA stress response in the human species.

It follows from this that the normal range of acute laboratory stressors to which we can ethically expose human participants are (with some exceptions usually involving social stress) unlikely to produce immune system effects which are mediated by the HPA axis, so straightaway we might expect differ-ences between experimental studies of acute stress, and those essentially correlational studies which have examined the impact of chronic stress on immune system measures. Chronic (and usually quite severe) stress, as we might expect, has been associated with HPA dysregulation as well as immuno-logical sequelae.

Empirical Studies of Chronic Stress

Having set the scene, we now move on to a consideration of some of the empirical evidence which has accumulated in regard to stress and the immune system. We shall begin by considering studies of chronic stress, by which we mean stress suffered over *periods* of time measured at least in weeks, but often months or even years. This contrasts with acute stress, which we define as *episodic* discrete events measured often in minutes or, at most, hours. Until the early 1990s, chronic studies tended to dominate the literature. They have been well reviewed in the past (see, for example, Herbert and Cohen, 1993). In this chapter, we shall be content merely to provide some good exemplars which tend to sum up the general conclusions to be drawn.

One important caveat which ought to be borne in mind is that earlier studies did not on the whole investigate the effects of stress (chronic or acute) on those vital molecular messengers of the immune system which we call cytokines (see Chapter 2). Indeed, appreciation of immune regulation at the level of cytokine influence was then in its infancy. However, our current knowledge of the role of cytokines will lead us, later in this chapter, to somewhat different, or at least more refined, conclusions about some of the effects which have been reported.

The early studies of chronic stress tended, with a few exceptions, to confine themselves to a few distinct immunological measures which have been outlined already in Chapter 4. The reader may wish to refer back to this chapter for more detailed discussion of the possible meanings of these measures in a wider context. While there has been some debate about the exact meaning of these measures in terms of broader immune system functioning, their widespread use has had the extremely positive consequence that by now we can be very confident that these particular immune responses to chronic stress are robust and reliable.

The most used measures can be divided into two categories. The first is enumerative measures (usually the number of circulating immune system cells of various types, but mostly T cells, B cells and Natural Killer (NK) cells) which are supposed to reflect the efficiency of the immune system in terms of its trafficking of important cells. The second category consists of what are called functional measures because they seek to mirror the efficiency of the immune system in responding to antigenic challenge. The most common functional measures have been, first, the capacity of lymphocytes to proliferate when challenged *in vitro* by substances called mitogens, and, second, the capacity of NK cells to 'kill' target cells *in vitro* (so-called cytotoxicity).

Two other measures have been used sufficiently in the chronic stress literature to merit further mention. Both involve antibodies. First, researchers have measured titres of specific antibodies to particular viruses which have the capacity to lie dormant or latent within the body's cells. The viruses have most often belonged to the Herpes family of viruses. This is a particularly good type of measure to take since a competent and vigilant cellular immune system should ensure that humoral involvement (production of specific antibodies) will be minimal. However, a virus that escapes cellular immune system curtailment will provoke humoral responding and lead to an increase in specific antibody titres.

The second measure which has been used sufficiently often in the research literature on stress for us to be able to draw robust conclusions is also enumerative and also involves measuring antibodies. Many researchers have measured levels of secretory immunoglobulin A (sIgA) which, as the name implies, is secreted on to all the mucosal surfaces of the body, and is therefore conveniently measured in saliva. In the case of this measure, the total concentration or secretion rate for all sIgA molecules is calculated regardless of antigen specificity. The rationale for the measure is that non-specific sIgA, by coating mucosal surfaces, acts as a competitive barrier against adhesion by any invading illness-provoking antigen.

Since effects involving all these particular measures have been very well documented and replicated across a number of studies, we shall not necessarily itemise them in detail in all the studies listed below. Suffice it to say that all measures have been reasonably consistent in showing that chronic stress is associated with down-regulated immunity: less trafficking of circulating lymphocytes (especially T cells, and more especially CD4+ cells as indicated by lower CD4/CD8 ratios), less efficient proliferation of lymphocytes in response to mitogen challenge, fewer circulating NK cells and lowered cytotoxicity, raised (specific) antibody titres to latent viruses, and lowered secretion of (nonspecific) sIgA.

However, the reader should not at this point jump to the conclusion that chronic stress is associated with a uniform down-regulation of all potential immune measures. We shall see later that there are indications that some aspects of humoral immune processes, in particular, may be up-regulated in chronic stress. It is worth emphasising that severe chronic stress may often be accompanied by depressed effect, withdrawal, and HPA dysfunction. Indeed, several of the chronically stressed groups mentioned in the studies below also exhibit high incidence of depressive disorders (for example, care-givers to spouses with Alzheimer's disease, divorced or separated individuals, and, as one would expect, those who have recently been bereaved). Interestingly, although the immunological profiles for chronic stress and diagnosed depression are similar in some respects (Natural Killer cells measures, for example) there are also important differences (in CD4+ T helper cell measures, for example). For that reason, depression and immunity is treated as a separate topic in Chapter 6.

The range of chronic stressors studied in relation to those most commonly used immune measures described above is impressive. Some of the earliest studies looked at the impact of a particularly severe source of stress: bereavement. In terms of life event research, bereavement is usually counted as the most stressful event on standard inventories of major events, and indeed is often used as an anchor-point for weighting other lesser events.

In a pioneering study of the impact of stress on the immune system, Bartrop *et al.*, (1977) compared a sample of twenty-seven recently bereaved persons with matched controls. The results showed a clear down-regulation of mitogen induced proliferation of both T cells and B cells in the recently bereaved compared with the controls.

In a further prospective study of bereavement as a stressor, Schleifer *et al.*, (1983) studied fifteen spouses of women with advanced breast cancer. Lymphocyte proliferation response to mitogen challenge was again significantly suppressed during the first two months following the death of the spouse, but this time (*cf.* the Bartrop *et al.* study) comparison was with the spouse's own pre-bereavement levels rather than with matched controls. A highly significant suppression was seen as early as one month after bereavement. During a four- to fourteen-month period after bereavement, proliferation scores were still lower than pre-bereavement but the effects not so pronounced.

Researchers have also looked at another major source of stress: divorce, separation and marital disharmony (Kiecolt-Glaser *et al.*, 1987; Kiecolt-Glaser *et al.*, 1993). In the first of these studies, women who had recently been separated from their partners scored significantly lower on both enumerative and functional immune measures than a group of demographically matched married controls. They also were significantly more depressed. Among those who were separated or divorced, the recentness of the separation experience and the level of prior attachment to their husband were both associated with poorer immunological functioning and greater depression.

In the second of these two studies, newlywed couples were invited to take part in a thirty-minute discussion of marital problems. Those who exhibited more negative or hostile behaviour during the discussion showed reduced NK cytotoxicity, reduced mitogen-induced proliferation, and higher antibody titres to latent Epstein-Barr virus, than their less negative and hostile counterparts. Although this study used an acute manipulation in the form of a discussion session designed to elicit thinking and talking about problems, the results can be interpreted in terms of more chronic differences between groups of individuals. It is likely that more negative and hostile behaviour in the discussion period reflected quality of interaction outside the experimental setting. However, it is worth pointing out that the more negative and hostile individuals actually showed a greater increase (over twenty-four hours following the manipulation) in the total number of T lymphocytes and, particularly, CD4+ T lymphocytes. As we shall see below, enumerative measures often do show increases in acute paradigms, and it seems that this particular finding reflected the acute aspect of the study.

It is also interesting to note that immunological effects were more evident for wives rather than husbands. This should remind us that the same stressor, measured in the same way in terms of what people said and how they behaved externally, does not necessarily 'mean' the same thing to different people. It is possible that differences in appraisal processes may explain the immunological differences between men and women in this study.

Caring for a demented relative is known to be a profoundly stressful and, by its nature, chronic life experience, and has provided PNI researchers with a useful model for studying the impact of stress on immune measures. In one of the first studies, Kiecolt-Glaser *et al.* (1991) showed that relative to controls, immunological deficits, particularly down-regulation of cellular immunity, were apparent over a follow-up period of thirteen months. The study also highlighted the role that social support can have in potentially buffering the effects of a powerful stressor. Immunological deficits were more apparent in those lacking good social support. This study also highlights yet again the importance of appraisal. Immunological deficits were more pronounced in those who reported greater personal distress occasioned by the symptoms of their spouse with dementia.

Another stressor which has proved very popular in PNI research has been academic examinations. The use of this stressor needs some qualification in regard to whether it is categorised as an acute stressor or a chronic one. As we shall see, in terms of immunological effects, results suggest that if measures are taken immediately before an examination and then immediately after, the profile does indeed match that of acute stressors. However, if the contrast is between measures taken at any time during an *exam period* and control measures taken at some other more distant and assumed 'relaxed' period, then the profile resembles that for chronic stress. We shall concentrate on the latter profile at this point.

An early classic study was that of Halvorsen and Vassend (1987). They looked at the effect of examination stress on functional measures, including mitogen-induced proliferation and enumerative measures (CD4+ and CD8+ T cells). Compared to control values six weeks before the examination, students showed a decline in lymphocyte proliferation through the examination itself and continuing down-regulation up to a fortnight after the examination. A decline in mitogen-induced lymphocyte proliferation has also been replicated in other studies of examination stress (for example, Gilbert *et al.*, 1996). The results from the enumerative measures were, however, particularly interesting since the researchers measured large and therefore probably activated T cells (see Chapter 2). These were lower at the time of examination compared with basal values, but circulating monocytes were higher.

This relatively early study also looked at cytokine function by measuring expression of the IL-2 receptor on cells. The expression of IL-2 receptors was shown to decline at the time of examinations. It will be remembered from earlier chapters that IL-2 is a cytokine which is strongly associated with Th1 activity and which therefore supports cellular-based immune processes rather than humoral-based ones. This experiment then gives an early indication of what we shall discuss a little later, that the effect of psychological stress is not so much an entire down-regulation of the immune system but rather a shift of bias from cell-mediated immune processes to humoral-based ones.

A similar study was carried out on first-year medical students (Glaser *et al.*, 1987) where it was shown that academic examinations led to raised titres of specific antibody to latent virus (Epstein-Barr). This was not the only measure in this study to point to a specific down-regulation of cell-based immunity. The researchers were also pioneering in the use of cytokine measures, and another finding was that production of IFN-γ by mitogen-stimulated lymphocytes was reduced at the time of examinations relative to the base measures taken a month before. It will be recalled from earlier chapters that IFN-γ is one of the key cytokines associated with Th1 cellular-based immunity.

Examinations have also been shown to be associated with lower levels of secretory immunoglobulin A (sIgA). Early work with this measure was difficult to interpret since researchers tended often to report only concentrations in saliva rather than secretion rates. Since the concentration depends crucially on the volume of saliva being secreted, it is imperative to control for volume or at least to report whether findings are volume dependent. More recent studies, which have done so, do, however, confirm earlier reports of lowered sIgA during periods of examinations (Deinzer and Schuller, 1998).

Another approach to studying the longer-term and more chronic impact of stress on immunity is to look at populations which have been exposed to natural disasters. McKinnon *et al.*, (1989) took immunological measures from chronically stressed individuals living near Three Mile Island where a nuclear power plant had been damaged with resulting high anxiety prevalent in the community. Compared with demographically comparable control subjects, Three Mile Island residents showed lower circulating lymphocyte levels (but raised numbers of neutrophils). They also had higher titres of specific antibodies to latent Herpes Simplex virus.

Similar lasting down-regulation of immune parameters has since been reported in the aftermaths of both earthquakes (Solomon *et al.*, 1997) and hurricanes (Ironson *et al.*, 1997).

Th1 to Th2 Shift in Studies of Chronic Stress

So far in our discussion, we have shown that chronic stress is associated with down-regulation on a number of commonly used immune system measures. We have, however, already cautioned that we should not on the basis of this accumulated evidence extrapolate to the entire immune system. There have already been clues in the presentation of the results above that chronic stress may actually be associated with shifts in the bias of certain immune system processes, rather than universal down-regulation.

We now shall consider evidence that this is indeed the case, and that the most salient aspect of bias concerns that crucial event in acquired immunity which happens when CD4+ lymphocytes meet antigenic targets. This is a key stage in the mobilisation of immune forces, the outcome of which will determine the degree to which effector mechanisms are directed towards assisting a predominantly (Th1) cellular immune response, or alternatively are directed to assisting a predominantly (Th2) humoral response (for more detail, refer back to Chapter 2).

While both humoral and cellular processes are normally involved in the total immune response, one process is usually dominant in any provoked challenge, and indeed any initial bias is reinforced by the fact that many of the different cytokines associated with Th1 processes actually inhibit Th2 processes and vice versa. Thus, when a bias is once in evidence it is very difficult to shift. A good example of this is in leprosy, where the nature of the pathology can be very different, and more or less severe, depending on whether the immune system has 'decided' initially to mobilise a predominantly Th1 cell-based response or a predominantly Th2 humoral response. Another example of the importance of potential shifting of bias is seen in HIV infection, where progression to full-blown AIDS is associated with a shift from a predominantly Th1 response to a Th2-response. The reader should refer back to earlier chapters for a more detailed discussion of the Th1/Th2 distinction.

The evidence that chronic stress involves not so much blanket down-regulation of immune processes but rather a shift, as in HIV infection, from Th1 to Th2 dominance is now very strong. We shall briefly describe some of that evidence. First, however, we may note that many of the studies already described point to stress being particularly associated with poorer cellular immune response. While T cell proliferation, as one of the most widely used PNI measures, is not an unambiguous indicator of Th1 functioning, raised titres of specific antibody to latent viruses is a clear indication of poorer cell-based immunity, as mentioned at the beginning of this chapter.

We can now point to another type of measure which has been used, especially more recently, in studies of stress and immunity. This involves the procedure of a skin test which experimentally introduces a previously encountered antigen in order to provoke a so-called delayed type hypersensitivity (DTH) reaction (see Chapter 4). Many readers may be familiar with an example of a DTH reaction in the form of the tuberculin test which is routinely given to children to see whether they have been previously exposed to tuberculosis infection. A characteristic small inflamed lump appears on the skin after a delay of a couple of days if prior exposure has taken place. The efficiency of a DTH reaction is a relatively pure measure of cellular immune system surveillance.

In terms of chronic stress studies, it has been shown repeatedly that DTH reactions are relatively poorer in people enduring long periods of isolation stress, such as space-station cosmonauts (Gmunder *et al.*, 1994), and scientists on Antarctic surveys (Tingate *et al.*, 1997). Similar suppressed DTH responding was found in a sample of military trainees undergoing stressful and intensive training over an eight-week period (Bernton *et al.*, 1995). The latter study was interesting in that it also showed that the effect is short-lived. Although suppressed cell-based immunity was evident at all sampling points within the eight weeks, DTH showed significant recovery within three days of the end of training.

Although the evidence so far clearly points to the role of stress in down-regulating Th1-orchestrated immune processes, we need to mention other more recent studies to provide a convincing case that the key effects of stress are to bias against Th1 and in favour of Th2 dominance. The studies that are most relevant have looked at the balance of Th1 and Th2 cytokines produced within organisms exposed to stress.

There have been relatively few cytokine studies of human beings exposed to chronic stress, and much of the evidence comes from experiments using restraint stress in animal models (for example, Iwakabe *et al.*, 1998). This experiment is typical in showing that stress causes a selective reduction in Th1 cytokines (in this case IFN-γ) and no change in Th2 cytokines (IL-4) thus altering the cytokine balance in favour of Th2 processes.

While many of the animal experiments might be described as acute stress manipulations, this is somewhat misleading in the context of the chronic/acute distinction we have made in regard to human studies. The acute stressors used by animal researchers are universally intense enough to ensure HPA activation, and as we shall explore later, Th1/Th2 shifting may well be one aspect of the effects of stress which is at least partially mediated by the HPA axis. As we indicated earlier, HPA activation is rare and, if it does occur, relatively weak in human studies of acute stress. Furthermore, human studies of acute stress are usually measured in minutes, both in terms of manipulations and immune system effects, while these so-called acute studies with animals are usually measured in hours with immune effects observable for days.

There is one stressor, studied in human subjects, which is similar in being somewhat intermediate on a scale of duration but high in intensity, and that is the event of a surgical operation. The father of modern stress research, Hans Selye, discovered many years ago that in addition to specific physiological effects of any particular surgical intervention, the trauma of the procedure itself was associated with activation of the classic stress systems, and researchers have continued to look at surgery as a stressor in relation to immune system effects. Studies have been done recently to see how the stress of surgery in human beings affects the Th1/Th2 balance of the immune system. There could of course be important implications of identifying a shift away from Th1 towards Th2 in this instance. Such a shift would potentially heighten vulnerability to infection in a population which is already vulnerable in this respect.

Two studies were carried out by Decker and colleagues (Decker *et al.*, 1996; Decker *et al.*, 1999). In both studies there was evidence of surgery inducing a Th1 to Th2 shift. In the first study, Th1 and Th2 activities were assessed by the cytokines IFN-γ and IL-4, respectively. Measures were taken from stimulated peripheral blood mononuclear cells (PBMCs). In the second study, Th1 and Th2 cells were themselves identified and quantified. What is particularly salient in identifying the impact of stress on immune function is that both studies also compared less invasive (so-called keyhole) surgical techniques with conventional ones: laparoscopic versus conventional surgery for cholecystectomy in the first study; endoscopic versus conventional surgery for hernia in the second study. In both cases, it was found that Th1 to Th2 shift was greater in the case of the more invasive and presumably more stressful conventional interventions.

Further evidence of stress induced Th1/Th2 shift comes from a study already mentioned (Bernton *et al.*, 1995). These researchers showed suppressed delayed type hypersensitivity reactions in stressed military trainees indicating suppressed Th1 functioning. However, in the same study, the trainees also showed increased circulating levels of immunoglobulin E (IgE). Increased switching (see Chapter 2) to this antibody class and its increased synthesis is a clear indication of Th2 processes being favoured in the internal milieu.

The implications of stress being associated with a shift from Th1 to Th2 bias we shall leave to our final chapter where we discuss health issues. But the implications for health may be quite important, especially in certain vulnerable groups. In this chapter it is more appropriate to ask how these stress-induced effects are mediated. There is a good deal of evidence from predominantly rodent studies that the HPA axis may underpin those down-regulated processes we see in stress and also perhaps the pattern of Th1/Th2 shift. We shall now look at HPA involvement.

The Role of the HPA in Stress–Immune Interactions

Important bidirectional communication between the central nervous system and the peripheral immune system has been well described earlier in this book (see Chapter 3) and so also has the crucial mediating role played by the HPA axis. At this point, and in the context of this particular chapter, we shall be using this basic knowledge to try to make some sense of the findings we have reported in relation to the effects of stress on the immune system.

It should be borne in mind that we will be presenting a simplified picture. Only some of the key cytokines and hormones are discussed, and the role of other hypothalamus-initiated axes (including the thyroid and gonadal axes) are not included. Nor should the reader assume that all effects of stress on the immune system are mediated by the HPA axis. For example, several *in vivo* studies suggest that some of the principal down-regulatory effects of stress on the immune system can still occur when adrenal activity is blocked. Equally, the immune system is known to be capable itself, at local level, of synthesising the key hormones (CRH and ACTH) which drive the main axis leading finally to the secretion of corticosteroids by the adrenal cortex.

We should also remember (see Chapter 3) that ACTH stimulates general steroidogenesis in the adrenal cortex, and the cortex also produces the androgen-type steroid DHEA, which tends to have opposite effects to glucocorticoids. DHEA may also be a significant factor in the overall stress response, although work in this area is at an early stage. Immunological consequences of stress may be more subtly dependent on the balance of glucocorticoid (principally cortisol in humans and corticosterone in rodents) and DHEA produced. It is known for example that severe trauma such as burns are associated with massively elevated cortisol and reduced DHEA. However, intense but non-injurious stress as seen in the study of military trainees mentioned above is accompanied by large elevations in cortisol and also moderate elevations in DHEA (Bernton *et al.*, 1995). Nevertheless, despite increasing evidence that the whole picture is indeed more complex than we are presenting here, most researchers would agree that the HPA does play a crucial and pervasive role in regulating activity of the immune system.

The first thing to note is the plethora of positive feedback loops that characterise the response of the immune system to antigen challenge. This is purposive. They are designed to *amplify* the initial response. Cytokines are not only released from one cell to activate another. There are also so-called 'autocrine' activities where a cytokine may provide feedback to stimulate its further release. We may further note that much inhibitory influence comes from glucocorticoids. Glucocorticoids are on the face of it potently and generally immunosuppressive, when studied both *in vitro* and *in vivo* (Falaschi *et al.*, 1999; Mastorakos *et al.*, 1999). However, in relevant physiological amounts the picture is more complex (see below). They suppress proliferation of immune cells to mitogen challenge; they reduce trafficking of most leukocytes, with the exception of the neutrophils. Neutrophils are the phagocytes which are produced rapidly and migrate to local areas of infection in the very earliest stage of the innate immune defence response. Glucocorticoids reduce all aspects of the inflammatory immune response. They reduce immune cell cytotoxicity. They also inhibit the production of most cytokines (for example, IL-1 through to IL-6, TNF-α and IFN-γ). Note this list includes cytokines such as IL-4 which supports Th2 response development as well as Th1 promoting cytokines. However, the evidence from studies involving physiologically relevant amounts of endogenous glucocorticoids, suggests that it is Th1 cytokines which are principally reduced, with little effect on or even up-regulation of Th2 cytokines (see Chapter 3).

Since the inhibitory effects of glucocorticoids, as we have noted, are in contrast to the generally amplifying nature of many other communications, we can reasonably assume that the HPA may have crucially evolved to provide a necessary brake on immune processes which, if activated in the absence of checks and balances, could be extremely harmful to an organism. Hence, cytokines which are produced by the immune system when infection is 'sensed' do indeed stimulate the HPA axis. The cytokines that are most responsible for acting as messengers from the immune system as sense organ to the brain which initiates the HPA cascade of events are IL-1, IL-6, and TNF. It is interesting that HPA stimulation by cytokines as a response to infection takes place over a longer period (several hours) than the HPA response to acute stress. Thus an immediate period of potent defensive inflammatory response is permitted prior to any significant glucocorticoid restraint. Equally, the earlier hormones produced in the HPA cascade (CRH and ACTH) are, in some respects, immuno-enhancing and pro-inflammatory. This should remind us that timing factors are crucial in the operation of what we should assume are normally adaptive systems.

Counter-regulation and homeostasis may not be the only factors in explaining why an activated immune system triggers the HPA cascade. The cytokines which stimulate the HPA also have other central nervous system effects, which result, for example, in fever and malaise (see Chapter 3). Raised temperature is adaptive since it tends to inhibit the multiplication of infectious microbes but facilitate defensive immune processes. However, raising the body temperature by a single degree Celsius involves a massive deployment of energy. Malaise and inactivity further encouraged by increased pain perception are therefore adaptive energy-saving consequences of infection which are orchestrated by the central nervous system and are particularly provoked by IL-1. However, as we have just said, this means that further reserves of energy are called upon in fighting an infection, and this is where the HPA is involved. One of the principal roles of glucocortocoids such as cortisol is gleaned from the generic term itself: these are steroids which promote the conversion of stored energy into a form (glucose) which can be used by the body.

Evidence is now clear that the HPA axis is involved in mounting and regulating the body's overall response to infection, and also guarding against excessive amplification of immune system effects, notably inflammation. Given such evidence, we may begin to see the HPA axis itself as peculiarly well adapted to these purposes. An illuminating speculation, therefore, is whether in fact these purposes were the *primary* factor in the evolution of the axis, and that its classic role in stress, although discovered and outlined earlier, is in fact a later development in evolutionary terms (for a review of this line of thinking see Maier and Watkins, 1998). As we know, the same consequences of energy mobilisation makes the HPA a peculiarly useful mechanism in coping with fight or flight emergencies. No matter that the energy is put to very different use in the context of response to stress, the need to release rapidly stored energy reserves is the same. There are also benefits, in the short term, in down-regulating the immune system, particularly inflammatory responses. Injuries such as sprains, for example, cannot be allowed to interfere with continued running, which may be a matter of life and death. The emphasis on 'short term' is important. As we have just mentioned, the HPA response to stress, particularly the peaking of glucocorticoid end-products, happens rapidly, unlike HPA activation via cytokines in response to infection. It will be a major discussion point in Chapter 9 whether chronic stress (and accompanying chronic HPA activation) is, in the natural scheme of things, a mostly human problem, and a modern one, to which we are not well adapted, and which may therefore have undesirable immunological consequences which impinge on our physical as well as psychological health.

Acute Stressors in Human Studies

We have suggested earlier that the effects of acute stress as evidenced in human studies may be different in key ways from the pattern we see in chronic stress. In this final section, we address this issue in more detail.

The sorts of acute stressors which have been looked at in laboratory studies have been a mixture of, on the one hand, mental tasks involving high demands on cognitive processes, and, on the other hand, social pressure, such as public speaking or confrontational role play. Sometimes the two types of stressor merge, as, for example, in a protocol where subjects are asked to perform mental arithmetic under conditions of harassment. From a good number of acute manipulation studies we can clearly state that such manipulations lead to an increase in certain immune cell trafficking, notably redistribution of NK cells and CD8+ cells into the blood circulation. Such effects have been reported for confrontational role play (Naliboff *et al.*, 1995), for mental arithmetic in several studies (for example, Naliboff *et al.*, 1991), and for public speaking (Mills *et al.*, 1995; Van der Pompe *et al.*, 1998).

Effects for B cells and T helper (CD4+) cells are minimal or non-existent (see Naliboff *et al.*, 1991). Thus measures such as the percentage of CD4+ cells or CD4/CD8 ratios tend to be reduced. Note that the elevation of NK cells and CD8+ cytotoxic T cells is an up-regulatory finding and contrasts sharply with the findings of reduced lymphocyte trafficking (especially for NK cells) in studies of those who are chronically stressed, or where the duration and consequences of an episodic stressor (such as surgery) are over a lengthier period than one measured in minutes. Typically, the sorts of stressors we are talking about here last for a few minutes and the effects have vanished within the hour.

Another consistent effect of acute stress is a pronounced elevation in the secretion of secretory immunoglobulin A (sIgA). Once again this contrasts with results from studies with a longer time horizon such as the stress of minor life events over weeks (Evans *et al.*, 1993) and exam periods (Deinzer and Schuller, 1998). In these circumstances, stress is associated with lower sIgA levels. By contrast, sIgA is elevated by stressors such as public speaking (Evans *et al.*, 1994), demanding computer games (Carroll *et al.*, 1996), mental arithmetic (Willemsen *et al.*, 1998), air traffic control sessions (Zeier *et al.*, 1996) and the very 'ecologically valid' stressor of being a soccer coach watching a crucial game (Kugler *et al.*, 1996).

One measure which seems to show a similar down-regulation in both acute and chronic studies is the proliferation response of lymphocytes to mitogen challenge (for acute studies see, for example, Sgoutas-Emch *et al.*, 1994; Cacioppo *et al.*, 1998).

So much for clear effects. One measure which seems to be more sensitive to complexity in acute manipulations is the activity, the actual cytotoxicity, of the NK cells. Although this has been examined in several studies, including many of those already reported above, it is a measure which can be confounded with the number of NK cells. The two measures are in effect correlated.

NK cell activity is generally reported as being increased by acute stress and this would be in line with the up-regulatory pattern reported for enumerative measures. However, this is not always the case when the often simultaneously increased number of NK cells is taken into account (see, for example, Cacioppo *et al.*, 1998). After adjustment for NK cell number, it has even been reported that a social stressor reduced NK cytotoxicity (Naliboff *et al.*, 1995). Similarly, a mental arithmetic stressor was shown to lead to an acute decrease in NK cell cytotoxicity among more chronically stressed persons (Pike *et al.*, 1997).

This last result suggests that whatever the mechanisms are that underpin changes in NK numbers, there are different mechanisms underpinning NK function. It further suggests that the effects on NK function may be importantly modulated by general and more chronic aspects of a person's emotional life. It is interesting to note that background emotional state has also been shown to modulate the effects of acute stress on NK numbers: those with worse emotional state over the week prior to the study showed less increase in NK numbers to the acute stressor (Naliboff *et al.*, 1995).

It seems from a number of studies that the mechanisms for some of the immune system effects of acute stress involve the sympathetic autonomic nervous system. It will be recalled that while HPA effects are small to non-existent for many of these stressors used in human studies, they do generally create significant autonomic arousal. It has been found that the degree of stressor-induced sympathetic activity, as measured by a sensitive cardiovascular index called pre-ejection period, is correlated with degree of NK cell activity (Uchino *et al.*, 1995). A recent meta-analysis of studies also shows a convincing relationship between cardiovascular and NK enumerative measures across a range of acute stressors indicating sympathetic nervous system involvement (Benschop *et al.*, 1998).

Studies of very acute stress in humans have not included direct measures of adaptive cellular immune system functioning as seen in the DTH test. However, one intriguing study has indicated that in rodents the effects of acute stress (two hours before antigen challenge) is to increase the efficiency of the DTH response, whereas more chronic stress in the week before challenge impairs it (Dhabhar and McEwen, 1997). The authors suggest that the facilitating effect of acute stress may be due to increased trafficking of immune cells to the skin.

Why might it be appropriate to up-regulate some aspects of immunity to deal with short-term stress? An answer may well be that it is adaptive in terms of fight or flight emergencies to mobilise rapidly for the possible ingress of infectious agents, either through wounds and grazed skin, or through the massively increased amount of potentially microbe-laden air which passes over mucosal surfaces to meet oxygen needs. It is interesting that all measures showing consistent up-regulation are enumerative. This points to the possible beneficial consequences of increased trafficking of cells under conditions of threat to barriers such as the skin, and of increased protection of mucosal surfaces in the case of elevated sIgA.

Conclusions

In this chapter we have reviewed a number of studies involving both chronic and acute stress, and their effect on a number of different immune system measures. By way of conclusion, the overall picture that emerges is presented in condensed form in Table 5.1.

Table 5.1 A summary of the effects of chronic and acute stressors on a variety of immune system measures

Measure	Description	Chronic	Acute
CD4+number	Trafficking efficiency	Down	0
CD8+number	Trafficking efficiency	Down	Up
NK number	Trafficking efficiency	Down	Up
B cell number	Trafficking efficiency	0	0
sIgA secretion	Mucosal protection	Down	Up
Mitogen challenge	Lymphocyte proliferation	Down	Down
EBV titres	Viral escape	Up	n/a
HSV titres	Viral escape	Up	n/a
DTH Test	Cellular immune efficiency	Down	Up
IgE	Humoral bias	Up	?
Th1 cytokines (e.g. IL-2)	Promote cellular immunity	Down	?
Th2 cytokines (e.g. IL-4)	Promote humoral immunity	0/Up	?
Cortisol	HPA activation	Up	0

Key:
'0' = inconsistent or no effect
'?' = unknown effects
'0/' = tendency but not always consistent
'n/a' = not applicable

The main conclusions are that chronic stress is clearly associated with down-regulation of a number of measures of cellular immune function, while humoral immunity is less affected, and, in some cases, may even be up-regulated. Putting together the findings, the effects of chronic stress are consistent with a shift in immunity from predominantly a Th1 type to a Th2 type. Acute stress, on the other hand, is associated with a rather different profile, which certainly involves increases in a number of enumerative measures (particularly NK cells, CD8+ cells, and secretion rate of sIgA), and may even temporarily up-regulate clear functional measures of cellular immunity (DTH reactions) via increased trafficking. Finally, we have speculated about why this may be.

We have not included in this chapter more recent studies of the effects of stress on such obviously health-related measures as time taken for wounds to heal, or response to clinical vaccination. These we leave to the final chapter of this book, where we shall discuss in detail the role of psychosocial variables, particularly chronic stress, in determining health outcomes.

6

Depression and the Immune System

Depression and Physical Illness

The belief that depression and susceptibility to certain physical illnesses are somehow linked reaches far back into history. Modern psychoneuroimmunology has set out to determine the validity of this belief and the possible mechanisms by which these factors may interact. Research has shown that progression of some diseases (for example, cancer, AIDS, cardiovascular disease) can be accelerated by depressed mood and that this relationship is mediated by dysfunction in both the immune and neuroendocrine systems. The evidence is presented below. Characteristic physiological changes which accompany depression occur in the brain (reduced monoamine neurotransmitter availability), various aspects of immune function (reduced NK cell activity and, paradoxically, activation of inflammation and the acute phase response) and the HPA axis (increased CRF and cortisol). It is considered that the complex relationships between behaviour, immune activity and the HPA axis were established early during vertebrate evolution and are adaptive for survival. Depression is associated with dysfunction in this triangular relationship. At present it is not clear whether the initial dysfunction may originate in the brain (mood change), the HPA axis (prolonged activation) or the immune system (prolonged inflammatory disturbance). What is clear, however, is that melancholic mood can both accelerate disease progression and is a *symptom* of immune activation and illness.

The link between depression and cancer has been the focus of much interest. The Greek physician Galen, practising in the second century AD, described how 'melancholic' women developed cancer more frequently than those of a more 'sanguine' nature. In the eighteenth century the surgeon Richard Guy identified women diagnosed with cancer as being 'of a sedentary, melancholic disposition of mind, who meet with such disasters in life as occasion much trouble and grief'. Others in the past have commented upon 'the influence of mental misery and the sudden reversal of fortune' as well as 'deep anxiety, deferred hope and disappointment' and occurrence of cancer. The problem with these early reports is that it is impossible to infer whether the melancholic disposition caused the onset of cancer, or vice versa.

Perhaps it is an indication of the striking link between depression and cancer that the first statistical study of this relationship was performed as early as 1893, many years before modern PNI research. This study (undertaken at the London Cancer Hospital) concluded that the relationship between depression and the cancers was too high to be attributable to chance. Others pointed to a relationship between bereavement and development of cancer. By the middle of the twentieth century there had been many reports in the medical press asserting that the link between depressed state of mind and occurrence of a wide range of cancer types was 'more than a coincidental finding' (Greer, 1983).

However, in reality it is very hard to perform controlled prospective studies designed to explore whether psychological characteristics predispose to a particular clinical condition. By the time a patient presents at a clinic for diagnosis the underlying condition may be well established. Cancer typically requires considerable time to develop or to be detected. These limits on our ability to detect very early-stage disease or to follow its slow early-stage development make it difficult to study the role of emotions in its aetiology. As we shall see later in this chapter, it is likely that the immune system's response to the disease may be able to influence the mood of cancer patients directly; the treatments may also provide a confounding factor. These methodological considerations mean that it is easier to explore the relationship between psychology and *progression* of the disease. Despite this, a few studies have tried to explore predisposition; however, they should be viewed with caution. In one much cited study the depression scores of over two thousand subjects were analysed seventeen years prior to a health assessment. There was a twofold increase in death from cancer among those who had previously scored high on the depression questionnaire (Shekelle *et al.*, 1981). A subsequent meta-analysis inferred 'a small but significant link between depression and the development of cancer' (McGee *et al.*, 1994). However, other studies have shown that while depression is associated with increased mortality, this mortality is primarily associated with accidents and suicide. Furthermore, a cluster of studies have demonstrated that the cause of death in depressed patients is not predominantly cancer (see Miller, 1998, for review).

Whilst the most recent studies agree that there is no conclusive evidence that depression does predispose to cancer, they are agreed that depression may influence the course of the illness once it has taken hold. Once cancer has been diagnosed, 'exceptional survival rates' have been associated with highly optimistic and positive psychological states (Roud, 1986). In addition it appears that emotional reactions and adjustment to diagnosis can affect progression (Helgeson and Cohen, 1996). Some of the strongest evidence of the impact of depression on cancer disease progression comes from intervention programmes. Psychosocial treatments have been shown to be helpful in improving mood in cancer patients and have also been reported to improve survival (Fawzy *et al.*, 1995; Newport and Nemeroff, 1998).

Depression has also been shown to contribute to increased mortality in cardiovascular disease (Frasure-Smith *et al.*, 1993). The link seems likely to be mediated by the effect of circulating hormones, known to be elevated in depression. For instance, cortisol and corticotrophin releasing factor (CRF) may induce tachycardia and increased arterial blood pressure. Dysregulation of other aspects of the sympathetic nervous system and central monoamine function could also contribute to increased morbidity from cardiovascular disease. Depression has also been shown to accelerate progression of HIV disease and AIDS. For example a study of 104 HIV+ individuals enrolled on the Oslo HIV cohort study suggested that negative affect was related to somatic symptoms associated with progression (Vassend *et al.*, 1997). Again, intervention programmes that reduced distress were shown to be beneficial in HIV (LaPerriere *et al.*, 1994).

In summary, studies indicate that depression, while it may not be associated with induction of a specific clinical syndrome, does interact with an individual's disease liability (for example, cancer, cardiovascular disease or AIDS) to significantly influence disease expression and progression. Recently it has been pointed out that PNI should not neglect the importance of individual genotype in disease susceptibility. In a twin study (in which the relative importance of genetic and environmental factors can be probed by comparison of identical and non-identical twins) the immune response to psychological distress (environmental factors) was substantially moderated by genetic influences (Hickie *et al.*, 1999). Notwithstanding this, it must be acknowledged that the psychological state of depression can, and does, have a physiological impact. This impact can be sufficient to influence disease progression. It is vital to understand how this effect is mediated. Only by understanding relevant mechanisms can effective treatments be developed.

Depression and Natural Killer Cells

The most likely way by which depression may be linked to cancer progression is via reduced immune competence. In this respect the role of NK cells is of prime importance. They respond in a relatively non-specific way to a variety of tumour and virally infected cells by general recognition of some significant change on the surface of a cell (see Chapter 2). It is thought that NK cells can therefore destroy cancer cells with immediate effect. Recall from Chapter 4 that determination of NK cell activity involves assaying their cytotoxic potency against tumour cell lines. Thus NK cells are certainly capable of fighting cancer. Notwithstanding their innate capacity to detect and destroy tumour cells, NK cells are part of the Th1 armoury (see Chapter 2) since they are sensitive to, and stimulated by, the Th1 cytokines IL-2 and IFN-γ. The importance of NK cells in defence against tumours is illustrated by the increased incidence of cancer in individuals with a genetic defect which results in impaired NK cell function (see Kuby, 1997). As a matter of interest, attempts to cure cancer by increasing immunocompetence (immunotherapy) are generally focused upon enhancing function of the NK cell population. On the other hand, AIDS progression is characterised by a shift from Th1 to Th2 domination (Clerici and Shearer, 1994). Therefore any psychological state that reduced the efficiency of Th1 defence could, in principle, compromise immunosurveillance by NK cells and accelerate morbidity.

The first report to consider the immune system in depressive disorders was published in 1978 (Cappel *et al.*, 1978). During the following twelve years an additional twenty human studies appeared in print. They used an array of enumerative techniques and functional assays to examine the effect of depression on the human immune system. These studies reported no *consistent* change in the representation of immune cell populations in the peripheral circulation of depressed patients. Of the functional studies, the two that received the most attention in this context were the *in vitro* lymphocyte proliferative response to mitogens and assay of Natural Killer (NK) cell activity (see Chapter 4). Unfortunately, again, there was no consensus of opinion as to the impact of depression on these measures. Although several groups reported reduced proliferation and decreased NK cell activity, others did not. Of course, these inconsistencies in the literature, which could be attributed to methodological issues, led to widespread confusion and some scepticism (for review see Stein *et al.*, 1991).

Depression: Diagnostic Considerations

The 1990s brought further research that has enlightened the entire area. There is now widespread agreement about the changes in immune system functioning commonly associated with depression of the 'melancholic' type. Before detailing these changes perhaps now is a good time to dwell on the significance of this last statement, that is, 'melancholic' type depression. The psychiatric diagnosis of depression largely relies on diagnostic criteria from the *Diagnostic and Statistical Manual of Mental Disorders* (*DSM-IV*) handbook (American Psychiatric Association, 1994). The diagnosis follows a semistructured interview that focuses on specific symptoms and symptom clusters. 'Mood' is defined as a person's relatively stable emotional state and is differentiated from brief fluctuations in emotion that may occur throughout the day. However, the appearance of 'depressed mood' alone is not sufficient, according to the *DSM-IV*, to make a diagnosis of major depression (MD). A diagnosis of MD requires not only a persistent depressed mood for more than two weeks, but also the concurrent appearance of a series of associated symptoms which disrupt the patient's level of functioning. The important point here is that these associated symptoms can be of totally different types. For example, a depressed patient can have predominantly psychological symptoms, such as self-reproach, difficulty in concentrating, loss of interest and recurrent thoughts of suicide. In contrast, another patient (also classified as MD) may have a completely different symptom profile with predominantly vegetative symptoms such as poor appetite and sleep disturbance, accompanied by psychomotor agitation or retardation. It seems unlikely that these different types of major depression share exactly the same aetiology and immune system changes.

The rating scales, used to measure the severity of the depressive symptoms, confound the problems over diagnosis. The most commonly used scale is the Hamilton Depression Rating Scale (HDRS). There are no clearly defined cut-off scores for levels of severity on this scale, rather it is a continuous scale. This allows correlations to be made between severity of depression and immune function but hampers comparisons between different studies where subjects may be classified as depressed with no reference to the HDRS score. It is valid to point out that, of the various items on the scale, only one specifically measures the severity of depressed mood. Other items rate symptoms not even included in the *DSM-IV* such as somatic anxiety, hypochondriasis, depersonalisation, distrust and obsessive/compulsiveness. Thus it is clear that people presenting with MD can rate similarly highly on the HDRS but present with quite different symptoms. In short, the rating scales do not use 'depressed mood' as the only, or indeed the main, criterion with which to rate patients. It is little wonder that the studies relating 'depression' to altered immune function were so confused and for so long.

It is apparent that the most marked immunological changes to accompany depression are associated with profound melancholia, the trait so accurately highlighted by Galen in the second century. Melancholic depression (synonymous with unipolar endogenous depression) is characterised by a lack of reactivity to the environment, a pervasive loss of interest in all or almost all activities, significant weight loss, diurnal variation in mood and early morning awakening. Melancholic depressed patients can also be characterised by the best response to antidepressant drug therapy. This final point may be very significant; it provides indirect evidence that the aetiologies of different types of depression are physiologically different.

Depression and Immune System Dysregulation

The view that depression is associated with less efficient immune system activity as a whole is far too simplistic. As we have seen in earlier chapters, the immune system has different aspects and is controlled by a variety of factors, many of which are counter-regulatory. What is clear is that this normally highly tuned system does become dysregulated in depression. In particular, those patients who present with severely depressed mood (melancholia) as well as being older, male and hospitalised, show the most marked immune system changes. The most widely reported of these changes is decreased NK cell activity (for example, Irwin and Gillin, 1987). In addition, reduced T cell proliferative response to mitogen stimulation (see Chapter 4) is often, but not always, documented (see, for example, Kronfol *et al.*, 1983). These changes do indeed suggest that major depression is accompanied by immunosuppression. However, this is only part of the story.

Strangely, perhaps, these changes (indicative of down-regulated Th1 activity) are accompanied by *activation* of cell-mediated immunity. This hint of a paradoxical immunological state in relation to depression first came to light in the late 1980s when depression was associated with an increased CD4+/CD8+ cell ratio (Tondo *et al.*, 1988). This has now been replicated many times and the size of the increased ratio (in relation to the normal) is significantly and positively related to the severity of melancholia. This change has been attributed to both an increase in the number of CD4+ cells and a reduction in the number of CD8+ cells. Others have found higher numbers of phagocytic cells; neutrophils and monocytes. Although it is not easy to interpret these enumerative data (see Chapter 4) the increase in circulating T helper cells (CD4+) challenges the notion of general immunosuppression.

However, perhaps one of the most striking changes seen in depression is the number of *activated* T cells. This is evidenced by the high level of IL-2 receptor binding sites on T lymphocytes (these receptors only appear during a state of activation). There are also high levels of soluble IL-2 receptors in the general circulation, another index of T cell activation. In fact, high levels of this soluble receptor have been linked with suicidal tendencies (Nassberger and Traskman-Bendz, 1993).

Consistently, it has been shown that cultured peripheral blood mononuclear cells (see Chapter 4) of melancholic depressed patients secrete more of the pro-inflammatory cytokines IL-1β and IL-6 when challenged with mitogen (Maes *et al.*, 1991). Additionally, plasma and urinary neopterin, a product of Th1 cell-mediated immunity, has repeatedly been shown to be elevated in depression. Critically, these same cells (T cells) lack normal sensitivity to the glucocorticoid dexamethasone (Maes *et al.*, 1991). Normally the production of both IL-1β and soluble IL-2 receptors is inhibited by glucocorticoids. However, these peripheral blood mononuclear cells in melancholic depressed patients are less inhibited than those of healthy control subjects. We will return to this very important characteristic of the immune system of depressed subjects later in this chapter.

Depression is also associated with increased plasma concentration of positive acute phase proteins (such as haptoglobin) alongside reduced negative acute phase proteins (such as albumin). It is known that elevated levels of acute phase proteins (and a drop in the negative proteins) are important indicators of acute or chronic inflammatory states. Consequently, these findings support the notion that some major depression patients (typically those with melancholia) suffer from a continuous activation of the 'acute' phase inflammatory response.

It has been hypothesised by Maes (Maes *et al.*,1995) that T cell activation and the increased secretion of IL-1β and IL-6, characteristic of melancholic depression, is the core event that mediates the reduction in NK cell activity (so vital in disease susceptibility). The reduction in NK cell activity may be the consequence of a combination of increased numbers of neutrophils, soluble IL-2 receptors, prostaglandins and the positive acute phase proteins (all under the influence of IL-1β and IL-6).

Thus, paradoxically, from an immunological perspective, depression is characterised by diminished NK cell activity and blunted lymphoproliferation responses in the *in vitro* stimulated T cell assay, but heightened indices of Th1 cell activation (in terms of cytokine production) together with a sustained acute phase response.

The Role of the HPA Axis

In order to understand how this unusual profile of immune activity is able to come about it is vital to appreciate the status of the HPA axis in depression; once again this response system is pivotal. In depression, unlike acute stress, the HPA axis is dysfunctional. Patients have enlarged pituitary and adrenal glands, the result of over activity: there is excessive secretion of both pituitary ACTH and adrenal cortisol. In addition, the PVN of the hypothalamus secretes excessive amounts of CRF, the key regulator of the stress response system. Thus, all three components of the HPA axis are performing at an unusually high rate. It is believed that the reason for this excessive activity is that the body becomes less efficient at regulating levels of CRF and cortisol. In non-depressed subjects acute stress-induced rises in these hormones are short-lived, as a result of negative feedback control. Depression, in contrast, is characterised by inadequate negative feedback, attributable to malfunctioning (desensitised) receptors for both CRF and cortisol. These receptors (located at strategic sites within the HPA axis) function like thermostats to monitor levels of each hormone. If levels above the 'norm' for the time of day are detected, production is checked so that levels return to that norm (the norm varies throughout the day due to distinct circadian rhythms in output). In summary, depression is associated with desensitised CRF and cortisol receptors the result of which is that over production remains undetected and unchecked. The result of this dysregulation is that the HPA axis secretes too much CRF and cortisol: hallmarks of melancholic depression.

As cortisol has powerful immunomodulatory influences (see Chapter 3), it is not surprising that it plays an important role in the connections between depression, the immune system and ill health. However, immunomodulatory influences of cortisol differ in depressed subjects compared with the characteristic relationship found in non-depressed subjects. In Chapter 3 we saw how the individual cells of the immune system to some extent mimic the entire HPA system. Individual cells possess receptors for a wide range of hormones, neurotransmitters and neuropeptides. The precise role of many of these receptors has yet to be fully determined, but we do know (see earlier in this chapter) that the cortisol receptors on the T cells of depressed subjects are desensitised to cortisol. So the cortisol receptors on both the HPA axis and the T cells have changed in the same way, that is, to be less sensitive to cortisol. As a result, Th1 activity of the immune system is less sensitive to cortisol inhibition. Thus depression is characterised by an unusual milieu of high cortisol (which would normally inhibit Th1 activity) but heightened Th1 inflammatory activity.

Excessive central CRF production may also have important peripheral influences. But whether CRF affects the immune system directly or indirectly via HPA axis and sympathetic nervous system activation is difficult to determine. Certainly, CRF administration to animals suppresses NK cell activity and lymphocyte proliferation responses whilst stimulating the release of pro-inflammatory cytokines (Torpy and Chrousos, 1996; Miller, 1998).

Thus, overactivity of the HPA axis, as seen in depression, accompanies stimulation of Th1 pro-inflammatory cytokine secretion and a cascade of events that has the effect of reducing NK cell activity and T lymphocyte proliferative response to mitogen, an index of cellular immunity. These indices of change in immune function could underpin accelerated disease progression in those diseases normally held in check by effective Th1 defences. The inflammatory cytokines produced also activate the HPA cascade, thus exacerbating the overdrive on this axis.

The described abnormalities of the HPA axis and Th1 branch of the immune system tend to co-exist in the same patients and are most obvious in those presenting with the melancholic (unipolar endogenous) form of depression. It seems that melancholic mood may be a result of the neuroendocrine and immune system changes. The question of whether the initial perturbation originates in the HPA axis or whether an initial dysregulation of the immune system could initiate the entire process remains to be fully answered (see Figure 6.1).

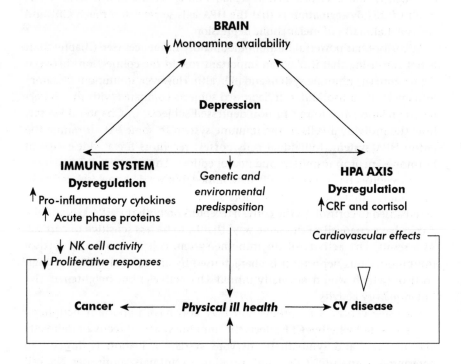

Figure 6.1 Simplified diagram showing relationship between the brain, the HPA axis and the immune system in melancholic depression. Depression is seen as a consequence of depleted monoamine availability in the brain, which may be induced by either excessive pro-inflammatory cytokines or excessive HPA axis activation. The relationship between the HPA axis and the immune system is bidirectional (see text). These changes can lead to physical illness, the nature of which is dependent on individual genetic and environmental predisposition

It seems likely that excessive stress activation of the HPA axis, in susceptible individuals, may lead to dysregulation of the entire neuroendocrine–immune axis. Once this system has lost sensitivity for negative feedback (in the brain and critical immune cells) the accumulation of cortisol and CRF would induce the immune system changes as secondary. However, it remains possible that primary overproduction of the Th1 pro-inflammatory cytokines (rather than prolonged stress) could be the cause of prolonged HPA activation with consequent dysregulation. For example, one large, prospective study (over 700 subjects) has shown an association between somatic illness in childhood and increased risk of major depression in adulthood. This study revealed an association between excessive drive in the immune system in early life with subsequent onset of major depression. This association was independent of prior depressive episodes and demographic covariates. Furthermore, the reciprocal relationship was also observed; depression predicted increased risk of future poor physical health. These associations were observed over a long time-period (a seventeen-year span) suggesting a causal relationship rather than short-term behavioural changes mediated by the illness itself (Cohen *et al.*, 1998a). However, regardless of the origin of the dysfunction (the HPA axis or the immune system), once a milieu of high levels of Th1 activity and pro-inflammatory cytokines, CRF and cortisol predominate, melancholia seems the likely outcome in terms of disturbance of effect.

The influence that pro-inflammatory cytokines can exert on the brain and HPA axis was discussed in Chapter 3. The role of these cytokines is to mobilise whole body responses, including behavioural changes that help to fight against infection. Fighting infection must take priority for the individual. One of the ways this is accomplished is to conserve energy normally expended on activity not relevant to the fight against infection. As a result, these cytokines induce a behavioural syndrome associated with withdrawal from social interaction, reduced sexual activity and appetite along with increased sleep. Healthy people given IL-2 and TNF-α (Th1 and pro-inflammatory cytokines) develop depressed mood, increased somatic concern, cognitive impairment and difficulties with motivation and flexible thinking (Maier and Watkins, 1998). These symptoms occur very quickly after cytokine administration and vanish soon after their removal, suggesting that they play a causal role in induction of the symptoms. However, the dose of cytokines given in these experiments is very large. Although they demonstrate the principle that a link exists between cytokines and mood, the most convincing evidence that this link is relevant to health comes from clinical studies. The most consistent psychological disturbance seen in infection (associated with increased circulating levels of pro-inflammatory cytokines) is depression. Again, individuals who suffer autoimmune diseases attributed to overactive Th1 activity (for example, multiple sclerosis and rheumatoid arthritis) display a high incidence of depressive disorders. Similarly, depression is twice as prevalent in females as males and females tend to be Th1 dominated. Furthermore, the increased production of IFN-γ in the winter months has been linked with seasonal affective disorder (SAD – depression in the winter months). Patients suffering from SAD can often be successfully treated with high-intensity light therapy. Wintertime darkness is associated with more prolonged melatonin production (a Th1 promoting agent) which can be reversed by bright light so that the shift towards Th1 can be minimised. Thus, the evidence is accumulating that not only is depression associated with raised levels of Th1 activity and pro-inflammatory cytokines but that these cytokines can induce depressed mood (see Connor and Leonard, 1998, for review).

The Role of Brain Monoamines

It is known that both psychological and physiological stressors produce alterations in noradrenaline (NA), serotonin (5HT) and dopamine (DA) levels in the brain. These are the neurotransmitters (collectively called monoamines) that operate in those parts of the brain that regulate mood, reward and vegetative function (appetite, sleep and reproduction). If the cytokines are to influence these behaviours (which is clearly evident) they must make an impact on monoamine activity. That is exactly what does happen. The changes in monoamine activity induced by a single administration of inflammatory cytokines are very similar to those induced by stress. Increased release and utilisation of monoamine levels in specific brain regions coincides with the peak of the immunological response to challenge (Besedovsky *et al.*, 1983). These changes can be blocked by pretreatment with immunosuppressive drugs, indicating they are the direct result of immune system activation. The problem with these experiments is that they determine effects following a single administration of cytokines or immunological challenge. In reality, inflammatory disease and depression are associated with elevated pro-inflammatory cytokines over protracted periods of time. It seems that an acute stressor or immunological challenge causes increased release and use of the monoamines, whereas repeated exposure to either leads to depletion. The brain is only able to synthesise limited quantities of neurotransmitters; if they are used up too rapidly there will be a shortfall. One consequence of depleted brain monoamines is depression.

Another, more indirect, way in which inflammatory cytokines can influence mood is via reduction in circulating levels of tryptophan. Tryptophan is an essential amino acid. This means that it cannot be synthesised in the body but must be consumed in the diet. The sorts of foods that contain quite high concentrations of tryptophan are bananas and chocolate. Once consumed in the diet, tryptophan circulates in the blood and is then actively taken up into the brain, where it is made into the neurotransmitter 5HT. All 5HT in the brain is made this way and to some extent levels of this neurotransmitter are dependent upon the tryptophan we consume in our diet (in this respect 5HT is unique). The system that transports tryptophan from the blood into the brain also transports other amino acids that are not capable of being converted into 5HT, these are known as competing amino acids (CAAs). Protein in the diet, such as meat, is broken down into just such amino acids, which compete with tryptophan for uptake into the brain. High levels of CAAs also cause an actual reduction in the levels of circulating tryptophan, by incorporating it into newly synthesised protein. As a result, high protein diets can cause mood disturbance due to compromised tryptophan transport and availability, and hence lower 5HT synthesis in the brain. Experimental reduction in peripheral tryptophan in normal healthy subjects (by administration of a drink rich in competing amino acids) causes depletion of blood 5HT levels and depressed mood (Ravindran *et al.*, 1999). Levels of tryptophan in the blood of depressed subjects have consistently been shown to be lower than matched controls. For a long time the reasons for this were not known, but it now seems clear that some inflammatory cytokines can decrease tryptophan availability to the brain by inducing its breakdown before being transported into the brain (Maes *et al.*, 1995). Plasma tryptophan levels are significantly and negatively related to IL-6 secretion, plasma levels of positive acute phase proteins and neopterin. Consequently, low tryptophan levels are probably a marker of the immune inflammatory response during major depression and may provide a link between the peripheral responses and mood (Maes *et al.*, 1997).

Even when tryptophan has entered the brain it is not guaranteed that all will be converted to 5HT. This conversion process requires a co-factor that is derived from neopterin. Although levels of neopterin are elevated in depression (a consequence of increased Th1 activity) its conversion to the essential co-factor is inhibited (this, of course, also contributes to the high levels of neopterin seen in depressed patients). So, once again we find a link between immune activation and brain neurotransmitter levels associated with mood (van Amsterdam and Opperhuizen, 1999).

The relationship between high cortisol levels and mood disturbance has attracted much attention. There is no doubt that the brain neurotransmitters NA, 5HT and DA play a crucial role in the regulation of mood and reward. Indeed, the initial theory of depression identified NA and 5HT as being the crucially depleted neurotransmitters. Drugs used to control depression increase availability of one or both of these neurotransmitters (for a comprehensive review see Trimble, 1996). More recently it has been suggested that the alterations in brain NA and 5HT, which result in the lowered mood, may be secondary to high cortisol levels (Dinan, 1994). The evidence that this peripherally circulating hormone can influence mood is quite compelling. Animal studies have demonstrated that when cortisol levels remain high for an extended length of time (as happens in depression), brain concentrations of monoamines are reduced.

Animal studies have also shown that direct administration of CRF to the brains of laboratory animals leads to a constellation of behavioural abnormalities reminiscent of intense anxiety and melancholic depression. These include social withdrawal, reduced appetite and sexual activity, alongside psychomotor agitation or retardation (depending on context). The behavioural effects of CRF can be obtained at doses too low to activate the HPA axis. In fact CRF is widely distributed throughout the brain where, it has been suggested, it plays a regulatory role in central monoamine function. Thus the high levels of CRF commonly associated with depression are thought to play a direct role in the symptoms of depression as well as acting to initiate the HPA cascade (Ritchie and Nemeroff, 1991).

A crucial fact to appreciate here is that NA and 5HT activate the HPA axis as well as regulate mood: increased levels of these neurotransmitters, in certain brain pathways, initiate the HPA cascade and increase cortisol concentrations in the circulation. Cortisol, in return, restrains HPA activity, not only by its direct negative feedback inhibition at the level of the hypothalamus and pituitary but also by inhibiting NA and 5HT availability. Under normal conditions, when cortisol levels are tightly regulated, this does not have any detrimental effect. The consequence of high cortisol levels over a prolonged time-period (as seen in depression) is to reduce substantially 5HT and NA availability, and hence lowered mood (Kvetnansky *et al.*, 1993; Pacak *et al.*, 1995). Thus one consequence of dysregulation of the HPA axis is melancholic mood (see Figure 6.2).

Cortisol also contributes to reduced availability of tryptophan. It does this in two ways. First, it also accelerates tryptophan metabolism (differently to inflammatory cytokines), shunting it away from the brain uptake mechanism. Second, a physiological role of cortisol is to mobilise energy required for fight and flight (stress) or fever and the acute phase response (infection). One way it does this is to stimulate the breakdown of muscle protein into amino acids. These amino acids compete with the tryptophan uptake mechanism, just like CAAs ingested in the diet.

To illustrate the long-term consequences of raised cortisol levels it is useful to look at the effects of Cushing's disease (CD) (a pathological condition characterised by hypersecretion of cortisol). The most common side effect of CD is mental disturbance and depression (Jeffcoate *et al.*, 1979). About one-third of patients with CD have significant psychiatric morbidity, two-thirds are depressed and approximately 10 per cent attempt suicide (Murphy, 1991). Direct involvement of cortisol in the induction of these mood changes is implied as the severity of the mood disorder in CD has been shown to correlate with the circulating cortisol level (Starkman and Schteingart 1981). Furthermore, treatment by adrenalectomy (which removes the source of cortisol) or pharmacological inhibition of cortisol effectively reverses the mood disorder (Zeiger *et al.*, 1993).

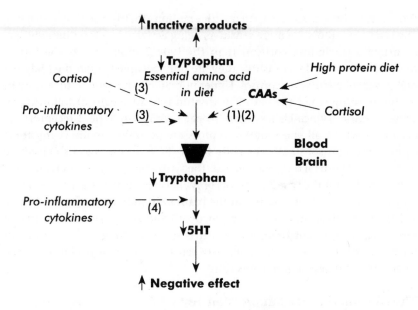

Figure 6.2 Simplified illustration to show how raised levels of cortisol and pro-inflammatory cytokines (as well as a high protein diet) can increase negative effect by reducing serotonin (5HT) availability in the brain. (1) Transport into the brain is reduced by competition with raised levels of competing amino acids (CAAs). (2) Raised levels of CAAs deplete tryptophan by inducing its incorporation in new protein synthesis. (3) Both cortisol and pro-inflammatory cytokines can deplete circulating tryptophan availability in the periphery by inducing its metabolic breakdown. (4) Conversion of tryptophan in the brain to 5HT is inhibited by pro-inflammatory cytokines (see text)

Dealing with Difficulties

The relationship between high cortisol and melancholia has been called into question by the evidence that administration of glucocorticoid drugs to subjects with normal adrenal function can lead to euphoria rather than depression (although there may also be irritability and sleeplessness) (Murphy, 1991; Brown and Suppes, 1998). This discrepancy has yet to be fully explained but may be associated with the fact that cortisol binds to two different types of cortisol receptor (types 1 and 2). These receptors mediate different effects and are also distributed in different brain areas. Type 2 is the classic form of the receptor being widespread in the brain, pituitary and immune cells (such as lymphocytes). On the other hand, the type 1 receptors are mainly found in those areas of the brain associated with emotion (that is, the limbic system). The type 1 receptors are more sensitive, being activated by ten times less glucocorticoid (including cortisol) than the type 2 receptors. As the type 2 receptors are much less sensitive they are only occupied when the body has high levels of circulating cortisol. Under normal circumstances this would be in the morning when the circadian rhythm is at its height or following an acute stressor. Typically, less than 10 per cent of the type 2 receptors are occupied, whilst all the type 1 receptors are occupied, maintaining tonic control over cortisol status. The body's own glucocorticoid (cortisol) binds to both types of cortisol receptor, whereas the synthetic glucocorticoids are more or less specific for the type 2 receptors only. This means they have little impact on the type 1 receptors located in the brain's emotional centres (see Dinan, 1994). As cortisol and synthetic glucocorticoid drugs work on different receptors, in different brain regions, it is not surprising that they induce different effects. The relationship between the body's own glucocorticoid (cortisol) and depression remains firm.

The Dexamethasone Suppression Test

Any discussion about depression and the role of the HPA axis must include a mention of the dexamethasone suppression test (DST). Dexamethasone (Dex) is an example of a synthetic glucocorticoid, acting mainly on the type 2 cortisol receptors. Under normal circumstances administration of Dex (which mimics the effect of high cortisol levels) acts on these receptors to suppress the production of cortisol. Non-suppression is an indication of poor negative feedback: desensitised receptors. In 1981 it was reported that melancholic depression could be simply diagnosed by non-suppression on the DST (Carroll *et al.*, 1981). As the DST was the first suggested biochemical marker for depression, it was greeted with great enthusiasm. A flood of papers, and controversy, quickly ensued: not all depressed patients were non-suppressors. Many of the problems stemmed from methodological considerations as different groups executed the test using different regimes and not always on 'melancholic' depressed patients (as discussed previously). However, it now seems clear that non-suppression is (usually) associated with high circulating cortisol levels. This led to the belief that depression could be categorised according to cortisol status; for example, high cortisol and non-suppression associated with greater melancholia (Evans *et al.*, 1983). Others have not demonstrated these relationships. What is clear is that non-suppression appears to be related to severity of depression. The rank order of non-suppression is striking: normal patients (7–8 per cent), grief reaction (10 per cent), minor depression (23 per cent), major depression (44 per cent), melancholia (50 per cent) and psychotic affective disorders (69 per cent) (Murphy, 1991).

Some dismiss the DST, claiming 50 per cent sensitivity to be meaningless. However, even if 50 per cent is accurate (bearing in mind the methodological problems) this means that half the incidence of one of the world's most rapidly growing afflictions of the mind can be associated with dysfunction of the HPA axis. Furthermore, the subjects who show most pronounced dysregulation of this axis also show the most marked changes in immune activation and are thus more susceptible to organic ill health. Recently an old idea has resurfaced: the possibility of identifying suicide-prone individuals by these physiological measures. As long ago as 1965 it was first predicted that high cortisol levels could give a good indication of suicidal intent (Bunney and Fawcett, 1965). Although not universally accepted as a simple tool it is recognised that high cortisol is associated with increased severity of depression. A recent paper linking suicidal intent with activation of Th1 immunity and pro-inflammatory cytokines may reopen this area for discussion (elevated Th1 activity and pro-inflammatory cytokines are known to co-exist with raised cortisol levels in depression (Mendlovic *et al.*, 1999)).

If, as we suggest here, cortisol is a factor in the generation of melancholia it would be reasonable to expect antidepressant drugs to lower its levels. Depression is treated, primarily, with drugs that block the re-uptake (inactivation) of NA and 5HT back into nerve terminals after release. This has the effect of prolonging the useful life of the neurotransmitters, as they are available in the synapse for longer. However, it has always been a mystery why antidepressant drugs take an average of three weeks to make any clinical impact. In reality, the action on the re-uptake sites is maximal after a couple of hours, but the patients feel no benefits. In contrast, other drugs, like the street drug, cocaine, with a similar mechanism of action (on DA nerve terminals), produce immediate effects on reward processes. One obvious difference here is that antidepressant drugs are given to clinically depressed individuals: those with high cortisol levels. It is known that in addition to their actions on the MA brain pathways antidepressants increase the sensitivity of cortisol receptors. As the receptors become more sensitive they detect the high cortisol levels and down-regulate production until concentrations fall within the normal range once more. Critically, the process of adaptation of the receptors during drug treatment takes about two to three weeks to occur and thus coincides with the clinical efficiency of the drugs. Thus it seems that one pathway by which antidepressant drugs are beneficial is to increase negative feedback sensitivity and hence reduce circulating cortisol. Direct anti-cortisol drug treatment is being developed to treat depression and the results look promising (see Sapse, 1997).

Depressed individuals that do not respond to drug treatment are sometimes treated with electroconvulsive therapy (ECT). This treatment has also been associated with reduced cortisol levels that fall in parallel with changed mood.

The most recent technique that has been employed to alleviate depression, in drug-resistant cases, is rapid transcranial magnetic stimulation (rTMS). This involves use of a magnetic coil to stimulate the brain through the intact skull with minimal pain and without the need for anaesthetic or muscle relaxants. In a small study of only twelve patients, all of which were non-suppressors on the DST, half responded to the treatment by reduced melancholia which was accompanied by normalisation (suppression) in the DST (Pridmore, 1999).

Bearing in mind what we have discussed about the three-way relationship between mood, the HPA axis and immunity, the need to treat depression, not only for its own sake but also because of its impact on physical health, becomes apparent. Of significance, and worthy of mention here, is the recent observation that antidepressant drug treatment also augments NK cell activity in subjects with low NK cell activity at baseline (Frank *et al.*, 1999). This latest finding indicates the importance of efficient diagnosis and treatment of depression in cancer patients as increased NK cell activity has been associated with slowed disease progression.

Conclusions

In summary, there is a triangular relationship between mood (brain monoamines), the immune system and the HPA axis. This relationship is evolutionary old and, under 'normal' circumstances, adaptive for survival. However, when one of the corners of this triangle becomes dysregulated the others are inevitably affected. Thus melancholia (disturbed mood) is characterised by changes in all three systems, that is, monoamine availability (depleted), aspects of immunity (reduced NK cell activity, inflammation and the acute phase response) and the HPA axis (increased CRF and cortisol). The systems are so intimately connected that it may be virtually impossible to determine which corner of the triangle initiates the dysregulation. Disturbed mood alters monoamine and sympathetic nervous system regulatory influences on the immune system and HPA axis, the immune system has effects on mood and the HPA axis and the HPA axis influences mood and the immune system. It should be no surprise therefore that disturbed mood (depression) is associated with accelerated progression in certain diseases as the parallel changes in both the immune system and neuroendocrine activity would mediate this. In the past the treatment of depression has focused almost entirely upon raising brain monoamine availability with virtually no attention paid to the other components of this triangle. In a similar way, clinicians treating physical illness frequently fail to recognise and treat accompanying depression, even though it has been shown that such treatment improves physical health. An understanding of the intimate relationship between mood and the immune and neuroendocrine systems should inform the development of new treatment strategies.

7
Conditioning of the Immune System

Significance of Conditioning of the Immune System for PNI

Some of the most powerful evidence for psychological influence over immunity stems from studies begun in the mid 1970s, long before the multiple connections between brain and the immune system (as outlined in Chapter 3) were known. This work explored the effect of classical Pavlovian conditioning on immune activity. The fact that the immune system could be conditioned, that is, learn to respond to a neutral stimulus previously paired with a stimulus with direct effects on some aspect of immunity, was perceived in the mid 1970s as truly extraordinary. Many experiments were undertaken to validate the claims that this could indeed happen. The early work focused on animals, mainly rodents, but humans were later shown to respond in the same way. Such experiments mainly observed the phenomenon: an understanding of how these processes could be mediated is only now beginning to emerge. However, together with the accumulating evidence that psychological effect could influence the immune system, these studies were influential in the establishment of PNI. It is now widely accepted that neutral associative processes (agents and procedures) can modify the immune system and that this is under the control of the brain, central nervous and neuroendocrine systems. The clinical significance of classical conditioning in the immune system, including its contribution to the placebo effect, is only now beginning to be fully appreciated.

Discovery

The first observation that the immune system could be conditioned arose incidentally. In the early 1970s Ader and Cohen had been working on conditioned taste aversion in rats. They provided fluid-deprived rats with access to a palatable, distinctly flavoured, but harmless, drinking solution (containing saccharin) thirty minutes prior to an intraperitoneal (i.p.) injection of toxic agent capable of making the animals feel unwell (due to temporary gastroin-

111

testinal upset). When the rats were re-exposed to the palatable and harmless saccharin solution their consumption was severely reduced. Classical conditioning theory states that pairing of an active agent (unconditioned stimulus: US) with a neutral agent (conditioned stimulus: CS) can result in the neutral agent acquiring the properties of the active agent (see Figure 7.1). During conditioning the signals generated by the US imprints a neural pathway located within the central nervous system and leaves behind a memory of the association between the US and CS. Thus in Ader and Cohen's experimental paradigm the rats associated the saccharin solution with feeling unwell so they avoided drinking it – conditioned taste aversion.

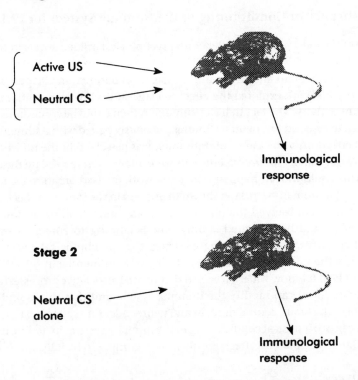

Stage 1

Active US

Neutral CS

Immunological response

Stage 2

Neutral CS alone

Immunological response

Figure 7.1   Diagram to illustrate acquisition of a conditioned response in immune function. During Stage I the neutral stimulus, known as the conditioned stimulus (CS), is paired with the active agent, known as the unconditioned stimulus (US). The change in immune response is measured. This pairing may occur only once or be repeated several times. During Stage 2 the neutral or CS alone is presented to the animal and the same immune response is observed.

The drug cyclophosphamide (CY), amongst several others, was effective in inducing conditioned taste aversion after just a single trial (pairing). However, CY is also an antimitotic agent, that is, it inhibits cell division (used in cancer chemotherapy; see later) and is therefore immunosuppressive (the acquired immune response, as we have learned already, requires rapid proliferation of lymphocytes). The crucial observation was that amongst those animals exposed to the uniform dose of CY there were some that unexpectedly died. It was noticed that the animals that had died prematurely were those that had consumed the largest volume of saccharin solution during the conditioning trial. This struck the researchers as strange as the saccharin itself had no detrimental effects on the animals. To account for this observation they hypothesised that pairing of the neutral solution of saccharin with CY, used to induce taste aversion but, as it happens, also an immunosuppressive agent, resulted in conditioning of immunosuppression (as well as taste aversion). Thus, in these conditioned animals the more of the neutral solution consumed, the more immunosuppressed they became. Ader and Cohen speculated that such immunosuppressed animals were more vulnerable to latent pathogens and hence premature death.

Ader and Cohen (1975) set out to explore this hypothesis. Following a period of adaptation to a water-deprived state (access for only fifteen minutes per day) animals were presented with the distinctly flavoured but palatable solution of saccharin and thirty minutes later given an i.p. injection of CY. Three days after conditioning, animals were injected with antigen (a suspension of sheep red blood cells) thirty minutes prior to re-exposure to the conditioned stimulus (saccharin). In this way they were able to test for immunosuppression directly by quantifying the antibody response to antigen challenge and how that was affected by the conditioned stimulus. The results were as they had predicted. Conditioned animals, previously exposed to a single dose of CY paired with the saccharin solution, showed a significantly reduced antibody response after re-exposure to the saccharin compared to placebo-treated, non-conditioned animals or conditioned animals (saccharin paired with CY) not subsequently exposed to the saccharin.

Furthermore, they demonstrated that the induction of taste aversion itself was not responsible for the observed effects on the immune system. They did this by performing a parallel set of experiments using the aversive agent lithium chloride (LiCl). LiCl is not an immunosuppressive agent but it is highly effective at inducing conditioned taste aversion. When animals were exposed to LiCl, in the same experimental paradigm to that used in the CY experiments, they did develop taste aversion but did not become immunosuppressed. They interpreted their results as clear evidence for the existence of behaviourally conditioned immunosuppression.

In an effort to discover the underlying mechanism for the observed behaviourally conditioned immunosuppression they measured plasma corticosterone levels at the time the animals were sacrificed (six days after injection of antigen and nine days after conditioning). They showed that there were no significant differences in corticosterone levels between the groups of conditioned and non-conditioned rats and that corticosterone levels did not relate to antibody titres at this time. Thus, this initial experiment failed to implicate the hypothalamic-pituitary-adrenal (HPA) axis in the induction of the conditioning.

A Robust Phenomenon

Many groups have replicated these initial findings. Most experiments re-exposed the animal to the CS (saccharin) *following* the challenge of an immunisation, indicating that the CS inhibited the activated immune system. Other work demonstrated that re-exposure to the CS *before* immunisation also depressed *in vivo* antibody production in rodents. This additional observation importantly demonstrated that an activated immune system was not a requirement for conditioning an immunosuppressive response. Using CY as the US it was also demonstrated that the CS could also depress *in vitro* splenic plaque-forming cell responses to antigen. This is a subtler test of immune response than the antibody titration method used in the initial experiments as it identifies and quantifies individual plasma cells secreting antibody in a spleen cell preparation. Thus, conditioned immunosuppression was a robust phenomenon that could be demonstrated across a variety of experimental paradigms (Cohen *et al.*, 1994).

The variety of different paradigms used and indices of immune function investigated mushroomed. Animals conditioned in the way described, but using injections of the immunosuppressive agent cyclosporine A (CsA, which specifically blocks IL-2 signalling in the immune system) as the US, displayed significant reductions in thymus, spleen and lymphoid organ weights, when examined at post mortem, after re-presentation of the CS (saccharin solution). This effect could last for up to seven re-presentations following an initial pairing of three consecutive trials, indicating that the conditioning was relatively hard to extinguish (Exton *et al.*, 1998b). The same study revealed that the CS could also significantly reduce the *in vitro* T cell proliferation response to Con A from isolated splenocytes, an indicator of functional status of Th1 mediated cellular immunity (see Chapter 4). Conditioning of the immunosuppressive influence of CsA has also been demonstrated in terms of leukocyte enumeration in the periphery, in response to behavioural conditioning (Von Horsten *et al.*, 1998).

Antibody response (AR) to presentation of antigen can also be conditioned. The normal progress of an immune response is an enhancement upon secondary presentation of an antigen (see Figure 7.2A). This is immunological

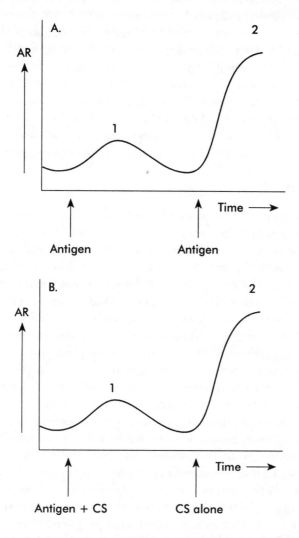

Figure 7.2   A. A primary challenge with antigen produces the initial primary response (1) followed by the secondary response (2) when re-exposed to the same antigen. B. The initial presentation of antigen is paired with a neutral conditioned stimulus (CS) and gives rise to the characteristic primary response (1). Representation of the CS alone induces the characteristic secondary antibody response (2) in the absence of antigen.

memory and the basis for the protective influence of vaccination (see Chapter 2). The antibody response to a soluble protein antigen is greater, more rapid and shows a characteristic isotype switch when the same antigen is given to an animal on a second occasion. In a remarkable study on the rat, a protein antigen was injected and paired with a gustatory CS. It was demonstrated that the characteristic secondary antibody response could be induced by representation of the CS alone (Alvarez-Borda *et al.*, 1995) (see Figure 7.2). Hence the signals required to recruit memory cells into an immune response, normally supplied by re-presentation of antigen, were triggered by the CS in the absence of antigen. This observation illustrates the remarkable degree to which the nervous system can regulate immune cell function. In addition this experiment demonstrated that conditioning of the immune system could induce enhancement of immune activity as well as immunosuppression.

Mechanisms

It has not been possible to identify a single physiological mechanism responsible for inducing the conditioned effects outlined above. This is probably because the conditioned effects are so varied that a number of related mechanisms are involved. For example, it has been shown that bilateral brain lesions of either the insular cortex or amygdala could abolish conditioned responses in antibody production (as described above) in rodents without having any effect on antibody generation *per se* (Ramirez-Amaya and Bermundez-Rattoni, 1999). These two brain structures are functionally and reciprocally interconnected and have been previously implicated in neural–immune interactions. Interestingly, the observation that lesions of the hippocampus did not interfere with the establishment of a conditioned response again mitigates against a dominant intermediary role for the glucocorticoids in this phenomenon (consistent with the early findings of Ader and Cohen, 1975). There is no doubt that the HPA axis is susceptible to classical conditioning (for example, Sabbioni *et al.*, 1997; DeVries *et al.*, 1998) so in some conditions it may play some regulatory role. However, conditioning of the HPA axis alone is not an adequate explanation to account for all types of immune system conditioning. Another study demonstrated parallel conditioning of both the HPA axis and numbers of peripheral blood mononuclear cells (PBMCs). However, these two conditioned responses did not appear to be causally related as increased numbers of PBMCs were found even on the fifth unreinforced trial day, whereas the conditioned cortisol response was lost after the initial unreinforced day (Buske-Kirschbaum *et al.*, 1996).

The available data suggest that the effects of conditioning may be mediated by a preferential effect on T cells. For example, in rodents conditioned suppression of the *in vitro* lymphoproliferative responses to the T cell mitogens Con A and PHA is more robust than for B cell mitogens. Other experiments also suggest that conditioning may be mediated by T cell changes. In these so-called 'adoptive transfer' experiments, splenocytes from conditioned or experimentally naïve animals were transferred into naïve recipients who have been manipulated so that their own immune systems cannot mount a response. The recipients' immune systems are reconstituted by the donor cells so that different contributions to the immune response by different cell populations can be revealed. This is a classical approach to immunological investigation. Such studies have revealed a central role for the T cell in mediating conditioned influences over immunity (see Ader and Cohen, 1993).

It has been suggested that T cells play an important role in conditioning of the immune system because the cell-mediated cytokine IL-2 is particularly sensitive to conditioning paradigms. Several investigators have demonstrated conditioned decreases in IL-2 production that could account for suppression of T cell proliferation. Although replacement of IL-2 did not normalise conditioned immunosuppression, others have shown IL-2 receptors to be down-regulated, suggesting that compromised ability to respond to IL-2 may be the key. Moreover, the conditioned reduction in cytokine production (induced using CsA as the US and saccharin solution as the CS) could be completely abrogated by surgical denervation of the spleen (cutting the splenic nerve). Thus it can be concluded that the nervous system rather than blood-borne products (like glucocorticoids; see above) are primarily instrumental in conditioning this aspect of immune function (Exton *et al.*, 1998a).

Perhaps one of the most frequently used immune measures in PNI is the behaviour of NK cells, both in terms of their trafficking and activity (see Chapter 4). One interesting experiment used stress (electric footshock) as the US paired with either auditory or visual cues as the conditioned stimulus. This study showed that the conditioned stimulus could cause a reduction in splenic NK cell activity, splenic T cell proliferation in response to mitogens and diminished levels of IFN-γ production by splenocytes. These are all indices of the strength of Th1 immunity. Furthermore, conditioned reductions in all these indices of immune function could be abolished by direct intracerebroventricular administration (that is, injection into the ventricles of the brain) of drugs that blocked opioid receptors (Perez and Lysle, 1997). Thus, this study indicated that the alterations of immune status produced by a conditioned stimulus, in this case cellular immunity, required activity of opioid-mediated circuits within the central nervous system. It is perhaps relevant here to remind the reader of the important role that the endogenous opioid β-endorphin plays (both centrally and peripherally) in inhibiting Th1 immunity (see Chapter 3).

Conditioned Up-Regulation of Immune Activity

Rodent NK cell numbers and activity have also been shown to be susceptible to *enhancement* by conditioning. One such study used arecoline (a substance capable of elevating the activity of preactivated NK cells) as the US and camphor odour as the CS. After pairing, the CS was able to elicit the same increased activity of NK cells as the US (Ghanta *et al.*, 1996). Another study investigated whether the somewhat impaired immune function of aged mice was susceptible to conditioning. Aged mice have been shown to have decreased spleen cell NK activity and NK cytotoxicity. This raised the question of whether psychological conditioning of an immune response (especially one involving NK cells) could be effective in old age and thus improve immune function. Again, camphor odour was used as the CS and injection of antigen (capable of activating NK cells) was the US. Both young and old mice were exposed to a series of pairings between CS and US. Mice were exposed to camphor odour alone seventy-two hours after the final association trial. The conditioned animals (both aged and young) showed statistically significant increases in spleen cell NK activity (Spector *et al.*, 1994). This interesting finding demonstrated the possibility of conditioning immune responses in old age, offering a valuable tool for attenuating age-related immune deterioration, possibly in humans.

Significance of Conditioned Immunosuppression: Animal Studies

The question as to whether the observed effects of conditioning of aspects on immune function have any biological or clinical *significance* needs to be addressed. Data of relevance to this question derives from animal models of human disease. In one excellent study using inbred mice that show a genetic predisposition to develop systemic lupus-erythematosus-like autoimmune disease, conditioned stimuli were substituted for half of the weekly treatments with CY (a beneficial immunosuppressive drug for this condition). The conditioned response was successful in delaying the onset of the disease, when used in conjunction with doses of CY that by itself was insufficient to have an impact on the disease (Ader and Cohen, 1982). Also in lupus-prone mice previously conditioned with CY and saccharin, re-exposure to the discontinued CS (saccharin) prolonged survival relative to those animals that were not re-exposed to the CS (Ader, 1985).

Similar beneficial results have been obtained using conditioning for the treatment of adjuvant-induced arthritis in rats (a widely used animal model of human rheumatoid arthritis). Adjuvant arthritis can be established by injecting complete Freund's adjuvant (a potent inflammatory agent) into a rat's hind paw. Within twenty-four hours this paw swells considerably. On about the twelfth post-injection day, the uninjected paw also starts to show signs of inflammation. Such animals benefited from reduced spread of inflammation to the uninjected paw following conditioned immunosuppression which had been acquired following a single pairing of the CS (saccharin/vanilla drinking solution) with CY (Klosterhalfen and Klosterhalfen, 1983). The failure to prevent the primary swelling in the injected paw was attributed to sub-sensitive quantitative indicators of extreme inflammation, and that the less severe secondary inflammation was more susceptible to both the uncondi-tioned and conditioned stimulus. The same authors speculated on the mechanism by which the demonstrated conditioned immunosuppression was effected. They concluded that changed levels of glucocorticoids were unlikely to have been responsible. Previous work had shown that exposure to social stressors or noise (known to elevate circulating glucocorticoid levels) before and after administration of the adjuvant had no reliable effects on the devel-opment of inflammation.

Conditioned immunosuppression has also been shown to be beneficial in retarding rejection of transplant tissues in animals. CY can impair the rejection of skin grafts in certain strains of mice that typically reject from other strains. Following pairing with CY the neutral CS was shown to have similar beneficial effects to CY, in terms of reduced tissue rejection (Gorczynski, 1990). Similarly, the survival of heart allografts in rats could be prolonged by behaviourally conditioned immunosuppression using CsA (the drug commonly used to prevent tissue rejection in humans) as the US in taste aversion conditioning Grochowicz *et al.*, 1991). Again, these authors speculated that the underlying mechanism mediating this effect was likely to be related to the action of CsA in inhibiting the release of IL-2 and IFN-γ at an early stage of T cell activation. Whatever the mechanism, these types of experiment clearly indicate the potential of conditioning the immune system; it is not a mere academic per-turbation. The amount of change in the immune system that can be induced by behavioural conditioning is sufficient to impact on physical conditions.

However, although conditioned immunosuppression may have beneficial influences in down-regulating autoimmune activity, such influences may be deleterious in other circumstances, for example, ability to withstand cancer. An animal model is illustrative of this. Mice conditioned to CY as the US showed accelerated mortality after artificial induction of cancer (inoculation with cells of a syngeneic plasmacytoma) when represented with the CS (Gorczynski *et al.*, 1985). Thus, in laboratory animals immune conditioning has the potential to retard or accelerate disease, depending on the nature of the underlying condition. Recall also that the initial serendipitous discovery of Ader and Cohen (1975) was that conditioned rats died prematurely.

Human Studies

The findings so far described, taken mainly from the animal literature, can be generalised to humans. Anecdotal clinical observation of such conditioning first appeared in the literature over a hundred years ago. A paper rose was observed to induce an allergic reaction in a susceptible individual (Mackenzie, 1896). Similarly, it had been reported that the picture of a hay field was sufficient to elicit a hay fever attack in very sensitive subjects (Hill, 1930). Subsequent laboratory studies in both humans and animals confirmed that exposure to symbolic, non-allergenic environmental stimuli (CS) previously associated with allergenic stimuli (US) was able to induce asthmatic symptoms in some subjects (Ottenberg *et al.*, 1958; Khan, 1977).

One of the first published scientific reports on humans examined the effect of conditioning on the delayed type hypersensitivity (DTH) response to tuberculin injection (see Chapter 4). In this study a small group of nine hospital employees were recruited to participate in what they were told was a study of the reproducibility of the tuberculin reaction. They were told that they would be given a tuberculin skin test on each arm monthly for six months, that the test would be the same each month and that the concentrations of tuberculin would be different between arms. They would be paid $25 for each test. The testing conditions were identical each month: the same office, same day of the week, same time of day, same nurse and same arrangement of office furniture. When a subject arrived for testing, he or she could see a red vial and a green vial on the desk. The contents of each vial were drawn into a syringe so that the subject could see that the content of the red vial was always applied to the right arm and the content of the green vial to the left arm. Subjects returned to the same office twenty-four hours and forty-eight hours after every administration, where the same nurse measured the extent of their reaction to the injection, always reading the right arm first. In fact the subjects were given an active dose of tuberculin to the right arm (red vial) and saline to the left arm (green vial).

This identical protocol was followed for five consecutive months, but on the sixth month (the experimental trial) without the knowledge of either the nurse or the subject, the contents of the vials were switched. Saline (now in the red vial) was applied to the arm that, for the previous five months, had been given tuberculin, and tuberculin (now in the green vial) was applied to the arm that had previously been given saline. As a control, on the seventh month the subjects were debriefed and a final dose of either tuberculin or saline (in their original colour of vial) was administered to the original arm. The results showed that the tuberculin injection caused a stable and measurable reaction for the first five months, whereas the saline injection caused no reaction. However, in the experimental month the arm that was given the tuberculin (misleadingly coloured) showed a very marked reduction in the intensity of its skin reaction. Saline injection to the previously exposed tuberculin arm caused no skin reaction. The following (control) week the reaction to tuberculin was as it had been in the initial five-month period. Thus, this experiment demonstrated that the delayed hypersensitivity response to tuberculin could be significantly diminished by psychological mediation, that is, the expectation that there would be no response in that arm (Smith and McDaniel, 1983).

The authors explained their findings in terms of behaviourally conditioned suppression of the immune response. In the experiment, the vials, the room, the day of the week and the nurse, as well as the idea that they would always be positive or negative (depending on arm), served as conditioned stimuli. In fact there were two conditioned responses (one in each arm): the positive response to tuberculin and associated stimuli and the negative response to saline with its associated stimuli. The experiment showed that the negative conditioned response inhibited the unconditioned response to tuberculin, whereas the positive conditioned response did not produce a response to saline. In this particular paradigm it was easier to inhibit the unconditioned response than to produce a response in the absence of the unconditioned stimulus. Since it has been shown that the skin DTH response can be modulated by neural regulation over leukocyte trafficking to the skin (see Chapter 5), it is easy to envisage how conditioning of autonomic processes could down-regulate this response. However, neural influences over cell trafficking clearly could not result in a DTH response in the absence of the provoking antigen.

Conditioning of lymphocyte cell trafficking has recently been demonstrated in a study on human subjects. An injection of adrenaline, capable of causing a transient increase in NK cell activity and circulating numbers in the periphery, was used as the US. It is known that adrenaline and/or stimulation of the sympathetic nervous system has this influence over NK cell activity and it can be blocked by β-adrenergic antagonists (see Chapter 4). This stimulus was paired with a sherbet sweet and white noise as the CS. After repeated co-presentation of the stimuli, re-exposure to the CS alone resulted in a significant increase in NK cell numbers as well as activity (Buske-Kirschbaum *et al.*, 1994). Hence in a study on humans it has been demonstrated that it is possible to directly condition recruitment of NK cells to the periphery and also possibly their contribution to immulogical defence.

The Th1 immunostimulatory agent IFN-γ has also been used to investigate the possibility of direct positive immune conditioning in normal human subjects. In this placebo-controlled, double-blind study of thirty-one normal volunteers, IFN-γ (the US) was paired with a neutral, orally given substance (CS), in a typical classical conditioning paradigm. During a four-week period the study group received progressively fewer injections of IFN-γ. By the final week these subjects received only the neutral stimulus. At the end of this regime the experimental group had higher levels of quinolinic acid and neopterin (a marker for IFN-γ stimulation of macrophage activity – indicators of Th1 activity; see Chapter 3) than those that had actually received the immunostimulatory agent all along (Longo *et al.*, 1999). These data strongly support the notion that the human immune system can be activated as well as down-regulated by classical conditioning.

Conditioned Immunosuppression: Clinical Implications

It is important to remember that classical conditioning can occur with pairings between inert substances (for example, sweets, as shown above) or procedures (for example, the colour of the vial) and the active agent. The more efficient and rapidly acting the active ingredient, the more likely it is that environmental cues or stimuli will be associated with that activity and hence induce a conditioned response. This suggests that as clinical medicine progresses with the development of sophisticated, potent drugs, the opportunity for conditioning will be dramatically increased. Some very exciting research on the significance of the clinical setting in the treatment of cancer has led the way in this area of research. It has been appreciated for many years that patients repeatedly exposed to nauseating cytotoxic drugs (such as CY for cancer chemotherapy) can develop 'anticipatory' nausea prior to drug exposure. Since CY and similar drugs are powerful immunosuppressive agents, the possibility for anticipatory (or conditioned) immunosuppression presents itself.

The first study to explore this investigated ovarian cancer patients after they had received at least three chemotherapy infusions. In the four-week interval between treatments they were telephoned to arrange a home assessment at least three days before their forthcoming treatment. In this session psychological tests were administered and a blood sample taken for determination of proliferative responses to mitogens and NK cell activity as well as complete blood counts and cell subset numbers. A similar blood sample was taken, and analysed, from patients on the occasion of their visit to the hospital, but before exposure to chemotherapy. The results showed that the *in vitro* proliferative responses to the T cell mitogens PHA and Con A were lower for the cells isolated from the hospital than from the blood collected in the patients' homes a few days earlier. NK cell activity was not significantly lower in the hospital than at home, nor were the number of white blood cells, percentage of lymphocytes or absolute number of lymphocytes. Although patients scored higher on measures of anxiety while in the hospital setting, the reduced proliferative response to mitogen could not be accounted for by anxiety alone. The authors of this study argued that their findings were a consequence of repeated pairing of the hospital stimuli (the conditioned stimuli) with immunosuppressive chemotherapy (the unconditioned stimulus) such that patients showed conditioned immunosuppression in the hospital setting (Bovbjerg *et al.*, 1990).

A subsequent study investigated breast cancer patients undergoing a form of chemotherapy that was less aggressive than that used in the ovarian cancer study described above (Fredrikson *et al.*, 1993). As before, blood was sampled in the patients' homes a few days before their fourth or fifth course of chemotherapy and in the hospital immediately before treatment. This time patients displayed *higher* numbers of white blood cells in the hospital, immediately prior to treatment, compared to two days earlier in their own home. This was due to an increased number of granulocytes in the peripheral blood. These authors were unable to replicate the reduced *in vitro* proliferative responses to T cell mitogens reported by Bovbjerg *et al*. The discrepancy in the results was explained by subtle differences in procedure between the two studies. In the original study patients arrived at the hospital the night before treatment whereas in the latter study they arrived just a couple of hours prior to treatment. It was hypothesised that conditioned immunosuppression may occur several hours after exposure to the conditioned stimuli and that the observed effects of the second study represented only the first stage in the treatment setting-induced effect. For example, an epinephrine-mediated increase in granulocytes may later be followed by the immunosuppressive effect of catecholamines.

Conditioning the Immune System and the Placebo Effect

The literature quite clearly indicates that conditioning of the immune system is a generalised phenomenon, occurring in different aspects of immune function and evidenced across a variety of stimuli. The more powerful and/or fast-acting the US, the greater the potential for conditioning of associated cues, be they agents or procedures. As a 'placebo' is defined as a presumably inert or neutral substance that elicits a therapeutic response, the possibility that this effect (or some part of it) may be attributable to conditioning of the immune system presents itself. Like conditioning, placebo effects are not limited to chemical treatments, but may include surgical and psychological therapies. Placebos may be useful in the therapy of a wide range of conditions, including some where the immune system is implicated (for example, cancer, arthritis, multiple sclerosis, coughs and the common cold). Many alternative hypotheses have been advanced to explain the mechanism of the placebo response. Some favour the 'suggestion' hypothesis, and others the 'reduction in anxiety' or 'expectancy' hypotheses. The 'classical conditioning' hypothesis of the placebo response has attracted the most attention. This theory stipulates that patients are particularly susceptible to conditioning as they are in a *health-deprived* state, just as Pavlov's dogs and Ader and Cohen's rats were in a food-

or-water deprived state. This state of health deprivation makes the individual selectively sensitised to certain health-related cues (for example, the healer, and associated substances and procedures) and therefore conducive to conditioning. It is therefore not hard to appreciate how the effects observed in the controlled experiments already outlined may be generalised within the clinical setting and substantially contribute to some types of the placebo effect.

Conclusions

The mechanism by which conditioning of the immune system occurs is not fully understood at present. However, what is clear is that a single mechanism could not possibly be responsible for all the observed effects. In truth this would be impossible as the intricate immune system is under the regulatory influence of myriad factors, each of which could be susceptible to classical conditioning. For example, it is clear that activation of the HPA axis and secretion of cortisol can be conditioned and that some of the conditioning paradigms described in this chapter condition its activation in conjunction with conditioning of an aspect of immunity. However, this does not imply that HPA axis conditioning alone is causally related to the observed immune conditioning, as some of these effects are not under the regulatory influence of cortisol and other factors have been shown to be important. In particular, it seems that the role of the central nervous system (rather than blood-borne products such as cortisol) is vitally important in behavioural conditioning. Experiments have demonstrated the role of certain areas of the cerebral cortex and limbic system (the insula and amygdala) in acquiring a conditioned response. Other experiments have implicated activity of endogenous opioids within the brain as being vitally important in acquisition of conditioned changes in immunity. Yet other experiments have revealed the role of direct autonomic innervation to organs of the immune system (for example, the splenic nerve).

What does seem clear, however, is that conditioning is mediated by a preferential effect on T cells. Conditioned suppression of lymphoproliferative responses in rodents, for example, has been more reliably observed in response to T cell than B cell mitogens. In addition, adoptive transfer experiments have demonstrated that if the T cells of a previously conditioned animal are transferred into a naïve animal the conditioning is also transferred. Several investigators have implicated a key role for IL-2 and its receptors in conditioned responses.

Examples of conditioned changes in immune function are found in both the humoral and cell-mediated branches of the immune system. Furthermore, the immune system can be conditioned to be inhibited or enhanced. These conditioned effects seem relatively easy to induce, sometimes after just a single pairing with the US. The more potent the US, the easier the conditioning. The observed conditioned responses have been shown to be of sufficient magnitude to impact on disease progression and mortality. As modern medicine produces more and more powerful pharmacological agents, the potential for conditioning of the immune system to cues within the clinical setting grows. The full impact of this phenomenon is only now beginning to be fully appreciated by the medical establishment.

8

Cerebral Lateralisation and the Immune System

The Brain, Emotion and Immune Function

We make the case throughout this book that the brain mediates the relationship between emotion and the immune system. This chapter takes this notion further as it postulates a differential role for each side of the brain in the regulation of immune function. For many years it was believed that the two hemispheres of the brain functioned (merely) as mirror images of each other, generally overseeing activities on the opposite side of the body. In fact the brain has many subtle asymmetries of function. Relevant to this chapter, however, is the view that, at the most basic level, motivation and emotion can be categorised as either 'positive' or 'negative' and that the left and right brain can be associated with these emotions and resultant behaviours, that is, 'approach' and 'withdrawal', respectively. In this chapter we present the evidence that this is the case and that left-hemisphere activation is preferentially associated with the Th1 branch of the immune system, whereas activation of the right hemisphere is associated with Th2 immunity.

Cerebral Lateralisation

The history of cerebral asymmetry has been marked by controversy. The first function to be identified as lateralised, by Broca in 1864, was language. At the time even this idea was greeted by many in the medical establishment with scepticism and distrust. Since then the literature on the subject has contained an unusually large amount of irreproducible and contradictory data. Consequently the notion of asymmetrical regulation of even straightforward processes like spatial processing was greeted with resistance. To this day there remains opposition to the notion that the left and right cerebral hemispheres have differential effects on immune function and that this may be linked to personality and emotion. However, the evidence to be reviewed in this chapter

126

points exactly to that conclusion: not only do the brain and emotions play a role in immune function, but that role is lateralised.

Cerebral Dominance and Handedness

Human cerebral asymmetry has been difficult to investigate. Marked individual differences in lateralisation exist and these differences are very difficult to identify. Some people's asymmetrical organisation is entirely opposite to others, and some people will be less asymmetrical than the rest. Cerebral 'dominance' (that is, the hemisphere largely responsible for language control) is a key determinant in the direction of lateralisation, but this too is not easy to determine. All too often the simple but blunt tool of handedness is used (the more reliable Wada test is difficult to execute and somewhat dangerous as it involves anaesthetising one of the hemispheres with sodium amobarbital). In theory, right-handed individuals will be left-hemisphere 'dominant' and left-handers will be right-hemisphere 'dominant'. In other words, left- and right-handed people are supposed to be opposite to each other in terms of the organisation of their cerebral asymmetry or lateralisation. The first problem with this is that handedness is not an 'all or nothing/right or left' phenomenon; there are degrees of being either right- or left-handed (determined by the Edinburgh Handedness Inventory). An additional problem of using handedness as an index of lateralisation is that although the majority of 'right-handers' (95 per cent) have left-hemisphere cerebral dominance, a majority of 'left-handers' (70 per cent) are also left-hemisphere dominant.

In reality, accurate determination of cerebral dominance from indices of handedness is impossible. This difficulty is one of the main reasons for the confused and sometimes contradictory literature on human asymmetry. Another reason is the unreliability of the methodologies used to investigate asymmetry experimentally. Until quite recently (see later) it has been technically difficult to directly stimulate the brain of normal volunteers without inducing considerable pain, as it is so well protected by the skull bones. As it is not ethical to operate (open the skull) of normal subjects, many conclusions have been drawn from brain-damaged patients, either by stimulation during routine surgery or, more commonly, following observation after a single hemisphere has been damaged, for example, following stroke or trauma. Although these studies are undoubtedly useful, it may be misleading to make conclusions about the functioning of the normal brain, where the two hemispheres are interacting, from what happens when a single hemisphere is failing.

Hemispheric Specialisation

Despite all these limitations the area of hemispheric specialisation has advanced and receives increasing attention. Hemispheric differences are no longer characterised by simple functional dichotomies such as verbal/analytic (left hemisphere) versus perceptual/intuitive (right hemisphere). There is a division of labour between the hemispheres whereby they complement each other and by necessity work together in many tasks. For example, the hemispheres can use different strategies when processing visual information: the left is superior in recognising categories of shape, whereas the right is relatively good at recognising specific shapes. Thus the hemispheres complement each other to work in harmony, rather than work in isolation on unrelated tasks.

The left and right hemispheres play different roles in the expression and control of emotion. In order to understand the differential effects of the hemispheres on the immune system it is necessary to review this asymmetry first. Patients who have suffered unilateral left-hemisphere brain damage/loss of function (right hemisphere intact) tend to experience more feelings of despair, hopelessness or anger compared to patients with similar but right-hemisphere damage. In contrast, right-hemisphere damage (left hemisphere intact) is associated with 'indifference-euphoric reaction' in which (perhaps surprisingly) minimisation of symptoms, emotional placidity and elation are common (Gainotti, 1969). Consistent with these findings are the results from non-traumatised individuals subjected to the Wada test (where one hemisphere is anaesthetised). Anaesthetisation of the left hemisphere (so only the right hemisphere is active) tends to cause dysphoric reactions, for example, crying, whereas the same procedure to the right (left hemisphere active) is associated with euphoria and well-being, for example, laughing (Terzian, 1964; Rossi and Rosadini, 1967). It is clear from observations such as these that differential activation of one or other hemisphere can elicit quite different emotional states.

One of the most influential people in the advancement of the lateralised approach/withdrawal theory of emotion is Richard Davidson, an electrophysiologist. Davidson has extensively studied activity in the brain by using recording electrodes placed on the skull. Sophisticated amplification devices magnify the signal so that the electrical activity in the brain beneath (caused by nerve cell firing) can be analysed. Different types of brain activity (for example, activity/relaxation) produce characteristic patterns of electrical activity. This technique usefully complements the studies described above as it is neither invasive nor painful, so can be performed in normal healthy individuals during experimental manipulation of emotion. Davidson discovered that the expression of emotion is associated with increased activity in the front part of the cerebral hemispheres, in particular in the 'frontal cerebral cortex'. The cerebral cortex is the outer layer of the hemispheres and therefore closest to the skull and easiest to record from (it is not possible to record what is happening deep inside the brain using electrodes placed on the skull). Significantly, however, he has shown that the left and right hemispheres are differentially active during positive and negative emotion. The left frontal region is more activated during positive, approach-related emotion, whereas the right frontal cortex is more activated during negative, withdrawal-related emotion (Davidson and Sutton, 1995).

Davidson has investigated individual differences in this asymmetrical activity of the frontal cerebral cortex during periods of no emotional experience: he proposes that we can all be classified according to whether we are predominantly 'right'- or 'left'-brain dominant. Some people show more left-brain activation at rest, whereas others show predominately right-hemisphere activation at rest (this is irrespective of language lateralisation). He has taken his theory even further by showing that emotional valance is related to this lateralisation. In experiments, 'left-brain-active' individuals reacted with more intense positive emotion to emotionally positive stimuli whereas the 'right-brain-active' subjects reacted with more intense negative emotion to emotionally negative stimuli (Wheeler *et al.*, 1993). In addition, subjects with greater basal left-brain activation tended to be more positive generally and minimise negative effect in their daily lives (in a similar way to the right-brain-damaged patients described above) (Tomarken *et al.*, 1992; Tomarken and Davidson, 1994). Davidson proposes that the left frontal cerebral cortex is part of a system that works to inhibit negative affect. Traditionally the physiology textbooks describe how the part of the brain responsible for emotion is the deep-seated 'limbic system'. This system is evolutionarily older than the cerebral cortex and comprises a group of sub-cortical interconnected structures with the hippocampus and amygdala at the core. Much has been written elsewhere about these structures, suffice it to say here that the amygdala has been shown to be influenced by activity in the frontal cortex – providing a route by which the frontal cerebral cortex can be involved in emotion (Drevets *et al.*, 1992).

Thus a body of evidence points to right-hemisphere activation being associated with negative (withdrawal) emotions, whereas left-hemisphere activation is associated with positive (approach) emotions. This provides us with a useful working hypothesis with which to explore the complex and conflicting literature regarding brain lateralisation and immune function.

Lateralisation and Immune Function

Some of the first studies to investigate the link between lateralised brain function and the immune system used handedness as the independent variable. We have already discussed how this is a far from ideal index of laterality, yet it has been the basis of many studies and has generated much controversy. The idea behind these studies is that the 'normal' condition of right-handedness (about 90 per cent of the population) involves greater activity of the left hemisphere as the left side of the brain controls the right side of the body and language function. Left-handers, in contrast, are assumed to be more right-hemisphere active (but remember the criticism of this assumption outlined above). Norman Geschwind first noticed in the early 1980s that left-handers were more susceptible to certain immune disorders (Geschwind and Behan, 1982). This first observation subsequently led to the GBG (Geschwind–Behan–Galaburda) model of cerebral lateralisation. The model proposed that left-handedness and altered immune function were related to each other and linked to excessive exposure to the hormone testosterone during critical stages of development in the womb (Geschwind and Behan, 1984; Geschwind and Galaburda, 1987). The theory suggested that testosterone slowed the growth of parts of the left hemisphere and the thymus (where T lymphocytes mature and are selected) during development, such that the right hemisphere develops more rapidly and the immune system is compromised. Bear in mind, however, that this is not the only theory that tries to explain the occurrence of left-handedness. Marion Annett has proposed the interesting 'Right Shift Theory' which links a dominant gene, responsible for the development of speech in the left hemisphere, with the increased probability of greater manual skills in the right hand. She has proposed a recessive form of this gene which results in absence of a systematic bias to one side, for either speech or handedness, about half of the people with this gene would become left-handed (see Annett and Alexander, 1996, for a fuller explanation of this theory). Yet others support the 'Birth Stress' hypothesis which postulates that left-handedness is essentially pathological in origin and that trauma occurring at birth, or birth stress, can account for most of it (Bakan, 1990).

Many studies have been carried out relating immune disorder to handedness. Certainly, being left-handed has not been shown to be associated with a massive failure of the immune system. What does seem apparent, however, is that left-handers (particularly female left-handers) are slightly more susceptible to allergy and asthma (see Bryden *et al.*, 1994; Kaplan and Crawford, 1994, for reviews) and less susceptible to Th1-mediated autoimmune disorders than right-handers. Asthma and allergy are manifestations of Th2 activity in which the immune balance is driven towards excessive IgE production (see Chapters 2 and 3), hence there is some evidence that left-handers are more Th2-dominated. On the grounds that left-handers may be less left cerebral hemisphere dominant, this may suggest that the right hemisphere may differentially promote Th2 activity.

Although there is no *direct* evidence to support it, the observation that the Th1 branch of the immune system is characteristically slightly suppressed in left-handers may be associated (through reduced immunosurveillance) with the reported reduced life expectancy in this group (London, 1989). Of course, there are many other possible explanations for the slightly decreased life-span of left-handers, not least their susceptibility to accident in a predominantly right-handed world.

However, the observation that left-handed females are slightly more prone to atopic (IgE-mediated) disorders than left-handed males requires further attention. Although many studies have shown no association between handedness and immune status, those studies that do report a positive link find that the link is often stronger in females (for example, McKeever and Rich, 1990). This is relevant here, as for a long time there has been evidence to suggest that females are generally less strongly lateralised than males (Lansdell, 1962; McGlone, 1978). There have been many reports on this topic and it has generated much controversy. Although some authors report no difference in lateralisation between the genders, there is sufficient evidence from a range of methodologies (clinical studies, behavioural research and brain imaging) to suggest that a degree of gender difference does exist. Critically, although some reports show no gender differences, there is a total lack of evidence to suggest that females may be *more* lateralised than males. It has been suggested that the greater bilateralisation of function found in females facilitated the skills required for successful female evolution (a blending of specialisations), whereas the 'hunter' male required excellent visuospatial skills specialised to a single and uncluttered hemisphere (Levy, 1978).

Some confusion lies in the observation that females in general are well known to be more susceptible to inflammatory autoimmune diseases, like multiple sclerosis and rheumatoid arthritis, which are indicative of overactive Th1 immunity (Whitacre *et al.*, 1999). If females are less strongly lateralised than males this would mean that in the female right-handed population in general the right hemisphere would be relatively more active than in the equivalent male population. If the right hemisphere preferentially oversees Th2 activity, this would predict that females in general would be more prone to atopic disorders like left-handers. Yet the evidence shows that only left-handed females are more prone to atopic disorders (Th2 domination). It is clear that lateralisation must be just one of a variety of factors that can exert some modulatory influence over the balance of the immune system. Certainly the hormonal milieu is also very influential. The possible explanation for the conundrum (although only speculation at this stage) is that in right-handed females the hormonal influences (absent in males) predominate over reduced asymmetry, but the left-handed females show more marked shift towards right-hemisphere domination (compared to male left-handers) such as to tip the balance in the opposite direction, towards Th2 activity and atopy.

Recently, there has been some very direct evidence published that lymphocyte trafficking is related to cerebral lateralisation. The language-dominant hemisphere of patients undergoing surgery for epilepsy was determined and immune status measured before and after surgery. There was a reduction in T cell indices (peripheral circulating total T cells including both CD4+ and CD8+ T cells) only in those patients who received surgery on the language-dominant hemisphere. There was an increase in these indices following surgery in the non-language-dominant hemisphere (Meador *et al.*, 1999). This study provides direct evidence to support the view that the language-dominant hemisphere (in the majority the left) may mediate up-regulation of some aspects of immune function, at least in terms of circulating lymphocytes. If the left hemisphere is damaged then that regulation is impaired and T cell mobilisation to the periphery is reduced. If the right hemisphere is damaged the left hemisphere can prevail, over the restraining influence of the right, and T cell indices rise.

Support for the notion that the left hemisphere mediates a stimulatory influence over Th1 immunity comes from the electrophysiological studies of Davidson and his group. Subjects were categorised according to the degree of their left-hemisphere activity as opposed to right-hemisphere activity. Those subjects who showed predominantly higher resting left frontal cortex activation had significantly higher levels of NK cell activity compared to pre-dominantly right hemisphere active individuals (Kang *et al.*, 1991).

The significance of these differences in immune function, mediated by cerebral lateralisation, to health has been investigated in terms of disease progression. Asymptomatic HIV+ men have been followed up for thirty months. It is known that AIDS progression is associated with a shift from Th1 to Th2 immunity (Clerici and Shearer, 1994). It was found that those individuals with greater left-cerebral dominance, implying more prolonged sustaining of Th1 defence, exhibited a slower disease progression and better mood (Gruzelier *et al.*, 1996). The maintenance of Th1 defence is crucial to the restraint that the body can exert over AIDS progression and physical decline (see Chapter 3). It seems therefore that lateralised control of immune function is not a redundant irrelevancy but fundamental to disease susceptibility; not just atopic disorder, but also life-threatening diseases like AIDS.

Differential Activation Effects

We have already discussed how difficult it is to investigate lateralised brain influences on immune parameters directly. Recently, however, a new technique has become available. Transcranial magnetic stimulation (TMS) is a non-invasive way of activating specific areas of the brain in healthy, conscious subjects. Using TMS it is possible to compare the effects of stimulation of identical areas of the left and right hemispheres. The technique is painless and involves generation of a magnetic field that triggers an electric current that can penetrate the skull without impedance to directly stimulate the intact cerebral cortex below.

This tool has been used to investigate lateralised brain influences on circulating immune parameters (Amassian *et al.*, 1994). TMS was used to stimulate a specific area of the left and right cerebral cortex (the border of the temporal, parietal and occipital lobes: the T-P-O cortex). Amassian *et al.* showed different effects on the immune system depending upon which hemisphere was activated. Although this study can be considered preliminary on a small population of five right-handed subjects, influences upon lymphocyte trafficking did seem to be lateralised. Left stimulation resulted in mobilisation of CD4+ T cells to the periphery acutely and CD8+ increases some hours later. Right-sided stimulation was much more variable in influence. The importance of this small study (which merits further investigation) is not the size or direction of effect, but that lymphocyte trafficking should be influenced (by TMS) at the level of the cerebral cortex at all, and that this aspect of regulation seems to be lateralised.

We have used this same technique (TMS) to investigate brain influences on levels of secretory IgA (sIgA). The secretion of sIgA is under the dual influence of the available reserves and active transepithelial transport (see Chapter 4), so it was hard to predict how differential activation of the left and right parts of the brain would influence its secretion. Using a paradigm based on the preliminary work of Amassian we have demonstrated that, in right-handed subjects, left-hemisphere activation caused increased secretion of sIgA into the saliva, an effect that was much less marked following right-hemisphere activation (see Gruzelier *et al.*, 1998). The observed effects were very rapid and transient, having returned to normal twenty minutes following cessation of the brain stimulation. The timing of the effect suggested that the transport of the antibody across the mucosal surface had been accelerated rather than actual production of antibody from plasma cells. These results therefore suggest that increased transport of sIgA, at least in the short term, is predominantly under left-hemisphere control. In contrast, availability of the antibody is believed to be predominantly under the influence of Th2-promoting cytokines, thought to be more associated with right-hemisphere activation. Experiments to date have not investigated the effect of prolonged right-hemisphere activation on levels of sIgA.

It is known that pleasant and unpleasant odours can differentially activate areas of the left and right cerebral cortex, respectively (work demonstrated by recording brain activity through the skull; see Martin, 1998). We utilised this knowledge to explore the effect of odours on the secretion of sIgA. Subjects were blindfolded and unaware of what odour they were about to be exposed to. Presentation of the pleasant smell of chocolate (known to activate the left hemisphere) caused increased sIgA secretion, whereas presentation of the unpleasant smell of rotten meat (right-hemisphere activation) caused the opposite effect. Again, the effect was immediate (during presentation of the odour) and transient (gone ten minutes later). So this experiment confirmed the results from the TMS study: an assumed left-hemisphere activation is associated with increased transport of the antibody sIgA across the mucosal surfaces.

Since left-hemisphere activity is associated with approach behaviour (as opposed to withdrawal) the teleological argument can be advanced that there is adaptive advantage associated with mobilisation of mucosal immunity (even in the short term), since exposure to pathogens will be greater during approach and exploratory behaviour. Hence left-hemisphere domination is associated with approach, socialisation, positive affect and adaptive mobilisation of mucosal defence.

Animal Studies

So far we have concentrated on examining the evidence for asymmetrical brain regulation of immune function in humans, but there is a large literature to complement this work from rodent studies. These studies are helpful as they have the potential to shed light upon the mechanisms that underpin the phenomena observed in humans. Most mice and rats have a preference for using either the left or right paw when reaching for food. The difference between rodents and humans, however, is that in rodents the ratio between left and right preference is 50:50. This suggests that whatever mechanisms determine cerebral dominance in rodents (including chance), they are evenly balanced; whereas in humans, 90 per cent of the population have preference for use of the right hand (there are theories relating this to the lateralisation of language to the left hemisphere). Despite this difference the rodent literature is broadly in agreement with the human studies demonstrating left-hemisphere domination for Th1 regulation. However, many of these early studies are impossible to interpret fully in terms of Th1/Th2 balance as this notion of how to view the immune system was not appreciated until recently.

Left-paw preference in mice has been associated with reduced Natural Killer cell activity (Betancur *et al.*, 1991), a finding consistent with the notion that right-hemisphere dominance potentiates Th2 activity (and consequent reduced Th1 activity). Another striking similarity to the human studies has been described in a specific strain of mice (New Zealand Black: known as NZB). These mice are prone to the development of a condition similar to systemic lupus erythematosus (SLE). This is a form of autoimmune disease associated with heightened Th2 activity (unlike organ-specific inflammatory autoimmune disorders that are Th1-driven). Female NZB mice are more susceptible to the development of this disorder and in females it runs a more aggressive course. This gender difference has been attributed to oestrogen. As in humans, where left-handed females show exaggerated Th2-related immune dysfunction, female left-paw-preference NZB mice develop the disorders earlier than their right-paw- preference littermates (Neveu *et al.*, 1989).

The opposite relationship also seems to hold. An association between pro-inflammatory cytokine-mediated sickness behaviour and left-hemisphere domination has recently been demonstrated. Right-pawed mice are more sensitive to sickness behaviour (reduced mobility, and so on) after administration of IL-1 (Neveu *et al.*, 1998). Hence the left hemisphere, as well as directing Th1-inflammatory immunity, seems more sensitive to peripheral inflammatory signals.

Bearing in mind the evidence that rodents have interindividual differences in lateralisation and that this has been related to differences in immunomodulation, it is surprising that much of the rodent literature, which does not take individual lateralisation into account, is so consistent. Many such studies have examined the effect of unilateral ablation of one or other cerebral cortex. These studies work on the premise that if one area of brain is removed the remaining areas will carry on working and reveal their true (uninhibited) function. In fact, these studies parallel the work carried out on brain-damaged humans and are subject to the same criticism.

This type of rodent study clearly demonstrates that lesions of the left or right cerebral cortex induce opposite effects on various immune parameters. For example, one of the earliest studies in this area found that NK cell activity reduced following left-hemisphere, but not right-hemisphere, ablation (Bardos *et al.*, 1981). Other studies looked at various T cell indices following left or right ablation. Typically, left ablation led to decreased activity in the mitogen stimulation test, and ablation of the right increased activity (for example, Neveu *et al.*, 1986; Barnoud *et al.*, 1988). No consistent results were found for antibody levels following ablation; some reported parallel changes to T cell indices and others no difference between hemispheres (for example, Neveu *et al.*, 1986; Barnoud *et al.*, 1988, respectively). Consistently, these studies demonstrate indices of Th1 immunity to be reduced following left-cortical ablation and increased following right-cortical ablation. It has been more difficult to clearly define the direction of changes in indices of the humoral immune system following unilateral cortical ablation (for review see Neveu, 1993).

So far we have merely described the phenomena indicating that the cerebral hemispheres appear to have distinct roles in relation to both emotion and regulation of the complex immune system. Evidence from across a range of techniques has implicated the left cerebral cortex in positive mood, approach-type behaviour and up-regulation of the cell-mediated immune system. On the other hand, the right cerebral cortex has been shown to be associated with negative mood, withdrawal-type behaviour and tendency to atopic IgE-mediated disorders. The question must therefore pose itself: how are these differences mediated and are these physiological mechanisms also lateralised?

Mediating Mechanisms

It is probable that any association between the cerebral cortex, emotion and the immune system is mediated via the autonomic nervous system (ANS). The sympathetic branch of the ANS, in particular, is known to have important influences on lymphoid tissue and the lymphocytes that inhabit it (see Chapter 3). Predictably, perhaps, asymmetrical hemispheric regulation of the ANS has been demonstrated. Substantial evidence of this effect has been derived from direct brain stimulation during neurosurgery. Stimulation of an area of cerebral cortex called the 'insula' in the left hemisphere resulted in bradycardia (slowing of the heart beat), whereas right insular stimulation caused tachycardia (increased heart beat) (Oppenheimer *et al.*, 1992). Consistent with this, right-hemisphere pathology (stroke), resulting in reduced function, has been associated with reduced sympathetic activation (Sander and Klingelhofer, 1995). Similarly, experimental strokes in cats and rats have provided evidence of right-sided dominance for sympathetic effects (Cechetto, 1993). Thus it is probable that asymmetrical cortical regulation of immune function may be mediated via an asymmetric autonomic nervous system. Indeed, the evidence suggests that sympathetic activation (dominant from the right hemisphere) will shift the balance of the immune system in favour of humoral Th2 (see Chapter 3). This asymmetry might explain both shifts in the Th1/Th2 balance and also mobilisation of the mucosal immune system that is known to be comprehensively regulated by autonomic processes (Chapter 3).

In addition, asymmetrical distribution of key neurotransmitters, known as monoamines, in the two hemispheres has been demonstrated. This group of neurotransmitters includes dopamine, noradrenaline and serotonin. The reason to highlight this group in particular is that they may provide the pivotal link between mood and the immune system. Dopamine is the brain's main reward substance. Addictive drugs like cocaine dramatically increase levels of dopamine in the brain. It is not just we humans who like to increase dopamine in the brain; rats will also relentlessly self-administer dopamine-boosting drugs. The other two monoamines (noradrenaline and serotonin) have been intimately linked to mood. Excessive levels are associated with anxiety and reduced levels are linked with depression. In fact, the well known antidepressant drug Prozac works to boost the brain's own supply of serotonin. Other antidepressant drugs enhance noradrenaline and some can boost both noradrenaline and serotonin. The point is that these neurotransmitters are key chemicals in mood and motivation. Bearing in mind what is known about the asymmetrical brain regulation of these psychological domains it is perhaps predictable that they too are asymmetrically distributed: higher concentrations of dopamine in the left hemisphere (approach motivation, pleasure) and higher concentrations of the other two in the right (withdrawal motivation, anxiety) (Barnoud *et al.*, 1990).

Apart from the ANS the other major system strongly implicated in immune regulation is the hypothalamic-pituitary-adrenal (HPA) axis. The relationship between psychological factors and activity of the HPA axis has been discussed in other chapters of this book. Increased levels of glucocorticoids (for example, cortisol) in the circulation following mood manipulation (usually unpleasant) provide evidence for this. The link here is that activity of the HPA axis is largely dependent upon relative levels of the monoamine neurotransmitters described above. Critically, central noradrenaline and serotonin can initiate the HPA cascade to cause release of cortisol (in humans). As the right hemisphere is especially rich in these neurotransmitters it seems likely that this hemisphere dominates in regulation of the HPA axis. High levels of circulating cortisol have an impact on the Th1/Th2 balance of the immune system (see Chapter 3). In short, cortisol promotes a shift to Th2. Thus differential activation of the HPA axis by the two hemispheres provides another mechanism for the immunomodulatory effects of cerebral lateralisation. Predominantly right-hemisphere individuals could preferentially activate the HPA axis and favour shifts towards Th2 and susceptibility to atopic conditions (see Figure 8.1).

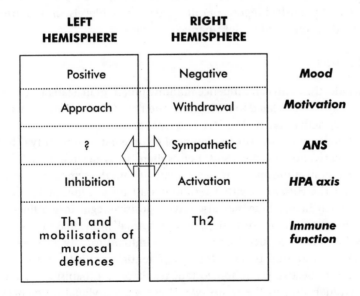

Figure 8.1 Simplified diagram to illustrate the relative importance of the left and right cerebral hemispheres in relation to mood, motivation, activation of the autonomic nervous system (ANS), the HPA axis and immune function (see text)

There is some direct evidence that the HPA axis is asymmetrically regulated in the direction suggested above. However, much less work has been carried out in this area, compared to asymmetrical regulation of the immune system itself. This is probably because explanatory mechanisms are usually explored after establishment of the initial phenomenon. However, the available evidence does point to right-hemisphere domination for glucocorticoid production. Rodent studies have demonstrated that removal of parts of the right cerebral cortex leads to down-regulation of both basal and stress-induced glucocorticoid levels, whereas removal of the identical area of the left hemisphere has no effect (Sullivan and Gratton, 1999). Consistent with this, it has been shown that left-pawed mice also have higher basal and stress-induced glucocorticoid levels compared to their right-pawed littermates (Neveu and Moya, 1997). In humans it has been shown that presentation of an aversive video (electroconvulsive treatment of a patient) to either the right or left visual field produced greater cortisol responses following right hemifield presentation (Wittling and Pfluger, 1990). Verbal self-reports of emotion, however, were not distinguished by hemisphere, emphasising the fact that physiological and self-report measures of emotional responding are not always consonant (see Chapter 1). Thus these data are consistent with right-side dominance for activation of the HPA axis. However, to our knowledge there have been no published reports of differential cortisol levels, or responses, in left-handed as compared to right-handed humans.

Conclusions

To conclude, the brain can influence immune processes in a lateralised, asymmetrical way that is related to motivation and mood. In 'normally' lateralised individuals, activation in the left hemisphere is broadly associated with approach motivation and up-regulation of cell-mediated immunity (Th1). In contrast, activation of the right hemisphere is associated broadly with withdrawal motivation and increased activity of both the sympathetic nervous system and the HPA axis, with a resultant shift toward humoral immunity (Th2). The left hemisphere may also have a positive regulatory influence on mobilising mucosal immunity (sIgA). In the 'normal' individual the two hemispheres are in balance such that neither is dominant for any great length of time. Transient stressors or rewards may differentially activate the right or left hemisphere respectively, but homeostatic regulatory mechanisms soon return the individual towards the *status quo*. However, individual differences are apparent in people's outlook and attitudes on life and this is reflected in relative hemisphere activation with a resultant impact on immune status. For example, optimistic individuals are characterised by greater left-hemisphere activation and this may have a bearing on their susceptibility to infection and disease (increased cell-mediated surveillance and a more effective secretory immune system). In evolutionary terms this would have facilitated the development of socialisation and exploration. Individuals with the unusual right-hemisphere lateralisation of language (poorly identified by left-handedness), and hence relatively greater right-hemisphere activation, tend towards predominant humoral-mediated immunity (Th2) which can result in atopic hypersensitivity disorders. Thus, an investigation of lateralised brain function has helped to illuminate the links between the brain, emotion and immune activity.

9
PNI and Health

One of the most frequently asked questions by those who have been most sceptical of the developing science of psychoneuroimmunology goes something like this: 'Yes, you may have evidence that psychological states and the like have detectable effects on the immune system, but what evidence have you that these immune system effects have any real relevance to health?' In the early years of PNI research, it was indeed difficult to point to such evidence. It was also a somewhat unfair question to ask when PNI research was in its infancy. However, researchers can now increasingly point to an accumulating pool of findings which address the issue of relevance to health.

Some of these issues have arisen naturally in the course of other chapters of this book, for example, the possible clinical implications of immune conditioning studies (see Chapter 7). Equally, the relevance of PNI to the clinical condition of depression has been discussed in detail in Chapter 6. Therefore, what we will be mostly dealing with in this chapter are the implications of the links which PNI research has underpinned between stress processes and immune processes, an area which was addressed in detail in Chapter 5. We did not at that point discuss implications for health, so these are the primary focus of this final chapter.

Psychosocial Variables and General Health

Although much of the evidence which we shall consider later in the chapter involves direct immune system measurement, we can begin by considering more global evidence that at the very least provides a plausible case for the pursuit of PNI research. Over many years epidemiologists have reported findings which suggest that psychosocial factors can be predictive of general morbidity and mortality in certain populations. Especially in the elderly, infections and cancer (both of which have direct relevance to the functioning of the immune system) make an appreciable contribution to all-cause morbidity and mortality. Such studies are therefore in the widest sense relevant to the agenda of PNI researchers.

In a recent prospective study, Korten *et al.* (1999) followed up a sample of people aged seventy or over living in a local community. Results indicated that poorer cognitive functioning was an independent predictor of mortality, even when obvious predictors such as baseline ill health and gender (males showing greater mortality) were controlled. Another recent study of the elderly in Germany by Maier and Smith (1999) showed essentially the same effect, and also linked 'dissatisfaction' with growing old to increased mortality. O'Connor and Vallerand (1998), in a prospective study of elderly residents in a nursing home, reported increased mortality to be associated with depression and lower self-esteem. Finally, Dalgard and Lund-Haheim (1998) presented evidence that the importance of psychosocial variables in predicting mortality may not be confined to just the elderly. In a large sample of adults of all ages, it was found that greater mortality was associated with less social interaction, fewer friendships and external locus of control.

Psychological Stress and Infectious Illness

While such studies indicate in the broadest fashion that psychosocial variables may impact on health, of more direct relevance to PNI are those studies which have linked psychosocial variables to infectious illness in particular. There are now sufficient studies of this type to draw fairly robust conclusions. Of course, such studies do not prove that psychosocial variables have their effects through modulation of immune system functioning, but they are at least suggestive.

One of the most tractable vehicles for studying the impact of psychosocial variables on infection has been the study of respiratory disorders such as the common cold and influenza. These disorders have two obvious desirable characteristics from the point of view of the researcher. First, they are frequent enough in most communities to enable researchers to conduct well controlled prospective studies, which are not prohibitively costly, on relatively small samples of people over relatively short periods of time. Second, the common cold at least is sufficiently mild an illness to enable researchers deliberately to expose volunteers to viruses in an ethical manner and thus gain the benefits which follow from using the experimental method. We describe first those studies which have looked at baseline psychosocial measures and sought to relate them prospectively to naturally occurring illness in a follow-up period.

An early study (Graham *et al.*, 1986) showed that a composite stress measure drawing on recent life events (major and minor) and psychological poor health predicted frequency of respiratory illness episodes over a period of six months. The same group (Graham *et al.*, 1990) have also reported (this time in a cross-sectional study) that maternal stress and family dysfunction are associated with children's proneness to respiratory infection. Although not prospective, the authors did show that the effects of stress were independent of a range of potentially confounding variables such as maternal smoking, early chest illness, number of siblings, occupation, sex, age, birthweight and parental history of respiratory illness. In a prospective family-based study, Clover *et al.* (1989) also investigated the effects of family functioning on incidence of influenza. Results again suggested that incidence was higher in dysfunctional families.

Cobb and Steptoe (1998) investigated stress and susceptibility to upper respiratory tract illness in an adult population using a prospective design. Not only did they find a predictive relationship between life event stress in the previous year and illness episodes over a subsequent fifteen-week period, they also showed that an avoidant coping style exerted a protective ('buffering') effect on illness vulnerability. Health behaviour variables such as smoking, sleep regimes and exercise did not account for differences in vulnerability, although alcohol usage was somewhat protective in its influence.

However 'Life Events' research in the context of naturally occurring episodes of common respiratory infections has to be treated somewhat cautiously. At least one study (Evans *et al.*, 1996) has shown that the overall tally of life events, positive and negative, predicts vulnerability. Indeed, when separated out, it was found that it was the number of positive, not negative, events which was the significant predictor. The reasons for this finding are not entirely clear, but one obvious factor may be that those who report more positive events lead more socially interactive lives and thus expose themselves more often to respiratory viruses. Controlling for exposure has not been a feature of this sort of study, despite the fact that the degree to which a person is exposed to viruses should be a relevant factor in determining the frequency of naturally occurring illness episodes.

Another way of addressing the linkage between psychosocial variables and respiratory illness is to look longitudinally and within subjects at when people have illness episodes. In three such studies (Stone *et al.*, 1987b; Evans *et al.*, 1988; Evans and Edgerton, 1991), researchers reported that episodes of common colds or influenza tended to be preceded around four days earlier by a distinct decline in the number of daily desirable events (or 'uplifts').

In most studies of naturally occurring colds and influenza, we should more rightly talk of respiratory illness rather than infection. Detection of virus is not a part of such studies. However, infection *per se* is clearly corroborated in studies which deliberately expose volunteers to respiratory viruses. Such studies have therefore been useful in providing converging lines of evidence for the role of psychosocial variables. In particular, studies by Cohen and colleagues have definitively shown that a composite stress measure, taken prior to virus exposure, predicts actual rates of subsequent infection in a dose-dependent fashion (Cohen *et al.*, 1991). More recently Cohen *et al.*, (1998b), in another viral exposure study, have shown that severe chronic stressors over a period in excess of a year are what predict susceptibility to the common cold, not acute stressors within a month of exposure, even though the acute stressors may themselves be severe.

Studies of Stress, Immunity and Respiratory Infection

Although most human studies of respiratory illness episodes and psychosocial variables have not examined immune measures, there are some exceptions. In a recent experiment, Cohen *et al.*, (1999) showed that symptomatology following influenza virus exposure was again more severe in those reporting more psychological stress prior to exposure. In addition, however, they showed that the effect of stress on symptom severity was also associated with increased production of the cytokine IL-6.

While the mechanisms through which stress may act on the immediate response to viral exposure are interesting, a central concern of PNI research in this area must be to demonstrate that stress does indeed undermine host resistance to infection through neuroendocrine-mediated changes in immune competence. There are few studies of this type but there is some evidence that levels of secretory immunoglobulin A (sIgA) may play a mediating role in the effects of stress on vulnerability to respiratory illness. We have already seen in previous chapters that sIgA is very sensitive to the effects of psychosocial variables, and we have also mentioned that immunologists have suggested that a prime function of sIgA is to provide a first line of defence against microbial entry via mucosal surfaces. Empirical evidence supports this view. Those rare individuals who lack the ability to produce sIgA do tend to suffer more from respiratory infections (Janeway and Travers, 1997). Retrospective studies (for example, Jemmott and McClelland, 1989) have linked lower sIgA to more self-reporting of respiratory infection, as well as more general symptom reporting (Evans *et al.*, 1995). In an early viral exposure study, it was also shown that symptom development following exposure was worse in those with lower levels of sIgA prior to exposure (Rossen *et al.*, 1970). Studies which have included measures of stress, sIgA, and respiratory infection are rare but do exist.

Deinzer and Schuller (1998), while examining the effects of examination stress on sIgA, also recorded incidences of common colds and influenza. Although the stressor was associated with lowered sIgA, there was no greater incidence of illness episodes in the exam condition and no association between illness and sIgA. However, the design is probably not well suited to testing a mediational hypothesis. First, sIgA levels are likely to be increased for a period in consequence of infection (Rossen *et al.*, 1970), which makes it difficult to test the hypothesis that low sIgA is associated with vulnerability. Second, given no overall association between the stressor and illness rates in the study, it is unlikely that mediational effects would be in evidence.

A study by Drummond and Hewson-Bower (1997) compared children with a history of recurrent colds and influenza to a control group of healthy children. They noted that the vulnerable children scored more highly on several dimensions of psychosocial stress and exhibited lower levels of sIgA. Although direction of causation cannot be established in a study of this type, it is nonetheless consistent with the view that prolonged stress impacts unfavourably on immune protection of mucosal surfaces and thus increases susceptibility to colds and influenza.

While the design of really persuasive human studies is difficult in this area, there are some interesting studies of rodents exposed to respiratory viruses. One particularly illuminating study (Dobbs *et al.*, 1996) examined the effect of restraint stress on both cytokine function and HPA activation in mice, who were exposed to influenza virus. The stressor was shown, as expected, to lead to elevation of corticosterone (the principal glucocorticoid produced in rats and mice). Results also indicated that the stressor suppressed the virus-specific production of Th1 cytokines (IFN-γ and IL-2) and IL-10 (a Th2 cytokine), indicating a down-regulation of both cellular and humoral response to infection, although, as we noted in Chapter 5, this is still compatible with a shift in balance from Th1 to Th2 in terms of an overall response. Also of interest was the finding that administration of a glucocorticoid receptor antagonist prevented the immune responses, thus indicating the mediating role of the HPA in producing stress-immune effects (see Chapter 5).

A similar experimental design was employed in a study by Hermann *et al.* (1993). Findings indicated that restraint stress was not only associated with suppression of cellular immunity and the natural inflammatory response, it was also associated, at least in one strain of mouse, with increased mortality following infection. The difference in end result depending on strain should remind us that the impact of stress on immune processes and finally health is likely to vary among individuals. We have seen examples both in this chapter and Chapter 5 of how variables such as appraisal, coping styles and social support can modulate or buffer the impact of stressors on both immune measures and health. This rodent study should remind us to add genetic factors to that list. Age has also been studied in this murine model, with senescence being shown to exacerbate the effects of stress on both the immune response to infection (CD4+ and NK cell function) and infection-induced mortality (Padgett *et al.*, 1998c).

Characteristic physiological responding to acute stress may also modulate the effects of more chronic stress on vulnerability to infection. This was seen,

for example, in a study by Boyce *et al.* (1995) which showed that the association between life stress and incidence of respiratory illness among nursery-aged
children was predicted by cardiovascular response to a laboratory stressor.

PNI and Other Infections

The studies so far described have dealt with (at least in the case of human
studies) relatively minor infection. However, such studies have been most
important in establishing fairly robustly the role that psychological factors,
such as stress, can play in the infection process, and the involvement of the
immune system in that process. The findings from this copious research
literature must strongly suggest that if one type of infectious illness can be
influenced by psychosocial variables, so might others which are far more
serious or life-threatening. For example, researchers have noted increased
incidence of tuberculosis in groups facing traumatic circumstances (for
example, refugees), and have speculated that this may have as much to do
with stress-induced changes in immune system functioning (notably a shift
from Th1- to Th2-promoting activity) as with exposure to pathogens (Rook,
1997). The same speculation has been made in regard to Gulf War syndrome,
where multiple Th2-provoking vaccinations were given under very stressful circumstances to troops (Rook and Zumla, 1997), where symptomology is
associated with a profoundly imbalanced immune system.

In terms of life-threatening infections, however, by far the most studies
have examined the role of stress (and also to some extent depression; see
Chapter 6) as a co-factor in determining the progress and outcome of HIV
infection. We have already suggested at various points that the very old may
be more vulnerable to the immunosuppressing and health-impairing effects of
stress. So those with HIV infection may also be considered a potentially high-
risk group for the deleterious effects of prolonged psychological stress. There
is indeed strong evidence that progression of HIV infection to full-blown AIDS
is characterised by a shift from Th1 to Th2 immunity, the exact profile which
we have seen is produced by chronic stress. We may ask, therefore, whether
there is any evidence that stress is associated with the swifter progression of
HIV infection.

Several studies have examined this question. Kemeny *et al.* (1995) examined
immune parameters in gay men who had recently suffered the bereavement
of a partner. Among HIV-infected men, immune system down-regulation
following bereavement was indicated by a mitogen-induced proliferation
measure. The down-regulation was independent of medication and recre-
ational drug use, including tobacco and alcohol.

In a more ambitious and wide-ranging study by the same group, Cole *et al.*
(1996) followed the progression of initially healthy HIV-infected gay men over

a period of nine years. They measured HIV progression in terms of critical reduction of CD4+ lymphocytes, time to AIDS diagnosis, and finally AIDS mortality. In terms of stress-relevant psychological variables, the best prediction of disease progression (and a dose-dependent one too) was the extent to which the individual concealed his gay identity. Interestingly, while the exact interpretation of this rather specific measure is not entirely clear, it showed itself not only to be independent of obvious control variables such as medication and health practices, but also independent of other psychological variables such as social support, anxiety and depression.

To the extent that Cole *et al.*'s measure of concealment implies a resigned acceptance of a stigmatic label rather than a more aggressive assertion of identity, there may be parallels with another study of HIV progression, once again by the same group (Reed *et al.*, 1994). In this study they showed that the subjects' resigned acceptance of their HIV status and its possible consequences was a significant predictor of decreased survival times. This very much echoes findings from some studies of cancer patients (see below).

Both of the above studies raise questions about the phenomenology of chronic stress, a difficulty which animal laboratory researchers can largely bypass. In Chapter 5 we pointed to an overlap between chronic stress and depression, and we might wish at this point to widen the experiential vocabulary to include something like passivity in the face of perceived uncontrollable sources of stress. Indeed, there is evidence from human studies that perception of control is important even in relatively mild acute stress. Brosschot *et al.* (1998), in a recent re-analysis of earlier data, have shown that decreases in CD4+ cell counts are only apparent in those perceiving low control over an interpersonal stressor. However, ratings of controllability or anything else can never get fully to the heart of the stress experience. Just what any questionnaire or interview measure homes in on is always going to be an essentially fuzzy concept and interpretation of predictions in this sort of research is likely to remain somewhat problematic and context-dependent. There is certainly a case to be made for more qualitative research methods in the area. At present there is a dearth of such studies.

PNI, Allergy and Autoimmune Disease

There is long history in the field of psychosomatics of attempts to link allergies to variables in the psychological domain. Asthma in particular has been the focus of much debate. From dubious psychoanalytic speculation that an asthmatic attack represents a repressed cry for help, to demonstrations by behaviourists that asthmatic responses can be classically conditioned to roses made of paper (see Chapter 7), the field has expanded to embrace the study of the role of stress.

Until recently, a hypothesis that stress could be a causative or aggravating factor in diseases such as asthma encountered some theoretical problems. Allergic reactions are themselves immune system reactions, albeit ones where the immune response is inappropriate and potentially dangerous. If chronic stress is simply immunosuppressive, stress should therefore inhibit rather than facilitate such conditions. From what has been said already in this and other chapters, the reader should now be aware that the theoretical problem has dissolved. We now believe that stress is not universally immunosuppressive. Instead it tends to shift the balance of the total immune response away from cellular immunity (which is therefore suppressed by chronic stress) towards a predominantly humoral response. Moreover, the switch, in so far as it potentiates the action of Th2 cytokines, such as IL-4, results in particular potentiation of the immunoglobulin E (IgE) response. It will be remembered from previous chapters that IgE binds to mast cells which are thereby stimulated to 'degranulate' and release powerful inflammatory agents, notably histamine. This type of response is potentially very useful for some purposes such as the removal of parasites. However, due to the greater prevalence in modern societies of allergy rather than parasites, most of our knowledge of immune processes involving IgE is grounded in pathology (Janeway and Travers, 1997).

So, stress, through encouraging Th1 to Th2 shift, could in principle facilitate allergic reactions. Although links between stress and asthma have been the focus of most attention, other possibly allergic disorders, such as irritable bowel syndrome (IBS), have also been a subject of interest in regard to stress being at least an aggravating factor (Gui, 1998), although the exact Th2 versus Th1 status of IBS is more controversial (Collins, 1996). In the case of asthma, at least, there has been speculation about the role of increased societal stress in partially accounting for the dramatic rise in asthma cases which has occurred in western countries, a rise which is in no way proportional to changes in environmental triggers such as pollutants (Rook, 1997). There certainly are studies which show that stress-related factors may be involved in both the course of long-term asthma and even its cause (see Wright *et al.*, 1998, for a review).

A recent empirical study (Gartland and Day, 1999) is interesting in that it followed a similar protocol to that seen in some of the studies of respiratory infection. These researchers looked at family functioning and its impact on the health of, in this case, asthmatic children. They found that the children of fathers who were more absent at weekends and more critical in their expression of emotion had higher incidence of symptoms, as indexed by both school absence and number of medical consultations. The mutual involvement of both stress and Th2 cytokine dominance has also been investigated recently in a study comparing asthmatic subjects and controls during stressful examination periods versus control periods (Kang *et al.*, 1997). In terms of stress being a trigger for asthma, it was noticeable that at the time of examinations asthmatic subjects released more IL-5 (a Th2 cytokine) while control subjects released more IL-2 (a Th1 cytokine).

An interesting question arises in regard to inflammatory disorder which is Th1-linked. Inflammatory autoimmune disorders such as rheumatoid arthritis (RA) and multiple sclerosis (MS) are of this type. The early use of corticosteroids as powerful anti-inflammatory agents in RA may suggest straightaway that hyperactivity of the HPA axis, associated with chronic stress and depression and with higher pervading levels of cortisol, may actually be protective against these kinds of autoimmune disease. Certainly, in the case of stress, there is some support for this from animal models of such disease. Whitacre *et al.*, (1998), for example, have recently shown that a regime of daily restraint stress can produce clinically significant suppression of an experimentally induced encephalomyelitis (EIE). EIE is routinely used as an animal analogue of human multiple sclerosis. Animal studies testify also to the fact that genetic differences between strains of rats, which lead to hyper- or hypofunctioning of the HPA axis, are also associated with differential response to analogue RA induction.

Evidence for the involvement of stress and HPA activity in human RA disease progression presents a mixed and somewhat confusing picture. It has been mentioned in Chapter 6 that depression as opposed to stress can be associated with a paradoxical picture of lowered aspects of innate immunity such as NK cell function, but increased Th1 cytokine activity, heightened inflammatory responding and acute phase protein release. However, there is, at the very least, no compelling evidence that chronic stress in itself is an aggravating factor in RA, and this is in strong contrast to infectious and allergic diseases. One complicating factor for human studies harks back to Chapter 5, where we noted that acute stressors can enhance aspects of cellular immunity. Since autoimmune diseases are characterised by patterns of relative health and relapse, it is therefore possible to speculate that acute stressful events could actually trigger illness episodes.

Vaccination and Wound-Healing Studies

An emerging line of research in the past few years has been to look at the effects of psychological variables on measures which reflect immune system functioning and at the same time have direct significance for health. There are two sorts of measures which fall into this category, and both have been introduced in Chapter 4. The first has looked at response to clinical as opposed to experimental vaccination. The second has looked at time taken for wounds to heal. This second paradigm has essentially been experimental, using volunteer subjects, although the results do have direct relevance to clinical settings. It is known that certain groups of the population who are to some extent immunologically compromised (such as the elderly) also exhibit longer healing times. The PNI research in this area has aimed to show that stress can also lead to impaired wound healing.

Beginning with vaccination studies, in one typical investigation, immunological response was monitored to influenza virus vaccine given to an elderly population as a routine seasonal precaution. Care-givers (for a spouse with progressive dementia) were compared with sociodemographically matched controls. There was clear evidence of compromised immunity in the chronically stressed population (care-givers). This was revealed in terms of both influenza-specific anti-viral antibody titres and indexes of cell-mediated defence, in particular virus-specific *in vitro* production of IL-1 and IL-2 cytokines (Kiecolt-Glaser *et al.*, 1996). A similar study (Vedhara *et al.*, 1999) has replicated the above findings in terms of antibody response, showing reduced specific IgG titres in a care-giver group compared to controls. Moreover, this latter study also implicates the HPA axis in producing the poor response. Care-givers exhibited more self-reported stress and higher cortisol levels, and, most pertinently, cortisol levels were predictive of poorer antibody response to vaccination.

In a study on a younger population, medical students underwent a routine hepatitis B vaccination programme. This coincided with a period of academic examinations. Levels of stress and anxiety experienced in relation to the exams were inversely related to the immune response to the vaccine (Glaser *et al.*, 1998). In terms of type of immunity affected, the use of hepatitis B vaccine needs some qualification. The vaccine is a recombinant protein, not a viable organism, and it cannot therefore result in antigen processing via the normal pathway. Therefore, in turn, it cannot trigger cell-mediated immunity. However, taking the findings of all studies together, they suggest that stress can have deleterious effects on both humoral and cellular aspects of acquired immunity, which in turn can affect in this case a clinically relevant outcome.

Alzheimer's care-givers were again compared with control subjects in a study, this time, of wound healing (Kiecolt-Glaser *et al.*, 1995). All subjects underwent the biopsy procedure described in Chapter 4 to create an experimental wound. Healing was assessed by strict objective criteria involving photographing the wound and observing the foaming response of the wound to hydrogen peroxide. A totally healed wound does not foam. Healing times were nearly 25 per cent longer in care-givers compared to controls, which is quite a large effect size. A relative failure of the normal immune inflammatory response was implicated in producing the results. Such a failure was indicated by differences which emerged between the groups in the IL-1 cytokine response to LPS antigen stimulation (see Chapter 4 for a fuller description of this measuring technique).

A second study (Marucha *et al.*, 1998) looked at the effects of examinations stress on wound healing. This time the researchers used a powerful within-subjects design, comparing the students' recovery times on two separate occasions for two separate wounds. One wound coincided with an examination period, the other with a vacation period. The results replicated the findings of the first study, and also implicated relative failure of inflammation processes in mediating the difference in healing times. Most importantly, using subjects as their own controls, the researchers were able to report an astonishing effect size: healing time was approximately 40 per cent longer at a time of fairly intense stress. The results were also very consistent: every single student took longer to heal at the time of examination compared to the time of vacation.

The same group recently added significantly to these findings by direct measurement of *in vivo* produced cytokines following the creation of blister wounds (Glaser *et al.*, 1999). The results clearly demonstrate that individual differences in stress are predictive of local cytokine production around the wound. In particular, subjects reporting more perceived stress showed less production of the pro-inflammatory cytokines IL-1 and IL-8. It is also noteworthy that more stressed subjects had higher levels of free cortisol, assayed in saliva. This is consistent with the view that hyperactivity of the HPA axis may be a factor mediating the relationship between perceived stress and cytokine production. More direct evidence, however, comes from an animal study (Padgett *et al.*, 1998b). Here, the investigators were able to confirm that, in mice also, wound healing took on average three days longer if accompanied by (restraint) stress. They also confirmed that local inflammatory response around the wound was less in the stressed mice, and finally that the stressed group had higher levels of corticosterone. However, by using an animal model the researchers were able to block the effects of glucocorticoids in a sample of stressed mice, using a receptor antagonist. When this was done, healing rates were comparable with controls. These findings argue persuasively that the effects of stress on wound healing are mediated by changes in HPA functioning. It is worth adding that groups mentioned earlier as having slower healing (such as the elderly) are also characterised by high levels of cortisol.

Stress and Cancer

Cancer in relation to depression has been dealt with in some detail elsewhere in this book (see Chapter 6). We have therefore seen already how difficult it is to test hypotheses about the role of depression in the aetiology of cancers, not least because it is usually impossible to pin-point a time when cancer begins. The same difficulties apply to any putative role of stress. However, there does seem to be some evidence from studies of human patients that psychological coping styles can be important in determining the course of cancers, though even here interpretation depends crucially on assumptions of equivalence in disease status at the time of psychological assessment. Survival times have been reported to be significantly longer, for example, in those with less resigned acceptance of their condition and those who exhibit something like 'fighting spirit' (Greer, 1983; Molassiotis *et al.* 1997).

Stress can alter immune function and particularly key immune processes (notably Natural Killer cell activity) which are thought to play a role in regulating tumour growth. However, the evidence that immune changes under stress are of the type and magnitude to influence tumour growth and metastasis is still questionable (Cohen and Rabin, 1998). Nevertheless, there are a few compelling animal studies from Ben-Eliyahu and colleagues which do suggest that the stress of surgery may have clinically significant deleterious effects on the development and metastasis of at least certain cancers, and that the effects involve NK cell mediation (see, most recently, Ben-Eliyahu *et al.*, 1999).

Conclusions and Implications

On the basis of the studies reported in this chapter, it would be fair to conclude that stress processes can significantly impact on health. We can also conclude that there is strong evidence that, in certain cases at least, associations between stress and health outcomes and health status are mediated by the effects of stress on the immune system.

What, then, are the implications of these findings? It may be convenient to consider implications for individuals and implications for a wider society separately. Too often, perhaps, there is a tendency to rush from a simplistic belief that stress is 'bad' for the individual to a conclusion that we must all, as individuals, do something about it (attend stress management courses, take up yoga or transcendental meditation, for example). Indeed, there are studies in the PNI literature which have shown that certain immune system measures are up-regulated following interventions such as relaxation training. However, it is more difficult to provide convincing evidence that *specific* interventions, by *specifically* influencing immune system functioning, are *specifically* health protecting or health promoting. Moreover, if studies, for example, are carried out to investigate the acute up-regulating effects of a meditation or relaxation session on the immune system, we should not forget that there are several studies (see Chapter 5) which indicate that certain aspects of immunity are actually up-regulated by acute stressors themselves. More importantly, some of the stressors that we have considered (examinations being a prime example) are likely to be viewed by many as an inevitable and normal part of life. The stress engendered, although it may temporarily compromise such processes as wound healing, may also have positive consequences in terms of concentration and motivation in meeting important challenges. Clearly, the extent to which individuals faced by the normal hurly-burly of life challenges ought to take seriously the stress–illness links which have been established will depend on an assessment not so much of their inevitable exposure to stressors, but the degree to which they have impact and over what course of time. We have emphasised at different points throughout this book the crucial importance of appraisal processes, coping mechanisms and other individual differences, in modulating the impact of stressors on both measures of immunity and health. Thus, notwithstanding our caveat against seeing all stress as 'bad', some individuals may be advised to take stress seriously as a factor in regard to their health. There is one recent example of a pilot study which provides some evidence that psychological intervention, in the form of hypnotherapy, may be therapeutic in reducing recurrence of symptoms in those infected with genital (HSV2) Herpes Simplex virus (Fox *et al.*, 1999). The study is potentially important because it also implicates psychologically induced changes in relevant immune system parameters as mediators of the therapeutic effect.

The situation with regard to certain other groups of individuals may be similar in suggesting the potential for therapeutic intervention. In particular, the evidence presented in this chapter in regard to those with HIV, or those suffering other severe chronic stress (as a consequence of living with and caring for a demented spouse, for example) suggests that psychological factors in such cases may be a very significant factor in regard to health. It is therefore a factor which merits attention by those responsible for the welfare of such people, although it is not part of this book's remit to consider the specific details of intervention programmes. The same may be said with regard to the links which have been established in regard to psychosocial variables in relation to cancer. It is certainly the case that depression, although common in cancer patients, often goes undiagnosed and untreated. However, it is known that depressed cancer patients have higher mortality rates, and though this may be partially due to less compliance with treatment regimes, impaired immunity may also be a significant factor (Newport and Nemeroff, 1998).

Another health message that emerges from some of the more recent PNI research described here is that there may be distinct *occasions* when it may be particularly prudent to consider the potentially negative effects of stress. The research described above would certainly lead us to highlight situations where surgery or vaccination is needed. The findings from animal studies that blocking aspects of the physiological response to stress can attenuate or prevent the negative impact of stressors suggests that acute pharmacological intervention to reduce stress may be able to play a role in ensuring a better clinical response in patients.

Although many psychologists will tend to think of stress as a fundamentally psychological state ideally to be 'managed' by addressing the person's psychological profile and social circumstances, PNI research is more neutral. Going right back to Chapter 1, the whole organism is involved, and if there is a chain from psychological stress to health outcomes via neuroendocrine and immune mechanisms, there is in principle therapeutic potential for intervention anywhere along the chain. It is also worth reminding ourselves yet again at this point of the bidirectional communication between the brain and the immune system. While we have placed a lot of emphasis on filling in the blanks, as it were, in the traditional belief of a route from disturbed 'mind' to disturbed 'body', we should not forget that it is a two-way street. We saw in Chapter 6 that immune and neuroendocrine dysfunction may not just be associated with depression, they may in some instances turn out to be a significant part of the underlying pathology. At a more mundane level, we may even ask ourselves whether our sometimes puzzling shifts and changes in mood state might have something to do with the continuous background activity of our immune system 'sense', rather than reflecting input to our external senses.

Finally, there is an important and very general health message which emerges from PNI research. In so far as PNI has begun to inform us of the actual mechanisms which can link psychosocial circumstances and health status, it is bound to reinforce and bolster the general argument that factors such as stress need to be taken seriously by society itself. In modern and rapidly changing societies, stress is not just a matter for individuals to deal with. It is entirely valid to ask certain pertinent questions. To what extent are modern societies evolving in ways which are increasing the burden of stress on their citizens? And, if so, to what extent is stress responsible for increases in certain types of disorder? Many occupational psychologists certainly believe that work stress is on the increase. However, even regardless of any changing picture over time, there are other societal issues in relation to stress which are beginning to emerge.

One such issue is health inequalities. It is well known that in terms of morbidity and mortality there is a social class gradient in the direction of lower social class being associated with higher morbidity and mortality rates. Aspects of this gradient may implicate stress as a factor in explaining, partially at least, some of the inequalities (Adler *et al.*, 1994). First of all, the gradient still exists when statistical control is exercised for purely material circumstances and differences between the classes in such obvious health-related behaviours as smoking and diet. Second, and also arguing against an explanation solely in terms of material factors, the gradient is relatively smooth. One's chances of being ill, or dying earlier, increase at every step down the social class ladder. This has led some researchers to ask the obvious question: if the gradient is not due to material circumstances, is it due to psychosocial ones? There is indeed reason to believe that important variables related to stress (job pressure, lack of personal control and low self-esteem, to give just a few examples) are in turn related to social class. Equally, there is good epidemiological evidence that longevity, at least in developed countries, is better predicted by how evenly and equitably wealth is distributed in a country, rather than by the absolute wealth of the country (Carroll *et al.*, 1994). This evidence becomes relevant to the general argument if one makes a (plausible) assumption that the perceived quality of life is better for the many in a society with less stark contrasts between rich and poor.

PNI, as we have said, has tangential relevance to these emerging large-scale issues by adding detailed and scientific support to the notion that our physical health cannot be considered independent of our 'mental' state and our social functioning. In so far as some immune measures have proven exquisitely sensitive to stress influences, research can actually go a step further, by considering these 'bio-measures' as possible proxies for stress, alongside conventional self-report or interview data, in large-scale survey work. This is as yet a largely undeveloped area, although we ourselves have recently published one study of secretory immunoglobulin A (sIgA) levels in a large survey sample. Lower levels of sIgA were, in this study, significantly associated with lower social class (Evans *et al.*, 2000).

The term 'psychoneuroimmunology' was coined only about twenty years ago to describe an embryonic interdisciplinary science. Alongside its growth, it has faced a fair degree of scepticism from some traditionalists in the scientific community. Despite the scepticism, or perhaps because of it, scientists have carried on researching and developing the area, devising improved protocols for their studies and vastly adding to our knowledge base. We hope that this book will have convinced you that the area of PNI is not only an exciting area of research but can also be informative to anyone seriously interested in the links between the domains of psychology and health.

Glossary

(Cross-referenced terms are given in italics)

-meric   units of structure; as applied to *antibody* structure – dimeric, two units; pentameric, five units

5-hydroxytryptamine (5HT)   a *monoamine* neurotransmitter substance

acute inflammatory response   rapid response to tissue damage and/or pathogen invasion. Orchestrated by inflammatory mediators, including *macrophage*-derived pro-inflammatory *cytokines* to induce physiological and behavioural adaptations to infection, the so-called *acute phase* response

acute phase proteins   *proteins* secreted by the liver in response to pro-inflammatory cytokines. These play a non-specific role in defence against infection but can be mobilised very quickly

adrenalin(e)   along with *noradrenalin(e)*, is an important catecholamine produced by the adrenal medulla. See also *SAM system*

adrenocorticotrophic hormone (ACTH)   also called 'corticotropin', released principally by the pituitary (but also some immune cells) and stimulates *corticosteroid* synthesis in the adrenal cortex. See also *HPA axis*

allergy   an excessive sensitivity to *antigen* (hypersensitivity) mediated by *IgE*, *mast cells* and *eosinophils*

allo-   pertaining to different forms of equivalent genes represented within the genotype of a population, as in allogeneic or allograft. Hence an allograft will be allogeneically different to the recipient. This is the most common form of human organ graft, where the donor is not genetically identical to the recipient.

amino acids   the primary building blocks of *peptides* and *proteins*

antibody   molecule secreted by *plasma cell* that can specifically bind to an *antigen*. It has a characteristic two heavy and two light chain structure organised into a Y shape.

antigen   recognised by the immune system as foreign or Non-Self and capable of generating an immune response. The term can be applied at the molecular or cellular level

atopic   pertaining to an *allergic* state or reaction

B cell   *lymphocyte* which can be stimulated to produce *antibody*. See also *humoral immunity*

basophil   circulating form of *mast cell*. This cell type, when involved in an immune response, releases mediators that stimulate *allergic* reactions.

beta-endorphin (β-endorphin)   an endogenous opioid molecule. Acts as a central neurotransmitter within the brain but also produced by pituitary *ACTH* releasing cells and certain immune cells. Thought to play a role in the immune system in promoting *Th2* activity.

CD4+   molecular marker for *Th* cells

CD8+   moelcular marker for *cytotoxic T cells (CTL)*

cell-mediated immunity   also cellular immunity or type1 immunity; the defence provided directly by cytotoxic cells – macrophages, *cytotoxic T cells* and *Natural Killer cells*

class switch   the switch during the course of an immune response from one *antibody* class to another. This refines the antibody response but specificity for antigen is retained

clonal expansion   rapid division of an *antigen*-specific *lymphocyte* to amplify the immune response

corticosteroid   the general term for steroids produced by the adrenal cortex

corticosterone   the principal *glucocorticoid* produced by rats and mice

corticotrophin releasing factor (or hormone) (CRF) (or CRH)   produced by *parvocellular* cells in the *PVN* of the hypothalamus (and some immune cells), and stimulates *ACTH* release by the pituitary. See also *HPA axis*

cortisol   the principal *glucocorticoid* produced by humans

cytokine   secreted molecule (small *protein*) that acts as a messenger within the immune system

cytotoxic T cell   same as *cytotoxic T lymphocyte*. See *CTL* and *CD8+*

cytotoxic T lymphocyte (CTL)   capable of recognising and killing a body's own cell that is making a foreign *protein* which advertises the cell as being abnormal

dehydroepiandrosterone (DHEA)   adrenal steroid hormone with generally opposing influences to those of *cortisol*

delayed type hypersensitivity (DTH) response   an inflammatory response to *antigen* introduced into the skin which takes several days to become apparent. It is a good index of the strength of *Th1* immunity.

dendritic cells   a cell type found in *lymphoid* organs that presents *antigen* to *lymphocytes*

dexamethasone (Dex)   synthetic *glucocorticoid*, often used in a diagnostic test for depression

domain structure   level of organisation that can give a *protein*, such as *antibody*, its biological activity

dopamine   a *monoamine* neurotransmitter substance

eosinophil   immune cell important in defence against helminthic worm parasites and *allergic* reactions

epitope   fine detail of molecular structure recognised by *lymphocytes*

Epstein-Barr virus (EBV)   responsible for glandular fever

glucocorticoids   general term for adrenal steroid hormones that play a role in maintaining blood glucose, also now recognised to have important influences over the immune system

Herpes Simplex virus (HSV)   type 1 associated primarily with cold sores; type 2 with genital Herpes

histamine   chemical released by *mast cells* that promotes *allergic* responses

Human Immunodeficiency virus (HIV)   infects and destroys *Th cells*

humoral immunity   *Th2* or type 2 immunity, mediated by *antibody*

hypothalamic-pituitary-adrenal (HPA) axis   the main stress neuroendocrine system, intimately involved in immune system functioning

immunoglobulin (Ig)   generic term for *antibody*. Antibody refers to protective functions. Immunoglobulin more properly describes the molecule since it is also the *B cell* receptor for *antigen*. Immunoglobulin is now recognised to be just one representative of a large family of molecules expressed on cell surfaces that play adhesion and recognition roles

immunoglobulin A (IgA)   the secretory form, *secretory IgA (sIgA)* is the most abundant *antibody* produced and defends mucosal surfaces

immunoglobulin D (IgD)   this class of *antibody* is found on the surface of *B cells* where it acts as an *antigen* receptor. It is not thought to have an effector function as a secreted molecule

immunoglobulin E (IgE)   this class of *antibody* plays an important role in *allergic* responses

immunoglobulin G (IgG)   the most important class of *antibody* in the blood, but can penetrate to extravascular spaces and is transported across the placenta to protect the foetus

immunoglobulin M (IgM)   very large antibody molecule because of its penta*meric* structure. It is produced early in an immune response but declines in importance later. It is considered to be primitive

interferons (IFNs)   molecules originally identified with anti-viral activity. Interferon gamma (IFN-γ) is an important *Th1 cytokine*

interleukin 1 (IL-1)   a pro-inflammatory *cytokine* produced by *macrophages* – plays an important role in the *acute phase* response and in signalling to the brain

interleukin 2 (IL-2)   an important *Th1 cytokine* – stimulates *T cell* proliferation and *NK cell* activity

interleukin 4 (IL-4)   an important *Th2 cytokine* – drives *antibody* production and *class switch* to *IgG and IgE*; promotes *Th2* activity

interleukin 5 (IL-5)   *Th2 cytokine*. Stimulates *eosinophils* and promotes *class switch* to *IgA*

interleukin 10 (IL-10)   *Th2 cytokine* important in counter-regulation as it inhibits activity of *Th1* cells

interleukin 12 (IL-12)   *cytokine* produced by *macrophages* and active *Th1 cells* – important in driving *Th1* type 1 immunity

isotype   An antibody class. The five human isotypes are designated IgA, IgD, IgF, IgG and IgM.

leukocytes   general term for all the white blood cells of the immune system

ligand   molecule that is recognised by a receptor

locus coeruleus   noradrenergic (*noradrenalin(e))* centre in the brain – important mediator of stress responses and controls the sympathetic nervous system

lymph nodes   *lymphoid organs* that act as filters of lymphoid vessels returning lymph to the blood vascular system. Trap and present *antigen* and provide the environment for *lymphocyte* activation

lymphocyte   the key cells of the immune system that uniquely can recognise *antigen* at the *epitope* level. Provide the immune response with specificity and memory

lymphoid organs   organs devoted to immune cell development, maturation and education – primary or central lymphoid organs; or *antigen*-driven activation – secondary or peripheral lymphoid organs.

macrophage   tissue equivalent of circulating *monocyte*. Important *phagocytic*, *antigen* presenting and pro-inflammatory cell. Intimately involved in *Th1* type 1 immunity

major histocompatibility complex (MHC) molecules   present *peptide epitopes* to *T cells*. T cells can only recognise epitopes displayed by these molecules and only if these molecules characterise the individual, Self MHC

mast cell   has *basophilic* granules containing substances which mediate *allergic* reactions

mitogen   a molecule that stimulates *lymphocyte* proliferation. These molecules bypass *antigen*-specific activation and can stimulate whole populations of *lymphocytes*. They are commonly used in *in vitro* proliferation assays of immunocompetence

monoamines   generic name for related neurotransmitter substances: *noradrenalin(e), dopamine, serotonin*

monoclonal antibody   *antibody* derived from a cloned *plasma cell* line. Plasma cells are normally short-lived but they can be immortalised in various ways so that they can be grown in culture. If cloned then a population can be derived from a single cell and all antibody produced will be identical with single specificity. Such antibodies have numerous clinical and research applications

monocyte   circulating equivalent of tissue *macrophage*

mucosal associated lymphoid tissue (MALT)   the largest mass of lymphoid tissue in the body – supports the *sIgA* mucosal immune defence system

Natural Killer (NK) cell   cytotoxic cell important in early defence against viral-infected and cancer cells. Strongly associated with *Th1* type 1 immunity

neopterin   a chemical produced by *IFN-γ* stimulated *macrophages*. Measurement in blood, urine or saliva is an index of *Th1* activity.

neutrophil   a *phagocytic* cell important in early defence against infection. Numbers in the circulation increase during the *acute phase* response

noradrenalin(e)   *monoamine* neurotransmitter. Also a circulating hormone released from the adrenal gland. Both central (brain) and peripheral noradrenalin(e) activity are important in the stress response

paraventricular nucleus (PVN)   region in the hypothalamus which produces *CRF*, and central to the stress response system

parvocellular cells   the cell population in the *paraventricular nucleus* that produce *CRF*

peptide   a small chain of *amino acids* (two to twenty or so) creating molecules which can have messenger and signalling functions

peripheral blood mononuclear cells (PBMCs)   *lymphocytes* together with *monocytes* isolated from a peripheral blood sample. These can be stimulated in various ways to reveal the activity of the immune system

phagocyte   cell that can engulf bacteria and destroy them internally

plasma cell   a *lymphocyte* that is a mature *anitbody*-secreting *B cell*

polypeptide   large chains of *amino acids*. May be physiologically active in their own right but can also be components of larger *proteins*. See also *peptide*

proliferation   cell division and expansion

protein   the expression of our genes. Proteins are large functional molecules composed of *polypeptide* chains but with several layers of molecular organisation. They direct biological processes

secretory immunoglobulin A (sIgA)   *immunoglobulin* class that defends mucosal surfaces

serotonin   also referred to as 5HT. *Monoamine* neurotransmitter, important in the brain in relation to mood, emotion and motivation, and also involved in the pathways that activate the *HPA axis*

spleen   organ in the abdomen that filters blood. *Lymphoid* tissue in the spleen responds to *antigens* that have penetrated to the vascular circulatory system

sympathetic adrenomedullary (SAM) system   one of the peripheral arms of the stresss response system. Induces physiological responses rapidly

T cell   T *lymphocyte*. Recognises *peptide epitopes* displayed by *MHC molecules* on other cells. *T helper (Th) cells* recognise cells expressing peptide epitopes displayed by MHC class II MHC molecules and activate these cells. *Cytotoxic T cells* recognise peptide displayed by class I MHC molecules and kill the target cell

T cell receptor (TcR)   recognises the *peptide epitope* – MHC signal. Expression of this receptor defines a *T cell*

T helper 1 (Th1) cell   a T helper population that drives inflammatory, type 1 immunity, also referred to as cellular or *cell-mediated immunity*

T helper 2 (Th2) cell   a T helper population that drives type 2 or antibody-mediated immunity, sometimes referred to as *humoral immunity*

thymus   central *lymphoid organ* responsible for *T cell* maturation and selection

tolerance   condition in which presentation to the immune system of an *antigen* results in specific immunosuppression rather than activation

tumour necrosis factor (TNF)   there are two forms: TNF-α is an important pro-inflammatory *cytokine*; TNF-β is a *Th1 cytokine*

Bibliography

Abbas, A.K., Murphy, K.M. and Sher, A. (1996) Functional diversity of helper T lymphocytes. *Nature* 383, 787–93.

Ader, R. (1985) Conditioned immunopharmacologic effects in animals: implications for conditioning model of pharmacotherapy, in White, L., Tursky, B. and Schwartz, G. eds *Placebo: Theory Research and Mechanisms*, pp. 306–23. New York: Guilford Press.

Ader, R. and Cohen, N. (1975) Behaviourally conditioned immunosuppression. *Psychosomatic Med.*, 37, 333–40.

Ader, R., Cohen, N. (1982) Behaviourally conditioned immunosuppression and murine systemic lupus erythematosus. *Science* 215, 1534–6.

Ader, R., Cohen, N. (1993) Psychoneuroimmunology: conditioning and stress. *Ann. Rev. Psychol.* 44, 53–85.

Adler, N., Boyce, T., Chesney, M., Cohen, S., Folkman, S., Kahn, R. and Syme, L. (1994). Socioeconomic status and health: the challenge of the gradient. *Am. Psychol.* 49, 15–24.

Agarwal, S.K. and Marshall, G.D. (1998) Glucocorticoid-induced type 1 type 2 cytokine alterations in humans: A model for stress-related immune dysfunction. *Journal of Interferon and Cytokine Research* 18, 1059–68.

Alvarez-Borda, B., Ramirez-Amaya, V., Perez-Montfort, R. and Bermudez-Rattoni, F. (1995) Enhancement of antibody production by a learning paradigm. *Neurobiol. Learn. Mem.* 64, 103–5.

Amassian, V.E., Henry, K., Durrkin, H., Chice, S., Cracco, J.B., Somasundarum, M., Hassan, N., Cracco, R.Q., Maccabee, P.J. and Eberle, L. (1994) Magnetic stimulation of left versus right temporo-parieto-occipital cortex acts differentially on the human immune system. *Journal of Physiology*, 459, 22P.

American Psychiatric Association (1994) *Diagnostic and Statistical Manual of Mental Disorders*, fourth edition (*DSM-IV*). Washington, DC: American Psychiatric Association.

Andersen, B.L., Farrer, W.B., GoldenKreutz, D., Kutz, L.A., MacCallum, R., Courtney, M.E. and Glaser, R. (1998) Stress and immune responses after surgical treatment for regional breast cancer. *Journal of National Cancer Institute* 90, 30–6.

Annett, M. and Alexander, M.P. (1996) Atypical cerebral dominance: predictions and tests of the Right Shift Theory. *Neuropsychologia* 34, 1215–27.

Bakan, P. (1990) Non right-handedness and the continuum of reproductive causality, in S. Coren ed., *Left-handedness: Behavioral Implications and Anomalies*. Amsterdam: North Holland Elsevier.

Bamberger, C.M., Else, T., Bamberger, A.M., Beil, F.U. and Schulte, H.M. (1997) Regulation of the human interleukin-2 gene by the alpha and beta isoforms of the glucocorticoid receptor. *Molecular and Cellular Endocrinology* 136, 23–8.

Bardos, P., Degenne, D., Lebranchu, Y., Biziere, K. and Renoux, G. (1981) Neocortical lateralisation of NK activity in mice. *Scand. J. Immunol.* 13, 609–11.

Barnoud, P., Le Moal, M. and Neveu, P. (1990) Asymmetrical distribution of monoamines in left and right-handed mice. *Brain Res.* 520, 317–21.

Barnoud, P., Neveu, P.J., Vitiello, S., Mormede, P. and Le Moal, M. (1988) Brain neocortex immunomodulation in rats. *Brain Res.* 474, 394–8.

Bartrop, R.W., Luckhurst, E., Lazarus, L., Kiloh, L.G. and Penny, R.S.O. (1977) Depressed lymphocyte function after bereavement. *Lancet*, 1 (16 April), 834–6.

Ben-Eliyahu, S., Page, G.G., Yirmiya, R. and Shakhar, G (1999) Evidence that stress and surgical interventions promote tumor development by suppressing natural killer cell activity. *Int. J. Cancer* 80(6) (15 March), 880–8.

Benschop, R.J., Geenen, R., Mills, P.J., Naliboff, B.D., Kiecolt-Glaser, J.K., Herbert, T.B., Van der Pompe, G., Miller, G.E., Matthews, K.A., Godaert, G.L., Gilmore, S.L., Glaser, R., Heijnen, C.J., Dopp, J.M., Bijlsma, J.W., Solomon, G.F. and Caciopppo, J.T. (1998) Cardiovascular and immune responses to acute psychological stress in young and old women: a meta-analysis. *Psychosomatic Med.* 60(3), 290–6.

Benschop, R.J., Oostven, F.G., Heijnen, C.J. and Ballieux, R.E. (1993) Beta 2-adrenergic stimulation causes detachment of Natural Killer cells from cultured epithelium. *Eur. J. Immunol.* 23, 3242–7.

Bergquist, J., Tarkowski, A., Ewing, A. and Ekman, R. (1998) Catecholaminergic suppression of immunocompetent cells. *Immunology Today* 19, 562–7.

Bernton, E., Hoover, D., Galloway, R. and Popp, K. (1995) Adaptation to chronic stress in military trainees: adrenal androgens, testosterone, glucocorticoids IGF-1 and immune function. *Annals of the New York Academy of Sciences* 774, 217–31.

Besedovsky, H., Del Rey, A. and Sorkin, E. (1983) The immune response evokes changes in brain noradrenergic neurones. *Science* 221, 564–66.

Betancur, C., Neveu, P.J., Vitiello, S. and Le Moal, M. (1991) Natural killer cell activity is associated with brain asymmetry in male mice. *Brain, Behav. and Immunity*, 5, 162–9.

Blalock, J.E. (1994) The syntax of immune-neuroendocrine communication. *Immunology Today.* 15, 504–11.

Blotta, M.H., Dekruyff, R.H. and Umetsu, D.T. (1997) Corticosteroids inhibit IL-12 production in human monocytes and enhance the capacity to induce IL-4 synthesis in CD4+ve lymphocytes. *Journal of Immunology* 158, 5589–95.

Born, J. and Fehm, H.L. (1998) Hypothalamic-pituitary-adrenal activity during human sleep: a coordinating role for the limbic hypocampal system. *Experimental Clinical Endocrinology Diabetes* 106, 153–63.

Bovbjerg, D.H., Redd, W.H., Maier, L.A., Holland, J.C., Lesko, L.M., Niedzwiecki, D., Rubin, S.C. and Hakes, T.B. (1990) Anticipatory immune suppression and nausea in women receiving cyclic chemotherapy for ovarian cancer. *J. Consult. Clin. Psychol.* 58, 153–7.

Boyce, W.T., Chesney, M., Alkan, A., Tschann, J.M., Adams, S., Chesterman, B., Cohan, F., Kaiser, P., Folkman, S., Wara, D. (1995) Psychobiologic reactivity to stress and childhood respiratory illnesses – results of two prospective studies. *Psychosomatic Med.*, 57(5), 411–22.

Brosschot, J.F., Godaert, G.L.R., Benschop, R.J., Olff, M., Ballieux, R.E. and Heijnen, C.J (1998) Experimental stress and immunological reactivity: a closer look at perceived uncontrollability. *Psychosomatic Med.* 60(3), 359–61.

Brouxham, S.M., Prasad, A.V., Joseph, S.A., Felton, D.L. and Bellinger, D.L. (1998) Localisation of corticotrophin-releasing factor in primary and secondary lymphoid organs of the rat. *Brain, Behav. and Immunity* 12, 107–22.

Brown, E.S. and Suppes, T. (1998) Mood symptoms during corticosteroid therapy: a review. *Harv. Rev. Psychiat.* 5, 239–46.

Bryden, M.P., McManus, I.C. and Bulman-Fleming, M.B. (1994) Evaluating the empirical support for the Geschwind-Behan-Galaburda model of cerebral lateralisation. *Brain Cogn.* 26, 103–67.

Bunney, W.E. and Fawcett, J.A. (1965) Possibility of a biochemical test for suicidal potential. *Arch. Gen. Psychiat.* 13, 232–9.

Buske-Kirschbaum, A., Grota, L., Kirschbaum, C., Bienen, T., Moynihan, J., Ader, R., Blair, M.L., Hellhammer, D.H. and Felton, D.L. (1996) Conditioned increases in peripheral blood mononuclear cell (PBMC) number and corticosterone secretion in the rat. *Pharmacol. Biochem. Behav.* 55, 27–32.

Buske-Kirschbaum, A., Kirschbaum, C., Stierle, H., Jabaij, L. and Hellhammer, D. (1994) Conditioned manipulation of natural killer cells in humans using discriminative learning protocol. *Biol. Psychol.*, 38, 143–55.

Cacioppo, J.T., Poehlmann, K.M., Kiecolt-Glaser, J.K., Malarkey, W.B., Burleson, M.H., Berntson, G.G. and Glaser, R. (1998) Cellular immune responses to acute stress in female caregivers of dementia patients and matched controls. *Health Psychology* 17(2), 182–9.

Cappel, R., Gregiore, F., Thiry, L., Sprecher, S. (1978) Antibody and cell-mediated immunity to herpes simplex virus in psychotic depression. *J. Clin. Psychiatry* 39, 266–8.

Carpenter, G.H., Garrett, J.R., Hartley, R.H. and Proctor, G.B. (1998) The influence of nerves on the secretion of immunoglobulin A into sub-mandibular saliva in rats. *Journal of Physiology* 512, 567–73.

Carroll, B.J., Feinberg, M., Greden, J.F., Tarika, J., Albala, A.A., Hasket, R.F., James N.M., Kronfol, Z., Lohr, N., Steiner, M., de Vigne, M.P. and Young, E. (1981) A specific laboratory test for the diagnosis of melancholia: standard-ization, validation and clinical utility. *Arch: Gen. Psychiat.* 38, 15–22.

Carroll, D., Davey Smith, G. and Bennett, P. (1994) Health and Socio-economic status. *The Psychologist* (March), 122–5.

Carroll, D., Ring, C., Shrimpton, J., Evans, P., Willemsen, G.H.M. and Huck-lebridge, F. (1996) Secretory immunoglobulin A and cardiovascular responses to acute psychological challenge. *Int. J. Behav. Med.* 3(3), 266–79.

Cechetto, D. (1993) Experimental cerebral ischaemic lesions and autonomic and cardiac effects in cats and rats. *Stroke* 24, 1–6.

Christeff, N., Gherbi, N., Mammes, O., Dale, M.T., Gharakhanian, S., Lortholary, O., Melchior, J.C. and Nunez, E.A. (1997) Serum cortisol and DHEA concentration during HIV infection. *Psychoneuroendocrinology* 22, S3–S10.

Clerici, M. and Shearer, G.M. (1994) The Th1–Th2 hypothesis of HIV infection: new insights. *Immunology Today* 15, 575–81.

Clover, R.D., Abell, T., Becker, L.A., Crawford, S., and Ramsey, C.N., Jr (1989) Family functioning and stress as predictors of influenza B infection. *J. Fam. Pract.* 28(5), 535–39.

Clow, A., Vellucci, S.V., Parrott, R.F., Hucklebridge, F., Sen, S. and Evans, P. (2000) Endogenous Monoamine Oxidase Inhibitory activity and HPA activation in the pig. *Life Sciences* 66, 35–41.

Cobb, J.M.T., and Steptoe, A. (1998) Psychosocial influences on upper respi-ratory infectious illness in children. *J. Psychosom. Research* 45(4), 319–30.

Cocke, R., Moynihan, J.A., Cohen, N., Grota, L.J. and Ader, R. (1993) Exposure to conspecific alarm chemosignals alters immune responses in BALB/c mice. *Brain, Behav. and Immunity* 7, 36–46.

Cohen, N., Moynihan, J.A. and Ader, R. (1994) Pavlovian conditioning of the immune system. *Int. Arch. Allergy Immunol.* 105, 101–6.

Cohen, P., Pine, D.S., Must, A., Kasen, S., Brook, J. (1998a) Prospective associ-ations between somatic illness and mental illness from childhood to adulthood. *Am. J. Epidemiology* 147, 232–9.

Cohen, S., Doyle, W.J. and Skoner, D.P. (1999) Psychological stress, cytokine production, and severity of upper respiratory illness. *Psychosomatic Med.* 61(2) (March–April), 175–80.

Cohen, S., Frank, E., Doyle, W.J., Skoner, D.P., Rabin, B.S. and Gwaltney, J.M. (1998b) Types of stressors that increase susceptibility to the common cold in healthy adults. *Health Psychology*, 17(3), 214–23.

Cohen, S. and Rabin, B.S. (1998) Editorial. Psychologic stress, immunity, and cancer. *Journal of the National Cancer Institute* 1 (7 January) 3–4.

Cohen, S., Tyrrell, D.A.J. and Smith, A.P. (1991) Psychological stress and susceptibility to the common cold. *N. Engl. J. Med.* 325(9), 606–12.

Cole, S. W., Kemeny, M.E., Taylor, S.E., Visscher, B.R., *et al.* (1996) Accelerated course of human immunodeficiency virus infection in gay men who conceal their homosexual identity. *Psychosomatic Med.* 58(3) (May–June), 219–31.

Collins, S.M. (1996) Similarities and dissimilarities between asthma and inflammatory bowel diseases. *Aliment. Pharmacol. Ther.* 10, Suppl. 2, 25–31.

Connor, T.J. and Leonard, B.E. (1998) Depression, stress and immunological activation: the role of cytokines in depressive disorders. *Life Sciences* 62, 583–606.

Dalgard, O.S. and Lund-Haheim, L. (1998) Psychosocial risk factors and mortality: a prospective study with special focus on social support, social participation, and locus of control in Norway. *J. Epidemiol. Community Health*, 52(8), 476–81.

Danzter, R., Laye, S., Goujan, E., Bluth, R., Konsman, J.P., Parnet, P. and Kelley, K.W. (1997) Mechanisms of action of cytokines on the central nervous system. Interaction with glucocorticoids, in Rook, G.A.W. and Lightman, S. eds *Steroid Hormones and the T-Cell Cytokine Profile*, Berlin: Springer-Verlag.

Darko, D.F., Gillin, J.C., Risch, S.C., Bulloch, K., Golshan, S., Tasevka, Z. and Hamberger, R.N. (1989) Mitogen-stimulated lymphocyte proliferation and pituitary hormones in major depression. *Biol. Psychiatry* 26, 145–55.

Davidson, R.J. and Sutton, S.K. (1995) Affective neuroscience: the emergence of a discipline. *Curr. Opin. in Neurobiol.* 5, 217–24.

Daynes, R.A., Dudley, D.J. and Araneo, B.A. (1990) Regulation of murine lymphokine production in vivo. II. Dehydroepiandrosterone is a natural enhancer of interleukin 2 synthesis by helper T cells. *Eur. J. Immunol.* 20, 793–802.

Decker, D., Lindemann, C., Springer, W., Low, A., Hirner, A. and von Ruecker, A. (1999) Endoscopic versus conventional hernia repair from an immunological point of view. *Surg. Endosc.* 13(4) 335–9.

Decker, D., Schondorf, M., Bidlingmaier, F., Hirner, A. and von Ruecker, A.A. (1996) Surgical stress induces a shift in the type-1/type-2 T-helper cell balance, suggesting down-regulation of cell-mediated and up-regulation of antibody-mediated immunity commensurate to the trauma. *Surgery* 119(3), 316–25.

Deinzer, R. and Schuller, N. (1998) Dynamics of stress related decrease of salivary immunoglobulin A (sIgA): relationship to symptoms of the common cold and studying behavior. *Behav. Med.* 23(4), 161–9.

DeKruyff, R., Fang, Y. and Umetso, D.T. (1998) Corticosteroids enhance the capacity of macrophages to induce Th2 cytokine synthesis in CD4+ve lymphocytes by inhibiting IL-12 production. *Journal of Immunology* 160, 2231–7.

DeVries, A.C., Taymans, S.E., Sundstrom, J.M. and Pert, A. (1998) Conditioned release of corticosterone by contextual stimuli associated with cocaine is mediated by corticotrophin-releasing factor. *Brain Res.* 789, 39–46.

Dhabhar, F.S. and McEwen, B.S. (1997) Acute stress enhances while chronic stress suppresses cell-mediated immunity in vivo: a potential role for leukocyte trafficking. *Brain, Behav. and Immunity* 11(4), 286–306.

Dhabhar, F.S. and McEwan, B.S. (1999) Enhancing versus suppressive effects of stress hormones on skin immune function. *Proc. Nat. Acad. Sci. USA.* 96, 1059–64.

Dinan, T.G. (1994) Glucocorticoids and the genesis of depressive illness: a psychobiological model. *Brit. J. Psychiatry* 164, 365–71.

Dobbs, C.M., Feng, Ni., Beck, F.M. and Sheridan, J.F. (1996) Neuroendocrine regulation of cytokine production during experimental influenza viral infection. Effects of restraint stress-induced elevation in endogenous corticosterone. *Journal of Immunology* 157(5) 1870–7.

Douek, I.F., Leech, N.J., Gillmore, H.A., Bingley, P.J. and Gale, E.A.M. (1999) Children with Type 1 diabetes and their unaffected siblings have fewer symptoms of asthma. *Lancet* 353, 1850.

Drevets, W.C., Videen, T.O., Price, J.L., Preskorn, S.H., Carmichael, S.T. and Raichle, M.E.A (1992). Functional anatomical study of unipolar depression. *Journal of Neuroscience* 12, 3628–41.

Drummond, P.D., and Hewson-Bower B. (1977) Increased psychosocial stress and decreased mucosal immunity in children with recurrent upper respiratory tract infections. *J. Psychosom. Research* 43(3), (September) 271–8

Dunn, A.J. (1998) Infection as a stressor: the role of cytokines, in Levy, A., Grauer, E., Ben-Nathan, D. and de Kloet, E.R. eds *New Frontiers in Stress Research*, Amsterdam: Harwood Academic Publishers.

Esterling, B.A., Keicolt-Glaser, J.K. and Glaser, R. (1996) Psychosocial modulation of cytokine-induced natural killer cell activity in older adults. *Psychosomatic Med.* 58, 264–72.

Evans, P. (1989) *Motivation and Emotion*. London: Routledge.

Evans, P., Bristow, M., Hucklebridge, F., Clow, A. and Pang, F.Y. (1994) Stress, arousal, cortisol and secretory immunoglobulin A in students undergoing assessment. *Brit. J. Clin. Psychol.*, 33, 575–6.

Evans, P., Bristow, M., Hucklebridge, F., Clow, A. and Walters, N. (1993) The relationship between secretory immunity, mood, and life events. *Brit. J. of Clin. Psychol.*, 32, 227–36.

Evans, D.L., Burnett, G.B. and Nemeroff, C.B. (1983) The dexamethasone suppression test in the clinical setting. *Am. J. Psychiatry* 140, 586–9.

Evans, P., Clow, A. and Hucklebridge, F. (1997) Stress and the immune system. *The Psychologist* 10, 303–7.

Evans, P., Derr, G., Ford, G., Hucklebridge, F., Hunt, K. and Lambert, S. (2000) The social patterning of mucosal immunity in a large community sample. *Brain, Behav. and Immunity* (in press).

Evans, P., Doyle, A., Hucklebridge, F. and Clow, A. (1996) Positive but not negative life events predict vulnerability to upper respiratory illness. *Brit J. Health Psychology* 2, 339–48.

Evans, P.D. and Edgerton, N. (1991) Life events and mood as predictors of the common cold. *Brit. J. Med. Psychol.* 64(1), 35–44.

Evans, P., Hucklebridge, F.H., Clow, A., and Doyle, A. (1995) Secretory immunoglobulin A as a convienient biomarker in health survey work, in Rodrigues-Marin ed. *Health Psychology and Quality of Life Research* (vol. 2), Alicante: University Press.

Evans, P.D., Pitts, M.K. and Smith, K. (1988) Minor infection, minor life events and the four day desirability dip. *J. Psychosom. Research*, 32, 533–53.

Exton, M.S., Von Horston, S., Schult, M., Voge, J., Strubel, T., Donath, S., Steinmuller, C., Seeliger, H., Nagel, E., Westermann, J. and Schedlowski, M. (1998a) Behaviourally conditioned immunosuppression using cyclosporine A: central nervous system reduces IL-2 production via splenic innervation. *Journal of Neuroimmunology*, 88, 182–91.

Exton, M.S., Von Horsten, S., Voge, J., Westermann, J., Schult, M., Nagel, E. and Schedlowski, M. (1998b) Conditioned taste aversion produced by cyclosporine A: concomitant reduction in lymphoid organ weight and splenocyte proliferation. *Physiol. Behav.* 63, 241–7.

Falaschi, P., Martocchia, A., Proietti, A. and D'Urso (1999) The immune system and the hypothalamus-pituitary-adrenal (HPA) axis, in Plotnikoff, N. P., Faith, R.E., Murgo, A.J. and Good, R.A. eds *Cytokines, Stress and Immunity*, London: CRC Press.

Fawzy, F.I., Fawzy, N.W., Ardnt, L.A., and Pasnau, R.O. (1995) Critical review of psychosocial interventions in cancer care. *Arch. Gen. Psychiat.* 52, 681–9.

Foulkes, R., Shaw, S. and Suitters, A. (1997) Immunological consequences of inhibiting dehydroepiandrosterone (DHEA) sulfatase in vivo, in Rook, G.A.W. and Lightman, S. eds *Steroid Hormones and the T-Cell Cytokine Profile*, Berlin: Springer-Verlag.

Fox, P.A., Henderson, D.C., Barton, M.S.H., Catalan, J., McCormack, S.M.G. and Gruzelier, J. (1999) Immunological markers of frequently recurring genital Herpes simplex virus and their response to hypnotherapy: a pilot study. *International Journal of STD and AIDS* 10, 730–4.

Frank, M.G., Hendricks, S.E., Johnson, D.R., Wieseler, J.L. and Burke, W.J. (1999) Antidepressants augment natural killer cell activity: in vivo and in vitro. *Neuropsychobiology* 39, 18–24.

Frasure-Smith, N., Lesperance, F. and Talajic, M. (1993) Depression following myocardial infarction: impact on 6 month survival. *J. Am. Med. Assoc.* 270, 1819.

Fredrikson, M., Furst, C.J., Lekander, M., Rotstein, S. and Blomgren, H. (1993) Trait anxiety and anticipatory immune reactions in women receiving adjuvant chemotherapy for breast cancer. *Brain, Behav. and Immunity*, 7, 79–90.

Friedman, E.M. and Irwin, M.R. (1997) Modulation of immune cell function by the autonomic nervous system. *Pharmacology and Therapeutics* 74, 27–38.

Gainotti, G. (1969). Reactions catastrophiqyues et manifestations d'indifference au cours des atteintes cerebrales. *Neuropsychologia* 7, 195–204.

Gartland, H.J., and Day, H.D. (1999) Family predictors of the incidence of children's asthma symptoms: expressed emotion, medication, parent contact, and life events. *J. Clin. Psychol.* 55(5), (May) 573–84.

Geschwind, N. and Behan, P. (1982). Left-handedness: association with immune disease, migraine and developmental learning disorders. *Proc. Nat. Acad. Sci. USA* 79, 5097–100.

Geshwind, N. and Behan, P. (1984) Laterality, hormones and immunity, in Geschwind, N. and Galaburda, N. eds *Cerebral Dominance*, Cambridge, MA: Harvard University Press.

Geschwind, N. and Galaburda, N. (1987) *Cerebral lateralisation: biological mechanisms, associations and pathology.* Cambridge, MA: MIT Press.

Ghanta, V.K., Demissie, S., Hiramoto, N.S. and Hiramoto, R.N. (1996) Conditioning of body temperature and natural killer cell activity with arecoline, a muscarinic cholinergic agonist. *Neuroimmunomod.* 3, 233–8.

Glaser, R., Kiecolt-Glaser, J.K., Malarkey, W.B. and Sheridan, J.F. (1998) The influence of psychological stress on the immune response to vaccines. *Annals of the New York Academy of Sciences*, 840, 649–55.

Glaser, R., Keicolt-Glaser, J.K., Marucha, P.T. MacCullan, R.C., Laskowski, B.F. and Malarkey, W.B. (1999) Stress-related changes in proinflammatory cytokine production in wounds. *Arch. Gen. Psychiat.* 56(5) (May) 450–6.

Glaser, R., Rice, J., Sheridan, J., Fertel, R., Stout, J., Speicher, C., Pinsky, D., Kotur, M., Post, A., Beck, M., *et al.* (1987) Stress-related immune suppression: health implications. *Brain, Behav. and Immunity* 1(1), 7–20.

Gmunder, F.K., Konstantinova, I., Cogoli, A., Lesnyak, A., Bogomolov, W., and Grachov, A.W. (1994) Cellular immunity in cosmonauts during long duration spaceflight on board the orbital MIR station. *Aviat., Space, Environ., Med.* 65(5), 419–23.

Gorczynski, R.M. (1990) Conditioned enhancement of skin allografts in mice. *Behav. Immun.* 4, 85–92.

Gorczynski, R.M., Kennedy, M. and Ciampi, A. (1985) Cimetidine reverses tumour growth enhancement of plasmacytoma tumours in mice demonstrating conditioned immunosuppression. *Journal of Immunology*, 134, 4261–66.

Gonzalez-Ariki, S. and Husband, A.J. (1998) The role of sympathetic innervation of the gut in regulating mucosal immune responses. *Brain, Behav. and Immunity* 12, 53–63.

Graham, N.M.H., Douglas, R.M. and Ryan, P. (1986) Stress and acute respiratory infection. *Am. J. Epidemiology*, 124(3), 389–401.

Graham, N.M., Woodward, A.J., Ryan, P. and Douglas, R.M. (1990) Acute respiratory illness in Adelaide children. II: the relationship of maternal stress, social supports and family functioning. *Int. J. Epidemiol.* 19(4), 937–44.

Granger, D.A., Schwartz, E.B., Booth, A., Curren, M. and Zakaria, D. (1999) Assessing dehydroepiandrosterone in saliva: a simple radioimmunoassay for use in studies of children, adolescents and adults. *Psychoneuroendocrinology* 24(5): 567–79.

Greer, S. (1983) Cancer and the mind. *Br. J. Psychiatry* 143, 535–43.

Grochowicz, P.M., Schedlowski, M., Husband, A.J., Kingman, M.G., Hibberd, A.D. and Bowen, K.M. (1991) Behavioural conditioning prolongs heart allograft survival in rats. *Brain, Behav. and Immunology*, 5, 349–56.

Gruzelier, J., Burgess, A., Baldewig, T., Riccio, M., Hawkins, D., Stygall, J., Catt, S. and Irving, G. (1996) Prospective associations between lateralised brain function and immune status in HIV infection: analysis of EEG, cognition and mood over 30 months. *Int. J. Psychophysiol.* 23, 215–24.

Gruzelier, J., Clow, A., Evans, P., Lazar, I. and Walker, L. (1998) Mind–body influences on immunity: lateralised control, stress, individual difference predictors and prophylaxis. *Annals of the New York Acadamy of Sciences*, 851, 487–94.

Gui, X.Y. (1988) Mast cells: a possible link between psychological stress, enteric infection, food allergy and gut hypersensitivity in the irritable bowel syndrome. *J. Gastroenterol. Hepatol.* 13(10), (October) 980–9.

Halvorsen, R. and Vassend, O. (1987) Effects of examination stress on some cellular immunity functions. *J. Psychosom.Research*, 31(6), 693–701.

Hammerlinck, F.F.V. (1999) Neopterin: a review. *Experimental Dermatology* 8. 167–76.

Helgeson, V.S. and Cohen, S. (1996) Social support and adjustment to cancer: reconciling descriptive, correlational and intervention research. *Health Psychology*. 15, 135–48.

Herbert, T.B., and Cohen, S. (1993) Stress and immunity in humans: a meta-analytic review. *Psychosomatic Med.* 55, 364–79.

Herbert, T.B., Cohen, S., Marsland, A.L. Bachen, E.A., Rabin, B.S., Muldoon, M.F. and Manuck, S.B. (1994) Cardiovascular reactivity and the course of immune response to an acute psychological stressor. *Psychosomatic Med.* 56, 337–44.

Hermann, G., Tovar, C.A., Beck, F.M., Allen, C. and Sheridan, J.F. (1993) Restraint stress differentially affects the pathogenesis of an experimental influenza viral infection in three inbred strains of mice. *Journal of Neuroimmunology* 47(1), 83–94.

Hickie, I., Bennett, B., Lloyd, A., Heath, A. and Martin, N. (1999) Complex genetic and environmental relationships between psychological distress, fatigue and immune functioning: a twin study. *Psychol. Med.* 29, 269–77.

Hill, L.E. (1930) *Philosophy of a Biologist.* London: Arnold.

Holgate, S.L. (1997) The cellular mediator basis of asthma in relation to natural history. *Lancet* 350, 5–9.

Hucklebridge, F., Clow, A., Abeyguneratne, T., Huezo-Diaz, P. and Evans, P. (1999) The awakening cortisol response and blood glucose levels. *Life Sciences.* 64, 931–37.

Hucklebridge, F., Clow, A. and Evans, P. (1998a) The relationship between salivary secretory immunoglobulin A and cortisol: neuroendocrine response to awakening and the diurnal cycle. *Int. J. Psychophysiol.* 31, 69–76.

Hucklebridge, F., Sen, S., Evans, P. and Clow, A. (1998b) The relationship between circadian patterns of salivary cortisol and endogenous inhibitor of Monoamine Oxidase A. *Life Sciences.* 62, 2321–8.

Hucklebridge, F.H., Smith, M.D., Clow, A., Evans, P., Glover, V., Taylor, A., Adams, D. and Lydyard, P.M. (1994) Dysphoria and immune status in postpartum women. *Biological Psychology* 37, 199–206.

Ironson, G., Wynings, C., Schneiderman, N., Baum, A., Rodriguez, M., Greenwood, D., Benight, C., Antoni, M., LaPerriere, A., Huang, H.S., Klimas, N. and Fletcher, M.A. (1997) Post traumatic stress symptoms, intrusive thoughts, loss, and immune function after Hurricane Andrew. *Psychosomatic Med.* 59(2), 128–41.

Irwin, M. and Gillin, J.C. (1987) Impaired natural killer cell activity among depression patients. *Psychiat. Res.* 20, 181–2.

Irwin, M., McClintic, J., Costlow, C., Fortner, M., White, J. and Gillin, J.C. (1996) Partial night sleep deprivation reduces natural killer and cellular immune responses in humans. *FASEB Journal* 10, 643–53.

Iwakabe, K., Shimada, M., Ohta, A., Yahata, T., Ohmi, Y., Habu, S. and Nishimura, T. (1998) The restraint stress drives a shift in Th1/Th2 balance toward Th2-dominant immunity in mice. *Immunol. Lett.* 62(1), 39–43.

James, W. (1884) What is emotion? *Mind* 9, 188–205.

Janeway, C.A. and Travers, P. (1997) *Immunobiology: The Immune System in Health and Disease.* London: Current Biology Ltd.

Jeffcoate, W.J., Silverstone, J.T., Edwards, C.R. and Besser, G.M. (1979) Psychiatric manifestations of Cushing's Syndrome: response to lowering plasma cortisol. *Quart. J. Med.* 191, 465–72.

Jemmott, J.B. and McClelland, D.C. (1989) Secretory IgA as a measure of resistance to infectious disease: comments on Stone, Cox, Valdimarsdottir, and Neale. *Behav. Med.* 12, 63–71.

Kang, D.H. Coe, C.L., McCarthy, D.O., Jarjour, N.N., Kelly, E.A., Rodriguez, R.R. and Busse, W.W. (1997) Cytokine profiles of stimulated blood lymphocytes in asthmatic and healthy adolescents across the school year. *Journal of Interferon and Cytokine Research* 17(8), (August) 481–7.

Kang, D. H., Davidson, R.J., Coe, C., Wheeler, R.E., Tomarken, A.J. and Ershler, W.B. (1991) Frontal brain asymmetry and immune function. *Behav. Neurosci.* 105, 860–9.

Kaplan, B.J. and Crawford, S.G. (1994) The GBG model: is there more to consider than handedness? *Brain Cogn.* 26, 291–9.

Kemeny, M.E., Weiner, H., Duran, R., Taylor, S.E., Visscher, B. and Fahey J.L. (1995) Immune system changes after the death of a partner in HIV-positive gay men. *Psychosomatic Med.* 57(6), (November–December) 547–54.

Khan, A.U. (1977) Effectiveness of biofeedback and counterconditioning in the treatment of bronchial asthma. *J. Psychosom. Research* 21, 97–104.

Kiecolt-Glaser, J.K., Dura, J.R., Speicher, C.E., Trask, O.J. and Glaser, R. (1991) Spousal caregivers of dementia victims: longitudinal changes in immunity and health. *Psychosomatic Med.* 53(4) (July–August), 345–62.

Kiecolt-Glaser, J.K., Fisher, L.D., Ogrocki, P., Stout, J.C., Speicher, C.E. and Glaser, R. (1987) Marital quality, marital disruption, and immune function. *Psychosomatic Med.* 49(1), 13–34.

Kiecolt-Glaser, J.K., Glaser, R., Gravenstein, S., Malarkey, W.B. and Sheridan, J. (1996). Chronic stress alters the immune response to influenza virus vaccine in older adults. *Proc. Nat. Acad. Sci. USA* 93(7), 3043–7.

Kiecolt-Glaser, J.K., Malarkey, W.B., Chee, M., Newton, T., Cacioppo, J.T., Mao, H.Y. and Glaser, R. (1993) Negative behavior during marital conflict is associated with immunological down-regulation. *Psychosomatic Med.* 55(5), 395–409.

Kiecolt-Glaser, J.K., Marucha, P.T., Malarkey, W.B., Mercado, A.M. and Glaser, R. (1995) Slowing of wound healing by psychological stress. *Lancet.* 346(8984) (4 November), 1194–6.

Klosterhalfen, W. and Klosterhalfen, S. (1983) Pavlovian conditioning of immunosuppression modifies adjuvant arthritis in rats. *Behav. Neurosci.* 97, 663–6.

Korten, A.E., Jorm, A.F., Jiao, Z., Letenneur, L., Jacomb, P.A., Henderson, A.S., Christensen, H. and Rodgers, B. (1999) Health, cognitive, and psychosocial factors as predictors of mortality in an elderly community sample. *J. Epidemiol. Community Health*, 53(2), 83–8.

Kronfol, Z., Silva, J., Greden, J., Dembinsky, S., Gardener, R. and Carroll, B. (1983) Impaired lymphocyte function in depressive illness. *Life Sciences* 33, 241–7.

Kruszewska, B., Moynihan, J.A. and Felton, D. (1997) The role of innervation of lymphoid tissue in the regulation of the Th1/Th2 dichotomy, in Rook, G.A.W. and Lightman, S. eds *Steroid Hormones and the T-Cell Cytokine Profile*, Berlin: Springer-Verlag.

Kuby, J. (1997). *Immunology* (third edition). New York: Freeman and Co.

Kugler, J., Reintjes, F., Tewes, V. and Schedlowski, M. (1996) Competition stress in soccer coaches increases salivary immunoglobin A and salivary cortisol concentrations. *Journal of Sports Medicine and Physical Fitness* 36(2), 117–20.

Kvetnansky, R., Fukuhara, K., Pacak, K., Cizza, G., Goldstein, D.S. and Kopin, I.J. (1993) Endogenous glucocorticoids restrain catecholamine synthesis and release at rest and during immobilisation stress in rats. *Endocrinology* 133, 1411–19.

Lansdell, H. (1962) A sex difference in the effect of temporal lobe neurosurgery on design preference. *Nature* 194, 852–4.

LaPerriere, A., Ironson, G., Antoni, M.H. and Schneiderman, N. (1994) Exercise and psychoneuroimmunology. *Med. Sci. Sports Exercise* 26, 182–90.

LeDoux, J. (1998) *The Emotional Brain*. New York: Weidenfeld and Nicolson.

Levy, J. (1978) Lateral differences in the human brain in cognition and behavioral control, in Buser, P. and Rougeul-Buser, A. eds *Cerebral Correlates of Conscious Experience*, New York: North Holland Publishing Co.

Levy, S.M., Fernstrom, J., Herberman, R.B., Whiteside, T., Lee, J., Ward, M. and Massaudi, M. (1991) Persistently low natural killer cell activity and circulating levels of plasma beta endorphin: risk factors for infectious disease. *Life Sci.* 48(2), 107–16.

London, W.P. (1989) Left-handedness and life expectancy. *Percept. Mot. Skills* 68, 1040–2.

Longo, D.L., Duffey, P.L., Kopp, W.C., Heyes, M.P., Alvord, W.G., Sharfman, W.H., Schmidt, P.J., Rubinow, D.R. and Rosenstein, D.L. (1999) Conditioned immune response to interferon-gamma in humans. *Clin. Immunol.* 90(2), 173–81.

Loria, R.M. and Ben-Nathan, D. (1998) Steroids, stress and the neuroimmune axis, in Levy, A., Grauer, E., Ben-Nathan, D. and de Kloet, E.R. eds, *New Frontiers in Stress Research*, Amsterdam: Harwood Academic Publishers.

McGee, R., Williams, S. and Elwood, M. (1994) Depression and the development of cancer: a meta-analysis. *Soc. Sci. Med.* 38, 187–92.

McGlone, G. (1978) Sex differences in functional brain anatomy. *Cortex* 14, 122–8.

McKeever, W.F. and Rich, D.A. (1990) Left-handedness and immune disorders. *Cortex* 26, 33–40.

Mackenzie, J.N. (1896) The production of the so called 'rose cold' by means of an artificial rose. *Am. J. Med. Sci.* 91, 45–57.

McKinnon, W., Weisse, C.S., Reynolds, C.P., Bowles, C.A. and Baum, A. (1989) Chronic stress, leukocyte subpopulations, and humoral response to latent viruses. *Health Psychology* 8(4), 389–402.

Maes, M., Bosmans, E., Suy, E., Vandervorst, C., Dejonckheere, C., Minner, B. and Raus, J. (1991) Depression-related disturbances in mitogen-induced lymphocyte responses, interleukin-1β and soluble interleukin-2-receptor production. *Acta. Psychiatrica Scandinavia* 84, 379–86.

Maes, M., Meltzer, H.Y., Bosmans, E., Bergmans, R., Vandoolaeghe, E., Ranjan, R. and Desneyder, R. (1995) Increased plasma concentrations of interleukin-6, soluble interleukin-6, soluble interleukin-2 and transferrin receptor in major depression. *Journal of Affective Disorders* 34, 301–9.

Maes, M., Stephens, W., Declerck, L., Bridts, C., Peters, D., Schotte, C. and Cosyns, P. (1993) A significant increased expression of T cell activation markers in depression: additional evidence for an inflammatory process during that illness. *Progr. Psychopharmacol. Biol. Psychiat.* 17, 214–55.

Maes, M. (1995) Evidence for an immune response in major depression: A review and hypothesis. *Progress in Neuro-Psychopharmacol. & Biol. Psychiat.* 18, 11–38.

Maes, M., Verkerk, R., Vandoolaeghe, E., Van Hunsel, F., Neels, H., Wauters, A., Demedts, P. and Scharpe, S. (1997) Serotonin-immune interactions in major depression: lower serum tryptophan as a marker of an immune-inflammatory response. *Eur. Arch. Psychiatry Clin. Neurosci.* 247, 154–61.

Mahoney, J. and Gordon, S. (1998) Macrophage receptors and innate immunity. *The Biochemist* (February). 12–16.

Maier, H. and Smith, J. (1999) Relationships of disability, health management and psychosocial conditions to cause-specific mortality among a community-residing elderly people. *J. Gerontol. B-Psychol. Sci. Soc. Sci.* 54(1), 44–54.

Maier, S.F., and Watkins, L.R. (1998) Cytokines for psychologists: implications of bidirectional immune-to-brain communication for understanding behavior, mood, and cognition. *Psychological Review* 105(1), 83–107.

Maier, S.F., Watkins, L.R. and Fleshner, M. (1994) Psychoneuroimmunology. The interface between behaviour, brain and immunity. *American Psychologist* 49, 1004–17.

Maisel, A.S. (1994) Beneficial effects of metaprolol treatment in congestive heart failure. Reversal of sympathetic-induced alterations of immunologic function. *Circulation* 90, 1774–80

Martin, I. (1998) Human electroencephalographic (EEG) response to olfactory stimulation: two experiments using the aroma of food. *Int. J. Psychophysiol.* 30, 287–302.

Marucha P.T., Kiecolt-Glaser, J.K. and Favagehi, M. (1998) Mucosal wound healing is impaired by examination stress. *Psychosomatic Med.* 60(3) (May–June), 362–5.

Marx, J.L. (1985) The immune system 'belongs in the body'. *Science* 227, 1190–2.

Mastorakos, G., Bamberger, C., and Chrousos, G.P. (1999) Neuroendocrine regulation of the immune process, in Plotnikoff, N.P., Faith, R.E., Murgo, A.J. and Good, R.A. eds *Cytokines, Stress and Immunity*, London: CRC Press.

Meador, K.J., Lecuona, J.M., Helman, S.W. and Loring, D.W. (1999) Differential immunologic effects of language-dominant and non-dominant cerebral resections. *Neurology* 53, 1183–7.

Meikle, A.W., Dorchuck, R.W., Araneo, B.A., Stringham, J.D., Evans, T.G., Spruance, S.L. and Daynes, R.A. (1992) The presence of dehydroepiandrosterone-specific receptor binding complex in murine T cells. *J. Steroid Biochem. Mollec. Biol.* 42, 293–304.

Mendlovic, S., Mozes, E., Eilat, E., Doron, A., Lereya, J., Zakuth, V. and Spirer, Z. (1999) Immune activation in non-treated suicidal major depression *Immunology Lett.* 67, 105–108.

Mestecky, J. (1993) Saliva as a manifestation of the common mucosal immune system. *Annals of the New York Academy of Sciences* 694, 184–94.

Miletic, I.D., Schiffman, S.S., Miletic, V.D. and Sattely-Miller, E.A. (1996) Salivary IgA secretion rate in young and elderly persons. *Physiol. Beh.* 60, 243–8.

Miller, A.H. (1998) Neuroendocrine and immune system interactions in stress and depression. *Psychoneuroendocrinology* 21, 443–63.

Miller, A.H., Spencer, R.L. Pearce, B.D., Pisell, T.L., Azrieli, Y., Tanapat, P., Moday, H., Rhee, R. and McEwan, B.S. (1998) Glucocorticoid receptors are differentially expressed in the cells and tissues of the immune system. *Cellular Immunology*, 186, 45–54.

Miller, W.L. and Tyrell, J.B. (1995) 'The adrenal cortex' in P. Fetig, J.D. Baxter and L.A. Frohman, eds, *Endocrinology and Metabolism*. 555–711, McGraw Hill Inc. New York.

Mills, P.J., Ziegler, M.G., Dimsdale, J.E. and Parry, B.L. (1995) Enumerative immune changes following acute stress: effect of the menstrual cycle. *Brain, Behav. and Immunity* 9(3), 190–5.

Molassiotis, A., Van Den Akker, O.B., Milligan, D.W. and Goldman, J.M. (1997) Symptom distress, coping style and biological variables as predictors of survival after bone marrow transplantation. *J. Psychosom. Research* 42(3) (March), 275–85.

Moynihan, J.A., Karp, J.D., Cohen, N. and Cocke. R. (1994) Alterations in interleukin-4 and antibody production following pheromone exposure: role of glucocorticoids. *Journal of Neuroimmunology* 54, 51–8.

Murphy, B.E.P. (1991) Steroids and depression. J. *Steroid Biochem. Molec. Biol.* 38, 537–59.

Murray, J.S. (1998) How the MHC selects Th1/Th2 immunity. *Immunology Today* 19, 157–264.

Naliboff, B.D., Benton, D., Solomon, G.F., Morley, J.E., Fahey, J.L., Bloom, E.T., Makinodan, T. and Gilmore, S.L. (1991) Immunological changes in young and old adults during brief laboratory stress. *Psychosomatic Med.* 53(2), 121–32.

Naliboff, B.D., Solomon, G.F., Gilmore, S.L., Fahey, J.L., Benton, D. and Pine, J. (1995) Rapid changes in cellular immunity following a confrontational role-play stressor. *Brain, Behav. and Immunity* 9 (3), 207–19.

Nassberger, L. and Traskman-Bendz, L. (1993) Increased soluble interleukin-2 receptor in suicide attempters. *Acta Psychiatrica Scandinavia* 88, 48–52.

Neveu, P.J. (1993) Brain lateralisation and immunomodulation. *Int. J. Neurosci.* 70, 135–43.

Neveu, P.J, Barnoud, P., Vitiello, S. and Le Moal, M. (1989) Brain neocortex modulation of mitogen induced interleukin 2, but not interleukin 1, production. *Immunol. Lett.* 21, 307–10.

Neveu, P.J., Bluthe, R.M., Liege, S., Moya, S., Michaud, B. and Dantzer, R. (1998) Interleukin-1-induced sickness behavior depends on behavioral lateralisation in mice. *Physiol. Behav.* 63, 587–90.

Neveu, P.J. and Moya, S. (1997) In the mouse, the corticoid stress response depends on lateralisation. *Brain Res.* 784, 344–6.

Neveu, P.J., Tahhzouti, K., Dantzer, R., Simon, H. and Le Moal, M. (1986) Modulation of mitogen-induced lymphoproliferation by cerebral cortex. *Life Sciences* 26, 1907–13.

Newport, D.J. and Nemeroff, C.B. (1998) Assessment and treatment of depression in the cancer patient. *J. Psychosom. Research* 45, 215–237.

Nishanian, P., Aziz, N., Chunh, J., Detels, R. and Fahey, L. (1998) Oral fluids as an alternative to serum for measurement of markers of immune activation. *Clinical and Diagnostic Laboratory Immunology* 5, 507–12.

Nistico, G. and De Sarro, G. (1991) Is interleukin-2 a neuromodulator in the brain? *Trends in Neuroscience* 14, 146–50.

Norbiato, G., Bevilacqua, M., Vago, T., Taddei, A. and Clerici, M. (1997) Glucocorticoids and immune function in the human immunodeficiency virus infection: A study in hypercortisolemic and cortisol-resistant patients. *Journal of Clinical Endocrinology and Metabolism* 82, 3260–3.

O'Connor, B.P. and Vallerand, R.J. (1998) Psychological adjustment variables as predictors of mortality among nursing home residents. *Psychol. Aging* 13(3), 368–74.

O'Leary, A. (1990) Stress, emotion and human immune function. *Psychological Bulletin* 108, 363–82.

Oppenheimer, S., Gelb, A., Girvin, J. and Hachinski, V. (1992) Cardiovascular effects of human insula cortex stimulation. *Neurology* 42, 1727–32.

Ottenberg, P., Stein, M., Lewis and J., Hamilton, C. (1958) Learned asthma in the guinea pig. *Psychosomatic Med.* 20, 395–400.

Ottoway, C.A. and Husband, A.J. (1994) The influence of neuroendocrine pathways on lymphocyte migration. *Immunology Today* 15, 511–17.

Pacak, K., Palkovits, M., Kvetnansky, R., Matern, P., Hart, C., Kopinm, I.J. and Goldstein, D.S. (1995) Catecholaminergic inhibition by hypercortisolemia in the PVN nucleus of the conscious rat. *Endocrinology* 136: 4814–19.

Padgett, D.A., Loria, R.M. and Sheridan, J.F. (1997) Endocrine regulation of the immune response to influenza virus infection with metabolite of DHEA-androstenediol. *Journal of Neuroimmunology* 78, 203–11.

Padgett, D.A., MacCallum, R.C. and Sheridan, J.F. (1998c) Stress exacerbates age-related decrements in the immune response to an experimental influenza viral infection. *J. Gerontol. A. Biol. Sci. Med. Sci.* 53(5), B347-53.

Padgett, D.A., Marucha, P.T. and Sheridan, J.F. (1998b) Restraint stress slows cutaneous wound healing in mice. *Brain, Behav. and Immunity* 12(1), (March), 64–73.

Padgett, D.A., Sheridan, J.F., Dorne, J., Berntson, G.G., Candelora, J. and Glaser, R. (1998a) Social stress and the reactivation of latent herpes simplex virus type 1. *Proc. Nat. Acad. Sci. USA* 95, 7231–5.

Panerai, A.E. and Sacerdote, P. (1997) B-endorphin in the immune system: a role at last? *Immunology Today* 18, 317–19.

Parrot, R.F., Velluci, S.V., Goode, J.A., Lloyd, D.M. and Forsling, M.L. (1995) Cyclo-oxygenase mediation of endotoxin-induced fever, anterior and posterior pituitary hormone release, and hypothalamic c-Fos expression in the pubertal pig. *Experimental Physiology* 80, 663–74.

Perez, L. and Lysle, D.T. (1997) Conditioned immunomodulation: investigations of the role of endogenous activity at mu, kappa and delta opioid receptor subtypes. *Journal Neuroimmunology* 79, 101–12.

Petrovsky, N. and Harrison, L.C. (1995) Th1 and Th2: swinging to a hormonal rhythm. *Immunology Today,* 16, 605.

Petrovsky, N. and Harrison, L.C. (1997) Diurnal rhythmicity of human cytokine production: a dynamic disequilibrium in T helper cell type 1/ T helper cell Type 2 balance? *Journal of Immunology* 158, 5163–8.

Pike, J.L., Smith, T.L., Hauger, R.L., Nicassio, P.M., Patterson, T.L., McClintick, J., Costlow, C. and Irwin, M.R. (1997) Chronic life stress alters sympathetic, neuroendocrine, and immune responsivity to an acute psychological stressor in humans. *Psychosomatic Med.* 59(4), 447–57.

Pridmore, S. (1999) Rapid transcranial magnetic stimulation and normalization of the dexamethasone suppression test. *Psychiatry Clin. Neurosci.* 53, 33–7.

Pruessner, J.C., Wolf, O.T., Hellhammer, D.H., Buske-Kirschbaum, A., von Auer, K., Jobst, S., Kaspers, F. and Kirschbaum, C. (1997) Free cortisol levels after awakening: A reliable biological marker for assessment of adrenocortical activity. *Life Sciences* 61, 2530–49.

Raghupathy, R. (1997) Th1-type immunity is incompatible with successful pregnancy. *Immunology Today* 18, 478–82.

Ramirez-Amaya, V. and Bermundez-Rattoni, F. (1999) Conditioned enhancement of antibody production is disrupted by insular cortex and amygdala but not hippocampal lesions. *Brain, Behav. and Immumity* 13, 46–60.

Reed, G.M., Kemeny, M.E., Taylor, S.E., Wang, H.Y. and Visscher, B.R. (1994). Realistic acceptance as a predictor of decreased survival time in gay men with AIDS. *Health Psychology* 13(4) (July), 299–307.

Ritter, M.A. and Ladyman, H.M. (1995) *Monoclonal Antibodies: Production Engineering and Clinical Application.* Cambridge: Cambridge University Press.

Rocken, M., Racke, M. and Shevach, E.M. (1996) IL-4-induced immune deviation as antigen-specific therapy for inflammatory autoimmune disease. *Immunology Today* 17, 225–31.

Romagnani, S. (1997) The Th1/Th2 paradigm. *Immunology Today* 18, 263–6.

Rook, G.A.W. (1997) The therapeutic potential of regulation of the Th1–Th2 balance. *Immunology News* (November), 226–8.

Rook, G.A.W. and Lightman, S. (1997) *Steroid Hormones and the T-Cell Cytokine Profile.* Berlin: Springer–Verlag.

Rook, G.A.W., Hernandez-Pando, R., Baker, R., Orosco, H., Arriaga, K., Pavon, L. and Streber, M. (1997) Human and murine tuberculosis as models for immuno-endocrine interactions, in Rook, G.A.W. and Lightman, S. eds *Steroid Hormones and the T-Cell Cytokine Profile,* Berlin: Springer-Verlag.

Rook, G.A. and Zumla, A. (1997) Gulf War syndrome: is it due to a systemic shift in cytokine balance towards a Th2 profile? *Lancet* 349(9068) (21 June), 1831–3.

Rose, S. (1997) *Lifelines: Biology, Freedom, and Determinism.* London: Penguin.

Rossen, R., Butler, W., Waldmann, R., Alford, R., Hornick, R., Togo, Y. and Kasel, J. (1970) The proteins in nasal secretion. *J. Am. Med. Assoc.* 211, 1157–61.

Rossi, G.F. and Rosadini, G. (1967) Experimental analysis of cerebral dominance in man, in Millikan C.H. and Danley, F.L. eds *Brain Mechanisms Underlying Speech and Language,* New York: Grune and Stratton.

Roud, P.C. (1986) Psychological variables associated with exceptional survival of terminally ill cancer patients. *Diss. Abstr. Int.* 46, 2051.

Sabbioni, M.E., Bovbjerg, D.H., Mathew, S., Sikes, C., Lasley, B. and Stokes, P.E. (1997) Classically conditioned changes in plasma cortisol levels induced by dexamethasone in healthy men. *FASEB Journal* 11, 1291–6.

Sander, D. and Klingelhofer, J. (1995) Changes of circadian blood pressure patterns and cardiovascular parameters indicate lateralisation of sympathetic activation following hemispheric brain infarction. *Journal Neurol.*, 242, 313–18.

Sapse, A.T. (1997) Cortisol, high cortisol diseases and anti-cortisol therapy. *Psychoneuroendocrinology* 22, S3–S10.

Schedlowski, M., Hosch, W., Oberdeck, R., Benschop, R.J., Jacobs, R., Raab, H.R. and Schmidt, R.E. (1996) Catecholamines modulate human NK cell circulation and function via splenic-independent B2-adrenergic mechanisms. *Journal of Immunology* 156, 93–9

Schleifer, S.J., Keller, S.E., Camerino, M., Thornton, J.C. and Stein, M. (1983) Suppression of lymphocyte stimulation following bereavement. *J. Am. Med. Assoc.* 250(3) (15 July), 374–7.

Schultz, P., Kirschbaum, C., Pruessner, J. and Hellhammer, D. (1998) Increased free cortisol secretion after awakening in chronically stressed individuals due to work overload. *Stress Medicine* 14, 91–7.

Sgoutas-Emch, S.A., Cacioppo, J.T., Uchino, B.N., Malarkey, W., Pearl, D., Kiecolt-Glaser, J.K. and Glaser, R. (1994) The effects of an acute psychological stressor on cardiovascular, endocrine, and cellular immune response: a prospective study of individuals high and low in heart rate reactivity. *Psychophysiology* 31(3), 264–71.

Shekelle, R.B., Raynor, W.J., Ostfield, A.M., Garron, D.C., Bieliauskas, L.A., Liu, S.C., Maliza, C. and Paul, O. (1981) Psychological depression and 17-year risk of death from cancer. *Psychosomatic Med.* 43, 117–25.

Sheridan, J.F., Dodds, C., Jung, J.H., Chu, X.H., Konstantinos, A., Padgett, D. and Glaser, R. (1998) Stress-induced neuroendocrine modulation of viral pathogenesis and immunity. *Annals of the New York Academy of Sciences* 840, 803–8.

Shirakawa, T., Enomoto, T., Shimazu, S.I. and Hopkin, J.M. (1996) The inverse association between tuberculin response and atopic disorder. *Science* 275, 77–9.

Smith, G.R. and McDaniel, P. (1983) Psychologically mediated effect on the delayed hypersensitivity reaction to tuberculin in humans. *Psychosomatic Med.* 45, 65–70.

Solomon, G.F., Segerstrom, S.C., Grohr, P., Kemeny, M., and Fahey, J. (1997) Shaking up immunity: psychological and immunologic changes after a natural disaster. *Psychosomatic Med.* 59(2), 114–27.

Spector, N.H., Provinciali, M., Di Stefano, G., Muzzioli, M., Bulian, D., Viticchi, C., Rossano, F. and Fabris, N. (1994) Immune enhancement by conditioning of senescent mice. *Annals of the New York Academy of Sciences* 741, 283–91.

Starkman, M.N. and Schteingart, D.E. (1981) Neuropsychiatric manifestations of patients with Cushing's syndrome. *Arch. Intern. Med.* 141, 215–19.

Stein, M., Miller, A.H. and Trestman, R.L. (1991) Depression and the immune system, in Ader, R., Feltery, D.L. and Cohen, N. eds, *Psychoneuroimmunology* (second edition).

Stevens-Felton, S.Y. and Bellinger, D.L. (1997) Noradrenergic and peptidergic innervation of lymphoid organs. *Chemical Immunology* 69, 99–131.

Stone, A.A., Cox., D.S., Valdimarsdottir, H. and Neale, J.M. (1987a) Secretory IgA as measure of immunocompetence. *Journal of Human Stress* 13, 136–40.

Stone, A.A., Reed, B.G. and Neale, J. (1987b) Changes in daily event frequency precede episodes of physical symptoms. *Journal of Human Stress* 13, 70–4.

Straub, R.H., Westermann, J., Scholmerich, J. and Falk, W. (1998) Dialogue between the CNS and the immune system in lymphoid organs. *Immunology Today* 19, 409–13.

Sullivan, R.M. and Gratton, A. (1999) Lateralised effects of medial prefrontal cortex lesions on neuroendocrine and autonomic stress responses in rats. *Journal of Neuroscience* 19, 2834–40.

Terzian, H. (1964) Behavioral and EEG effects of intracarotid sodium amytal injection. *Acta Neurochirurgia.* (Vienna), 12, 230–9.

Thomasi, T.B. (1992) The discovery of secretory IgA and the mucosal immune system. *Immunology Today* 13, 416–18.

Tingate, T.R., Lugg, D.J., Muller, H.K., Stowe, R.P. and Pierson, D.L.(1997) Antarctic isolation: immune and viral studies. *Immunol. Cell. Biol.* 75(3), 275–83.

Tomarken, A.J. and Davidson, R.J. (1994) Frontal brain activation in repressors and non-repressors. *J. Abnor. Psychol.* 103, 339–49.

Tomarken, A.J., Davidson, R.J., Wheeler, R.E. and Doss, R.C. (1992) Individual differences in anterior brain asymmetry and fundamental dimensions of emotion. *J. Personal. and Social Psychol.* 62, 676–87.

Tondo, L., Pani, P.P., Pellegrini-Bettoli, R., Milia, G. and Manconi, P.E. (1988) T-Lymphocytes in depressive disorder. *Med. Sci. Res.* 16, 867–8.

Torpy, D.J. and Chrousos, G.P. (1996) The three way interactions between the hypothalamic-pituitary-adrenal and gonadal axes and the immune system. *Baillieres Clinical Rheumatology* 10, 181–98.

Trimble, M.R. (1998) *Biological Psychiatry*, Chichester: Wiley, pp. 241–81.

Tsigos, C. and Chrousos, G.P. (1996) Stress, endocrine manifestations and disease, in Cooper, C.L. ed. *Handbook of Stress, Medicine and Health*, New York: CRC Press.

Uchino, B.N., Cacioppo, J.T., Malarkey, W. and Glaser, R. (1995) Individual differences in cardiac sympathetic control predict endocrine and immune responses to acute psychological stress. *J. Personal and Social Psychol.* 69(4), 736–43.

van Amsterdam, J.G. and Opperhuizen, A. (1999) Nitric oxide and biopterin in depression and stress. *Psychiat. Res.* 18, 33–8.

Van der Pompe, G., Antoni, M.H., Visser, A. and Heijnen, C.J. (1998) Effect of mild acute stress on immune cell distribution and natural killer cell activity in breast cancer patients. *Biol. Psychol.*48(1), 21–35.

Vassend, O., Eskild, A. and Halvorsen, R. (1997) Negative affectivity, coping, immune status and disease progression in HIV infected individuals. *Psychol. Health* 12, 375–88.

Vedhara, K., Cox, N.K., Wilcock, G.K., Perks,P., Hunt,M., Anderson, S., Lightman, S.L. and Shanks, N.M. (1999) Chronic stress in elderly carers of dementia patients and antibody response to influenza vaccination. *Lancet* 353 (9153) (20 February), 627–31.

Visser, J., Boxel-Dezairre, A., Methorst, D., Brunt, T., deKloet, E.R. and Nagelkerken, L. (1998) Differential regulation of interleukin-10 and IL-12 by glucocorticoids in vitro. *Blood* 91, 4255–64.

Von Horsten, S., Exton, M.S., Schult, M., Nagel, E., Stalp, M., Schweitzer, G., Voge, J., del Rey, A., Schedlowski, M. and Westermann, J. (1998) Behaviourally conditioned effects of cyclosporine A on the immune system of rats: specific alterations of blood leukocyte numbers and decrease of granulocyte function. *Journal of Neuroimmunology*, 85, 193–201.

Watkins, L.A. and Maier, S. (1998) Stress and cytokine–brain interactions, in Levy, A., Grauer, E., Ben-Nathan, D. and de Kloet, E. R. eds *New Frontiers in Stress Research*, Amsterdam: Harwood Academic.

Weigent, D.A. and Blalock, E.J. (1999) Bidirectional communication between the immune and neuroendocrine systems, in *Cytokines, Stress and Immunity*, eds Plotnikoff, N.P., Faith, R.E., Murgo, A.J. and Good, R.A. London: CRC Press.

Wheeler, R.E., Davidson, R.J. and Tomarken, A.J. (1993) Frontal brain asymmetry and emotional reactivity: a biological substrate and affective style. *Psychophysiology*, 30, 820–9.

Whitacre, C.C., Dowdell, K. and Griffin, A.C. (1998) Neuroendocrine influences on experimental autoimmune encephalomyelitis. *Annals of the New York Academy of Sciences* 1 (840) (May), 705–16.

Whitacre, C.C., Reingold, S.C. and O'Looney, P.A. (1999) A gender gap in autoimmunity. *Science* 283, 1277–8.

Wilkens, T. and De Rijk, R. (1997) Glucocorticoids and immune function: unknown dimensions and new frontiers. *Immunology Today* 18, 418–24.

Willemsen, G., Ring, C., Carroll, D., Evans, P., Clow, A. and Hucklebridge, F. (1998) Secretory immunoglobulin A and cardiovascular reactions to mental arithmetic and cold pressor. *Psychophysiology* 35, 252–9.

Wittling, W., Pfluger, M. (1990) Neuroendocrine hemisphere asymmetries: salivary cortisol secretion during lateralised viewing of emotion-related and neutral films. *Brain Cogn.* 14, 243–65.

Wright, R.J., Rodriguez, M. and Cohen, S. (1998) Review of psychosocial stress and asthma: an integrated biopsychosocial approach. *Thorax* 53(12), 1066–74.

Wyke, S., Hunt, K. and Ford, G. (1998) Gender differences in consulting a general practitioner for common symptoms of minor illness. *Soc. Sci. Med.*, 46(7), 901–6.

Zajonc, R.B. (1984) On the primacy of affect. *Am. Psychol.* 39(2), 117–23

Zeier, H., Brauchli, P. and Joller-Jemelka, H.I. (1996) Effects of work demands on immunoglobulin A and cortisol in air-traffic controllers. *Biol. Psychol.* 42(3), 413–23.

Zeiger, M.A., Franker, D.L., Pass, H.I., Nieman, L.K., Cutler, G.B., Chrousos, G.P. and Norton, J.A. (1993) Effective reversibility of the signs and symptoms of hypercortisolism by bilateral adrenalectomy. *Surgery* 114, 1138–43.

Zovato, S., Simoncini, M., Gottardo, C., Pratesi, C., Zampollo, V., Spigariol, V. and Armani, D. (1996) Dexamethasone suppression test: corticosteroid receptors regulation in mononuclear leukocytes of young and aged subjects. *Ageing, Clinical and Experimental Research* 8, 360–4.

Index